FRENCH EAST INDIA COMPANIES

A Historical Account and Record of Trade

Donald C. Wellington

Hamilton Books
A member of
The Rowman & Littlefield Publishing Group
Lanham · Boulder · New York · Toronto · Oxford

Copyright © 2006 by
Hamilton Books
4501 Forbes Boulevard
Suite 200
Lanham, Maryland 20706
Hamilton Books Acquisitions Department (301) 459-3366

PO Box 317
Oxford
OX2 9RU, UK

Library of Congress Control Number: 2006923845
ISBN-13: 978-0-7618-3475-5 (paperback : alk. paper)
ISBN-10: 0-7618-3475-3 (paperback : alk. paper)

Dedicated
To
my wife, Jean
And
my daughter, Evelin

Contents

List of Tables

Preface

This book serves two purposes. Part I, chiefly based on the French secondary literature, gives a succinct history of the two principal companies, the Compagnie des Indes Orientales (1664-1719) and the Compagnie des Indes (1719-1763). Each company largely monopolized French trade with the Orient. Although this historical account is mainly concerned with these two companies, its first chapter covers their precursors and the last records the aftermath.

Part II provides an economic analysis of the companies' import trade. It is primarily based on statistical data that I accumulated from many archives in France, including many municipal and departmental collections. The handbills issued by the companies listing the commodities available at their auction sales were particularly useful.

Acknowledgments

I wish to thank the University of Cincinnati for financial assistance in the preparation of the book. It gave me a sabbatical leave and its Louise Taft Semple Fund generously gave me travel funds.

I wish also to thank particular persons. Professors Thomas J. Zinn and Jeffrey A. Mills of the University of Cincinnati gave excellent statistical assistance. Monsieur René Estienne, archivist at the Service Historique de la Marine in Lorient, guided me through the gathering of the statistical data. The staffs at the Archives Nationales, the Bibliothèque Nationale and the British Library were very helpful. Ms. Cynthia Browne did most of the typing. Mrs. Geri Kirchner, Mrs. Susan Burns and Ms. Huda Kebede did the rest. All translations were done by the author with the help of Monsieur Robert Fogels. Susan Stites proofread the manuscript. The final preparations of the camera ready copy were done by John Wallrodt.

Most importantly, I must thank my wife, Jean Susorney Wellington, for her encouragement and bibliographic assistance.

Part One:

Brief History

Chapter 1
Beginnings of French Trade

The French East India companies were the creatures and later the creation of the French state. The honor goes to a prince of the Church, Armand Jean du Plessis, Cardinal Richelieu.

Armand Jean du Plessis de Richelieu was born in 1585. He entered the priesthood at an early age, initially devoting himself to clerical duties, but later became the political adviser, first to the queen mother, then to the king. He became the chief minister of Louis XIII in 1624 and remained in office until his death in 1642. He is more famous in political than economic history. His great accomplishments were the unification of the French state and the maintenance of German disunity. He accomplished the first through the suppression and destruction of a Protestant state-within-a-state in France, and he accomplished the second goal through the subsidization of the Protestant cause in Germany, thereby ruining the chance of a possible unification under the Habsburgs.

His achievements in the realm of economics were less noteworthy, less significant and less long lasting. They were not, however, unimportant. They did not involve any direct involvement in French trade with India. They were more crucial. They established a French naval power, without which a commerce could not survive against suppression at the hands of the armed might of foreign powers and their chartered companies.

The French saw outlets for their overseas trade being closed to them on all sides, while on the other hand foreigners, whether Dutch, Spanish or English (but especially the Dutch), had access to French ports, where they were establishing a commercial monopoly.

The French merchant fleet was not large enough to cope with France's maritime trade and was in no position to take risks in the absence of protection from the

King's navy. 'The navy was at that time so neglected that Your Majesty had not a single ship left.' The decadent condition of the navy, positively frightening in the case of a country which was bordered by the sea on three sides, was undoubtedly one of Richelieu's main anxieties when he assumed power (Tapie, 1975, 142).

As the *Testament politique* was to put it later: 'It is a prerequisite of our armed strength that the king should not only be strong by land but also powerful at sea.' Richelieu's attempt to put this policy into effect thus dates from as early as 1625: to secure the safety of those of his subjects who trade with the Levant and in order to uphold his reputation and dignity in the eyes of foreigners, the king is to have forty galleys available in French ports which are to be ready for action in summer and winter alike (Tapie, 1975, 150-151).

French attempts at trading with the East predate Richelieu by more than a century. The first recorded effort was launched in 1503 from Honfleur by Paulmier de Gonneville in a ship named the *Espoir*. The ship encountered a storm and only reached Brazil.

The next effort, in 1529, at least reached an Eastern destination. It consisted of two ships provided by Jean Ango, a merchant from Dieppe, and commanded by two brothers, Jean and Raoul Parmentier. The ships were the *Pensée* of two hundred tons and the *Sacre* of one hundred twenty tons. They put into Madagascar where some of the crew were massacred by natives, then sailed on to Sumatra where the two captains died of sickness. The disasters prevented the ships from voyaging on to their planned destination of China.

Although the sixteenth century expeditions were not successes, they at least aroused the interest of the French crown, and a number of royal proclamations in favor of the trade were declared in 1537, 1542 and 1578. The French religious wars inhibited any effective action by the government until the crowning of Henry IV brought an end to the warring.

Before the Crown acted, some merchants of Saint Malo, François Pyrard de Laval and Martin de Vitré, formed a company capitalized at 48,000 ecus on November 13, 1600. Its purpose was to trade with the Moluques and Japan. It equipped two ships, the *Croissant* commanded by Nicolas Frotet de la Bardelière and the *Corbin* commanded by François Grout du Clos-Neuf. The ships left Saint Malo with a crew of one hundred eighty men, and sailed in the company of three Dutch ships. One of the Dutch ships was commanded by a Frenchman whom the Dutch later executed for helping the French.

The route of the voyage became the commonly used one of sailing to the island of Saint Helena, then past the Cape of Good Hope and into the Indian Ocean. The French ships arrived on the west coast of Madagascar, which soon proved an unhealthy place where forty-one of the Frenchmen died. The *Corbin* was wrecked off the Maldive Islands during the summer, and the *Croissant* sailed on towards Sumatra where the French were granted an audience with the king of Achin. He gave them the right to trade, and some meager trading continued for five months. It yielded only a small cargo, valued at two million livres, for the *Croissant*. It sailed for France without its captain who had died on November 22, 1602. The ship almost reached France, but was leaking badly off Cap Finistere in Spain and was captured by Dutch ships on May 21, 1603.

The expedition was a failure: both ships lost, many soldiers died and the returning cargo confiscated by the enemy. Nevertheless, it gave French merchants, captains and sailors much information about shipping and commerce with the East, which was complemented with accounts by François Pyrard de Laval and François Martin de Vitré. The information later helped in the development of French navigation and trade with the East.

Soon afterwards, the French state intervened. Henri IV gave monopoly rights to a company on June 1, 1604. It was organized by a Flemish captain, Girard de Roy, and a French financier, Antoine Godefroy. Its right to a monopoly of trade in the Indian Ocean was to last for a period of fifteen years. It had the right to raise capital through stock subscription with the minimum subscription being three thousand livres. Brest was to be its port.

It accomplished nothing. Although it was permitted to buy ships and recruit sailors abroad, Dutch opposition inhibited its purchase of ships and recruitment of crews from the best source, which was Holland. It did not send a single successful expedition. One ship did sail in 1613, but its captain, who was an Englishman, surrendered his ship to the English.

The monopoly rights passed to a new company in July 2, 1615 when two merchants, Jacques Muisson and Ezéchiel Cahen from Rouen, founded the company later named Compagnie des Moluques. The letters patent gave the company the monopoly rights for twelve years dated as of the departure of the first ships. The company accomplished nothing in the way of dispatching its own ships, which meant that its monopoly rights did not go into effect. Its tentative attempts at organization may, however, have helped others to organize expeditions.

One expedition left in 1616. Its organizers were French and Flemish merchants, one of the latter being Pierre Brasseur who was residing in Saint Malo. The merchants from the Flemish town of Anvers were Jean Breughel, Georges Henriquès and Diego de Arthe. They advanced a loan of 455,691 livres. The rest was contributed by French merchants, Armel Martin de la Parisière, Le Fer, Briand la Choue and Jean Pépin. The sums were used to equip two ships, the *Saint Louis* commanded by Nicolas Frotet de la Bardelière and the *Saint Michel* commanded by Louis Hans de Decker.

The ships left in 1616, stopped for supplies on the way and reached the Cape of Good Hope within four months. They sailed to the Red Sea and the Persian Gulf before continuing to Ceylon where they parted company. The *Saint Michel* sailed for Achin on the island of Sumatra. Notwithstanding Dutch power in the East Indies, its captain purchased a cargo of pepper.

The *Saint Louis* sailed along the Coromandel coast, where it received a warm welcome from the ruler at Pondichéry, who allowed the French to store their goods in his fortress as well as giving the French permission to establish a post in Pondichéry. Cargoes of cotton cloth, gems and other goods were collected before the *Saint Louis* sailed to join the *Saint Michel*. They left their joint cargoes at Bantam while they sailed to the other islands in search of trade.

Disaster struck when the Dutch governor, Laurent Real, ordered an attack on the *Saint Michel*. His two ships, the *Bantam* and the *Nassau*, overpowered the French ship and captured it. The governor arrested the *Saint Michel's* captain and sixteen of its crew as Dutch deserters. More significantly for the French company, he confiscated the ship and its cargo valued at two million livres. He even confiscated the French officers' uniforms.

All attempts to revoke the confiscations through diplomatic means failed, and the *Saint Louis* had to return alone to France. Although only twenty-eight men out of an original crew of two hundred survived and disembarked at Saint Malo, the expedition did yield a cargo valued at a million and a half livres to the company. It consisted of pepper, indigo, cotton and silk cloth, and diamonds.

Besides its financial returns, the voyage highlighted the nature of the trade. It involved the ships stopping on route both to resupply provisions, and to sell goods and buy other goods for sale elsewhere. Ivory could be purchased on the coast of Guinea in Africa and on the Coromandel coast in India; cloth and precious stones in Surat; indigo and cloth on the Coromandel coast; cloth could be sold at Achin and the other East Indies islands where pepper could be purchased. In other words, some goods were used in an intra-Eastern trade, with the result of expediting the purchase of goods for shipment to France.

Success led to plans for even larger expeditions. A sum of six million livres was to be raised to acquire sixteen ships, with the plan being that eight ships would sail each year. Each set of eight ships were to include two smaller ones designed for the trade between India and the Indies, and six heavily gunned ships, equivalent to warships of the first rank, for service between France and the East.

Raising the necessary funds proved difficult. Nor was the company's capital plant in ships much in existence. Its remaining ship, the *Saint Louis* burned in a fire in the port of Saint Malo, and the *Saint Michel* was lost. The company did get some compensation for it, but the sum amounted to only five hundred fifty thousand livres.

The next expedition left Honfleur in 1619 and consisted of three ships, the *Montmorency*, the *Espérance* and the *Hermitage*. They were commanded by Augustin de Beaulieu and carried a crew of two hundred seventy-three men. The ships coasted leisurely along Africa and Madagascar, making geographic, geological and ethnographic observations on the way. In Madagascar, treaties were made to allow the French to buy land. In Sumatra, the French were well received by the king of Achin, but the Dutch counteracted. They burned the *Espérance* in the port of Batavia, and its captain died in the fire. The *Hermitage* sailed among the Indies and the Philippines, and picked up a cargo valued at about one million livres. It and its cargo were seized by the Dutch. Only the *Montmorency*, carrying a cargo and Beaulieu, left for France in February 1622.

The mostly abortive expeditions clearly revealed that a rich trade was possible, and its pattern would fall into quite a well-ordered format. Outgoing ships would stop along the coast of Africa to re-supply and pick up some cargo such as ivory. The ships would proceed to Surat where cloth and precious stones were bought, then stop at the Coromandel coast to purchase indigo and additional cloth before sailing to the East Indies where the cargo of goods and specie would be sold and a variety of products purchased for return to France. The most important purchase was pepper, but other goods included nutmeg, cloves, diamonds, pearls, perfume, resin and silks (Roncière, 1913, 54-55).

The French colony in Madagascar was of little use in the trade. More significantly, force would be required to counter the depredations of the Dutch East India Company. At the moment, the French situation was mostly one of paper assets. Treaties with local rulers gave the right to set up trading posts in Madagascar and on the Persian Gulf. Territory for a fortified post had been ceded at Pondichéry. An alliance existed with the king of Achin in Sumatra.

Cardinal Richelieu came to the rescue. At the December meeting of the Assembly of Notables in 1626, he said that to succeed, it was necessary to set up a large company and oblige merchants to join it, giving them important privileges. Without it, each merchant would traffic on his own in mostly small ships so poorly equipped that they would be the prey of pirates and enemies. (Barbier, 1919, 7-8).

The groundwork for the realization of Richelieu's plans had been laid two years earlier in 1624 when the Dutch government had requested French support against the pretensions of the Habsburgs. Richelieu had agreed and negotiated an alliance sealed by the Treaty of Compiègne signed on July 20, 1624. The treaty provided that the Dutch stop creating obstacles to French trade and instead give assistance to French traders in both the East and West Indies. The French were to choose places for trade with complete freedom and security from Dutch attack, and could initiate joint sailings with the Dutch.

Richelieu endorsed the establishment of a company, to be named the Compagnie du Morbihan or Cent Associés, with a proposed capitalization of one million and six hundred thousand livres. It was to operate out of Brittany, but the Breton parlement refused to register the required edict, and Richelieu did not force the issue.

Nevertheless private traders from Dieppe sent out expeditions after the monopoly of the Compagnie des Moluques had lapsed in 1627. One expedition, led by Gilles Rézimont, left in 1633. It was quickly followed by subsequent expeditions. Their success led to a reconstitution of the monopoly, as of June 24, 1642, in the form of the Compagnie d'Orient. Its directors were Rézimont and Nicolas Rigault, and its charter was to last for ten years. Its objective was trade with Madagascar and its colonization. This island's land was considered fertile enough to grow the same spices controlled by the Dutch in the East Indies, and the colonists were to be settled on the land and proceed to raise the desired crops.

The company's first ship, the *Saint Louis*, sailed from Dieppe in March 1643. It was commanded by Captain Coquet, and carried a small band of a dozen colonists under the direction of two company agents, Jacques Pronis and Jean de Foucquembourg. The ship reached the island of Bourbon, which Pronis claimed in the name of the king of France, and passed on to Madagascar where the crew found a dozen French sailors at Sainte-Luce bay. Unfortunately, the ship ran aground and its captain perished.

A second ship, the *Saint Laurent* commanded by Rézimont, left Dieppe in November 1643 and arrived in Madagascar in May 1644. It brought seventy more colonists who found that a third of the French settlement had died in the unhealthy climate at Sainte-Luce bay. Pronis decided to move the colony southward, and established the new base, called Fort Dauphin on the southeast coast. In September, the colony was reinforced with ninety men, who arrived on the third ship, the *Royal*.

The ships were loaded with return cargoes of ebony and hides. The *Saint Laurent* sailed in 1645 and the *Royal* in 1646, the latter carrying Foucquembourg who was murdered and robbed of some gems while travelling to Paris. Nor did events go well in Madagascar. The colonists revolted against Pronis and put him in chains from which he was only freed and restored to command when the *Saint Laurent* returned in July 1646. Once again in command, Pronis made the unfortunate decision to accede to the request of the Dutch governor of the island of Maurice and sell a hundred native slaves to him. The result was to further arouse general hostility among the natives to the French colony.

The *Saint Laurent* took another cargo of ebony and hides to France and later returned in 1648 carrying a new governor. He was Etienne de Flacourt who was one of the large shareholders in the company. He found the colony in dire straits: little food supplies and surrounded by hostile natives who had killed five colonists. A large body of colonists had abandoned their posts, and trekked across the island to the western coast where they found an English ship that took them back to Europe.

Flacourt resolutely took charge. He had the colonists plant rice, methodically explored the surrounding countryside for suitable goods for export, tried to inveigle the return of colonists who had gone to Bourbon, which may have been a wise decision considering that Flacourt had reported to the company that the island had fertile land. His efforts brought some fruition in that the *Saint Laurent* returned to France laden with a more varied cargo including sandalwood and gum.

In the longer term, however, the enterprise came to naught. No ships were sent during the next four years, and the colonists languished with a dwindling complement of European-made provisions. At the end of 1653, Flacourt gave up hope, left command of the post to an assistant, Antoine Couillard, and sailed away in a small bark with a few colonists in the hope of reaching France. Contrary winds, however, drove them back to port. His next recourse was to send a message to Saint Augustin bay where a Dutch ship happened to be lying at port and took the message with it to Europe.

Letters did not help. The Compagnie d'Orient was in no position to give assistance because its finances were in desperate straits. It had borne large expenses in the efforts of colonization while the value of return cargoes had been too small. Nor could it obtain government support. Cardinal Mazarin did look upon its efforts with favor, but he was too occupied with the revolt of the Fronde to subsidize the company.

The colony did, however, receive succor from another source when two ships, the *Saint Georges* and the *Ours*, arrived in July 1654. The ships were commanded by La Forest des Royers, and one ship carried Pronis. They had been sent by the duc de la Meilleraye who was a marshall of France and governor of Nantes. He had received permission from the Crown to send the two ships into the Indian Ocean and Red Sea.

Flacourt was unsure of his situation. He was an officer of the company, and yet now was expected to submit to another authority. He decided to return to France and left Pronis in charge of the colony. On arrival in France, he found that the company's charter had been renewed for another fifteen years. The company had not been taken over by Charles de la Porte, the duc de la Meilleraye, but he had royal permission for his own enterprise, the Compagnie de la Meilleraye, to infringe on the company's monopoly. In 1655, Meilleraye sent a small fleet of four ships, the *Duchesse*, the *Maréchale*, the *Grande Armand* and a smaller ship. The fleet reached Fort Dauphin, but sickness had decimated its crew and it could provide little assistance to the colony. Meilleraye's next effort was a ship that sank in a storm at port. He did not give up hope, and another ship reached Madagascar and safely returned.

In the meantime, the company renewed its efforts. Its ship, the *Vierge*, left Dieppe in May 1660 and reached Fort Dauphin. Flacourt took passage on its return, but the ship was attacked by Barbary pirates off Lisbon, burned and exploded with the loss of Flacourt. The company's disaster led to its complete inactivity, whereas Meilleraye continued to send out ships until his death in 1663. The ships' destinations were, however, India. Only in 1663 did one ship stop at Fort Dauphin.

The entire French enterprise, from 1604 to 1663, proved to be largely an abortive effort to establish a colony in Madagascar. Its purpose was to grow and raise crops rather than trade with the natives. Although nearly five hundred colonists were sent by the company and Meilleraye, only one hundred remained in 1665. Their circumstances were miserable. They were surrounded by hostile natives, and their farming raised little for subsistence or export.

Nevertheless, the Crown had a rosy picture of the economic prospects of Madagascar. Its location was considered a good stopping-off point on the voyage to the East and its land was evaluated as good and fertile enough to yield crops and provisions. If these estimations had been valid, a French colony on the island could have come to serve a good entrepôt for the Eastern trade: the French ships could have used it to reprovision and possibly obtain additional cargo for either direct shipment to France or trade elsewhere in the East for goods in demand in France (Froidevaux, 1905, 81-85).

Chapter 2
Company Organization

The French state acted by establishing a new company, la Compagnie Royale des Indes Orientales. It was founded in 1664 under the aegis of Colbert, the great minister of Louis XIV and the most famous practicing mercantilist in history.

Jean Baptist Colbert was born in Reims on August 29, 1619. Although his father was a cloth merchant, the son entered government service rather than following a career in business. His youth was devoted to the service of Cardinal Mazarin, the de facto regent of France during the minority of Louis XIV. He remained loyal to his patron and the Crown during the Fronde uprising between 1648 and 1653 when he worked diligently to restore the royal authority. After the death of his patron, he was appointed to a series of important posts in the royal administration before becoming intendant of finances in 1661, and secretary of state and minister of the marine in 1669. His position in government allowed him to ceaselessly pursue mercantilist policies to encourage and direct the French economy. He worked to unify and codify French law, impose strict regulations and controls over commerce and industry, protect them with tariffs on imports, establish royal manufactories of carpets, glass and textiles, recruit and subsidize the immigration of foreign skilled labor into France. He was particularly concerned about stimulating the expansion of French shipping and shipbuilding, the founding of chartered companies for foreign trade being one means to accomplishing that end. The Compagnie Royale des Indes Orientales was one such company. Its purpose was to replace foreign intermediaries in the trade between France and India.

He prepared the grounds for the establishment of the company with a public relations campaign that included a fifty-seven-paged brochure, entitled, *Discours d'un fidèle sujet du Roi touchant l'établissement d'une Compagnie française pour le commerce des Indes Orientales, adressé à tous les Français*, prepared by François Charpentier, who was one of his proteges and an academician pensioned by the Crown. It was published in April 1664 and outlined the benefits and advantages to France of the prospective company, the extent of its operations, and its formal organization and structure. The brochure enthusiastically highlighted the Crown's support and encouragement for the establishment of the company.

The French merchant community was not greatly impressed with the company's prospects, largely because they had observed the lack of success of the defunct Compagnie de la Meilleraye. Nevertheless, the founding meetings, held in Paris between May 21 and May 28, 1664, brought together a large contingent of rich merchants, influential officials and aristocratic courtiers. They set out the company's articles of incorporation which were presented to the assembled dignitaries and received their consent before being presented to the king at a royal audience on May 29, 1664 at the palace at Fontainebleau. The king made annotations on the document before returning it on May 31.

An organizational conference followed on June 5. The assembly included more than 300 men. They nominated twelve provisional syndics who were to act as directors of the company. The principal task was to set up the company in accordance with the articles of incorporation. One primary problem was the Compagnie d'Orient, which had trading rights extending until 1667. It wanted an indemnity of 90,000 livres, but accepted 20,000 livres worth of shares in the new company. The duc de Mazarin subscribed 100,000 livres less the value of the cannons, munitions and effects at Madagascar.

The company's charter was registered by the parlement of Paris on September 1, by the Cour des Comptes on September 11, and the Cour des Aides on September 12, 1664. It officially set out the rights and obligations of the company. It consisted of forty articles and conditions. An early English translation reads (British Library, London: I/1/1, Part 1):

Articles and Conditions

Whereupon the Trading Merchants of this Kingdom do most humbly beseech your Majesty to grant them his Declaration, and the Graces therein contained, for the Establishment of a Company for the Commerce of the East Indies.

1. First, that his Majesties Subjects of what quality or condition soever shall be taken into the company for the sums they please, without loss either of nobility or privilege, his Majesty granting them in that particular his royal dispensation: provided, that under a thousand livres no share shall be admitted: nor any augmentations under five hundred; for the sale of accompts, divisions, and sales of actions; a third part whereof shall be paid down presently, and go to the furnishing of the first expedition; and the two other thirds within two years after, by equal portions, under pain of losing what is already advanced, to any man that shall fail of paying in his full proportion within the said time: the money so forfeited remaining to the benefit and stock of company.

2. That all strangers (be they the subjects of what prince or state soever) shall have free admittance into the said company, and such of them as shall have twenty thousand livres in stock, shall be reputed as natives, without and further need of

naturalizing, by which means their kindred, though strangers too, shall have a right of inheritance to what effects they shall be possessed of in this kingdom.

3. That no part or portion belonging to any particulars in the said company, of what nation soever, shall be either seized by the king, or confiscated to his profit, even though they be subjects of some prince, or state, in open hostility against his majesty.

4. That the directors of the said company, shall not be molested either in their persons, or estates, for, or concerning the affairs of the said company: nor shall the estate of the said company be liable either to be made over, or seized upon the accompt of any debt due to his majesty from any of the particular members thereof.

5. That such officers as shall have 20,000 livres in the said company shall be dispensed their residence, to which otherwise they are obliged by his Majesties declaration of december last, at the treasury-offices, and other places of their establishment: enjoying all their rights, allowances, and fees, as if they were present.

6. That all such as shall have to the sum of 8000 livres in the said company, shall enjoy the privilege of burgers in the towns where they live; unless Paris, Bordeaux, and Bayonne: in which places they shall not acquire their freedom, unless they have the interest of at least twenty thousand livres in the said company.

7. That all such as shall be willing to enter into the said company, shall be obliged to declare themselves within six months to commence from the reading, and registering of the declaration in the Parlement of Paris: after which time no more shall be admitted. And they that shall have furnished their parts, and declared themselves accordingly, shall have liberty within three months after the registering of the said declaration to nominate, and establish on moyety of the directors of Paris for the Chamber-General of the said company, and the rest shall be named within the aforesaid term of six months.

8. That there be established a chamber of Direction-general of the affairs of the said company in the town of Paris only, to consist of one and twenty directors, and no more: twelve whereof to be of Paris, and the other nine, of the provinces; to be named, and chosen: that is, the twelve by persons concerned in the town of Paris, and the other nine, by the interested persons in the said provinces, every one in his division; for every town or province shall have a right of nomination, which shall be ordered by the chamber of direction-general after the settlement of it, in proportion to the stock that every town shall have brought into the said company, or otherwise, as shall be thought convenient; and for the future, the elections shall be always made after this manner.

9. In the meantime, till the said company shall be established as aforesaid; for the first time, the said nine directors for the provinces shall be chosen, and named by the interested parties in the said towns and provinces respectively; (but provided, that it may not be drawn into consequence for the time to some other.) That is to say, one from each of the towns of Rouen, Nantes, St. Malo, Rochelle, Bordeaux, Marseilles, Tours, Lyons and Dunkerque, or such other towns of the kingdom, as shall have the most considerable interest in the company. And in case, that any of the said towns shall be found without some interested person in it, there shall be two named out of such other town, as shall be chosen by the six directors named for Paris: And it shall be lawful for the parties interested in each of the said towns

respectively, to name their cashier of the town of Paris; who shall be named for the first time by the said six directors of Paris, and so to continue till the Chamber-General shall be established.

10. That none shall be capable of being directors, but merchants trading, and without office, except such of the King's secretaries as have dealt formerly in commerce: Only it shall be lawful to admit two burgers into the number of the directors, although they have never meddled with traffique: Provided, that they be persons that have no offices, and that no more be taken into the said chamber upon any ground whatsoever; the company being perpetually to consist at the least of three fourths of negotiating merchants, and without offices: Neither shall any man have a vote in the election of the directors, unless he has at least ten thousand livres in the company: Nor be chosen a director for Paris without twenty thousand livres at least; nor for the provinces under ten thousand livres; all in the interest of the said company.

11. That it shall be lawful for the chamber of direction general to constitute chambers of particular direction, in such numbers and places as they find most agreeable to the interest and benefit of the said company; and likewise to regulate the number of the directors of the said particular chambers.

12. That the accompts of the chambers of direction particular of the provinces, shall be sent from six months to six months, to the chamber of direction general at Paris; where the accompt-books shall be viewed, examined, and stated, and the profits afterward divided by the said chamber of direction general, as they shall think meet.

13. That the said chamber of direction general, and particular, shall name such officers as shall be found necessary for keeping the cash, books, and papers of accompts, for buying and selling; for taking care of all provisions, and equitage, paying of wages, and other ordinary expenses, every man in his proper place.

14. That the first directors, shall continue in power for the first seven years, after which time there shall be two changed every year at Paris, and one in the other chambers; and the first, second, third, fourth, and fifth changes of those that go out, shall be made by lot: and in case of death of any of the directors, within the first seven years, the other directors shall have power to fill the vacancy with a new choice, and it shall be permitted to chuse the same director again, after six years respite from the execution of his office: nor shall it be lawful for father and son, or son-in-law; nor for brothers and brothers-in-law to be directors at the same time; and his Majesty shall be further supplicated to confer upon the said directors certain titles of honour and privileges, that may descend to their posterity.

15. That the directors of the said chambers general and particular, shall reside by turns, each man his month, to begin with the antientest, in each of them severally.

16. That the said chamber of general direction shall be empowered to make statutes, and rules for the benefit and advantage of the said company, which in case of need shall be most humbly preferred to his Majesty, for the obtaining of his royal commission.

17. That the said chamber shall make a general accompt every six years, of the estate of the said company, and no man shall be suffered to withdraw himself, unless by the sale of his action to some one or other of the said company, who shall always uphold and maintain the same right, so that the stock be not diminished.

18. That his Majesty will grant to the said company (to the exclusion of all other his subjects) the sole power and faculty of traffique and navigation from the Cape of Good Hope throughout all India, and the Eastern Seas: Nay even from the Straight of Magellan, and the Maire throughout the Southern Sea, for the term of fifty years, to begin from the setting out of the first shipping from this Kingdom; during which time his Majesty shall be desired expressly to inhibit all other persons from entering upon the said voyage, and commerce; under pain of forfeiting all their vessels, arms, munitions, an merchandise, to be applied to the profit of the said company. To which company, his Majesty shall grant license to send gold and silver as much as shall be thought needful, both into the Isle of Madagascar, and the East-Indies, and other places of the said commerce, all laws and ordinances to the company notwithstanding.

19. That his Majesty shall be likewise requested to grant unto the said company, the propriety, and the lordship of all those lands, places, and Isles, which they shall either gain from the enemies of his Majesty, or otherwise make themselves masters of whether as abandoned, uninhabited, or in the possession of barbarians.

20. That his Majesty shall comprehend in the said concession, the propriety of the Isle of Madagascar, or Saint Laurence, with the neighbouring islands, forts, habitations, and colonies belonging unto any of his subjects: concerning which, his Majesty shall be most humbly desired to permit the company to come to a fair treaty, with those who may have formerly obtained the Grant thereof from his Majesty; or if not, that commissioners may be appointed for the examination of the interest of all parties there in concerned for the indemnification of the proprietors, that the company may quietly enjoy the fame.

21. That the propriety of the said Isles and things belonging to the said company, may remain unto them after the expiration of the grant, to dispose of according to their own pleasure and as their proper inheritance.

22. That his Majesty shall vouchsafe to give and grant to the said company, over and above the jurisdictions annexed to the seignory and propriety heretofore granted, for the said Isle of Madagascar and others round about it, full power and authority to establish judges for the exercise of sovereign justice, throughout the whole extent of the said countries, and such other as they shall subject to the obedience of his Majesty; even over the French themselves who shall there inhabit; provided, always, that the said company shall name to his Majesty the persons whom they shall chuse for the exercise of the said sovereign justice, who shall swear allegiance to his Majesty; and execute justice, and issue out all their orders and decrees in his Majesties name, even all privileges of justice and admiralty in matters concerning the sea affairs throughout the whole extension of the said countries. To which effect, his Majesty (if he pleases) shall empower and authorize them by patent, or commission under his great seal.

23. That for the execution of decrees, and for all Acts where his Majesty's seal shall be necessary, there shall be one established, and put into the hands of him that shall preside over, the said sovereign justice.

24. That the officers constituted for the said sovereign justice shall be authorized to constitute likewise such a number of subordinate officers, and in such places as they shall think meet, to be by them supplyed with commissions under the name and seal of his Majesty.

25. That for military command, the said company shall name to his Majesty a governor-general of the company, and of each other countries as shall be subdued; whom his Majesty shall be humbly desired to authorize with a commission, and to receive his oath of fidelity. And in case that the said company shall not be well satisfied with his conduct that they may be at liberty to name some other, to be likewise impowered by his Majesty.

26. That his Majesty will be pleased to grant to the said company the power and authority of settling garrisons in all the places before-mentioned and in such other as shall be conquered or built; consisting of what numbers the company shall think necessary: and therein to put arms, canon, and ammunition; and to cast guns and other arms in what place soever, and in what quantity soever they shall think needful; with his Majesties arms imprinted upon them, and underneath them the arms of the said company; which shall be authorized to provide for the safety of the said places as by them shall be thought expedient. The officers and commanders of the said places to be totally dependent, and put in or out at the pleasure of the said company; provided always, that they shall all swear allegiance to the King, and after that, take a particular oath to the said company, in consideration of traffique and commerce.

27. That his Majesty shall vouchsafe to authorize the said company to send ambassadors in his Majesties name to the Kings of India, and to treat with them, either upon peace or truce or even to declare war with them, and to do all other acts which shall be deemed by the company to be the advantage of the said commerce.

28. That the directors of the chamber-general and particular shall keep register-books of all the wages and salaries, which they shall give to their officers, servants, clerks, workmen, soldiers, and others, which books shall be good evidence in court, and serve for the decision of questions upon any demand or pretention against the said company.

29. That of all differences that shall arise upon what cause forever concerning the said company, betwixt two or more directors, or interested persons, and any one particular, touching the affairs of the said company, the circumstances and dependences shall be judged and determined by the consular justice to the exclusion of all others, whereof the sentence and judgments shall be executed sovereignly and without appeal, as far as 1500 livres; and in cases of a higher concern, the judgments and sentences shall be executed notwithstanding all oppositions and appeals whatsoever: the appeal to be brought before the ordinary judges that are properly to take cognizance of the matter: to which effect his Majesty shall be desired to establish the consulary justice before spoken of, in the town where it is not, and wheresoever else his Majesty shall find it necessary.

30. That all criminal matters wherein any of the said company shall be a party, whether as plaintiff or defendant, shall be determined by the ordinary judge, provided always that for no cause or pretext whatsoever, the criminal shall ever carry along with it the civil, which shall be still judged as is aforesaid.

31. That his Majesty shall have the goodness to promise to the said company protection and defense against all opposers, and by force of arms, to maintain them upon all occasions in the entire freedom of their commerce and navigation, and the fee them repaired in case of any injuries or affronts offered them. And in case further of any design against the said company, to appoint them such convoys both

forward and backward, at his proper charge and expense, as may be sufficient to secure the company not only over all the coasts of Europe and Africa, but even as far as India itself.

32. That his Majesty shall be pleased to advance at present out of his own coffers, a fifth part of the whole expense for the three first expeditions, so that so soon as ever the person authorized for receiving of the moneys shall be named by the company, his Majesty shall cause to be delivered into his hand three hundred thousand livres, and upon his receiving of four hundred thousand livres from the persons engaged, his Majesty shall cause to be delivered three hundred thousand more, and so forward to three fifths, for the first year, which comes to one fifth upon the whole; (his Majesty furnishing nothing at all for the two following years) by virtue of which advance his Majesty will give a foundation to the establishment of the said company, which will be of so great advantage to the state.

33. That his Majesty shall be graciously pleased to lend the said summe to the said company, without interest; and even without any participation in the said adventure, his Majesty contenting himself with the companies obligation of paying back the said summe without interest at the end of ten years, to reckon from the day whereupon the said company shall have perfected their first capital stock; and in case that at the end of the said ten years, it should appear by a general accompt then to be made, that the said company had lost of their capital, that the whole damage shall fall upon that summe which his Majesty shall have advanced. And his said Majesty shall be more humbly desired upon valuation of the estate of the company (to see whether they have gained or lost) not to reckon upon immovables, fortifications, canon, and ammunitions, and to content himself with such accompt as shall be stated by the company, without bringing them to any further reckoning before the chamber of accompts, or elsewhere.

34. That the merchandises that shall come from the Indies and be consumed in France, shall pay but half the duties charged upon them by his Majesties rates, for his rights of the five gross farms; which moyety shall be regulated at so much per cent. And for such commodities as shall be sent into foreign countries, or countries exempt from custom, whether by sea or land, they shall pay no duties at all, either in or out: and shall be deposited in their store-houses; as to the exemption of all duties; the valuation of commodities unknown, by the Chamber General, and the Regulation of the Rights upon them at three per cent. And in regard that the discharge of one half of the duties of Entry cannot be entered in a manner as is desired, for the reasons which have already appeared upon the debate, there shall be allowed instead thereof a certain sum upon the return of each vessel coming from the Indies, according to the regulation that shall be made thereupon any such; and where there are none, they laden with lead, and laid up, till they are to be taken away, which places an account of them shall be given to the persons interested, or to the clark of the said five gross farms, signed by one of the directors of the said company: And upon their removal elsewhere there shall be an obligation of bringing back within a certain time a receipt with proof that they are arrived: and as to merchandise unknown, and not as yet rated, they shall pay three per cent according to the valuation that shall be made of them by the chamber-general of the said company.

35. That wood, and other necessaries for the building of the ships of the said com-

pany shall be exempt from all the duties of entry; the vessels and merchandise free from the duties of the admiralty and wood; and the munitions of war, victuals, and other things necessary for victuallings and embarquing requisite for the said company, shall be free from all rights of in and out, during the term of the present privilege.

36. That his Majesty shall order the furnishing of the said company for their provisions and equipage with the quantity of a hundred measures of salt, or what other number the said company shall have occasion for, in the town of Havre de Grace, by the hand of the clark of the store of that town, and at the merchants price: provided always, that the company shall deal fairly in the business, without abusing the grant.

37. That his Majesty shall permit the said company to settle ecclesiasticks in the said Isles of Madagascar, and other places where they shall plant themselves, in such number and of such quality as the company shall judge convenient.

38. That his Majesty shall be most humbly desired not to grant any letters of protection, respit, evocation, or delay, to any that shall have bought the goods of the said company, or sold anything due to their use and service, that so the company may through condition to compel their debtors to make just compense according to the form and tenour of their obligations.

39. That his Majesty shall be most humbly desired, to vouchsafe that the Sieurs Pocquelin Père, Maillet Père, le Brun, de Faverolles, Cadeau, Samson, Simonet, Tabac, and Scot, merchants; may present these articles, and receive his pleasure thereupon: This establishment being of infinite advantage both to his Majesties Kingdom, and all his subjects, who shall redouble their vows and prayers for the long continuance of his Majesties health.

40. That his Majesty be most humbly desired, by the deputies above-named, to vouchsafe, that in case anything shall appear to be omitted in these present articles, they may be allowed to deliver memorials of them, to what persons he shall be pleased to appoint, to make report thereof to his Majesty, and to be made use of in his declaration, which shall be issued in consequence of this present petition. *Done and Resolved at the Assembly held by his Majesties Gracious Permission at the House of Monsieur Faverolles, Merchant at Paris, Tuesday, May 26, 1664.*

The most important right was the monopoly of the trade between France and the world between the Cape of Good Hope and the Strait of Magellan at the southern tip of South America. The trade was subject to French tariffs on imports which was set at three percent of value except for the importation of material required for construction and armament, which could be imported free of duty. The Crown paid a subsidy of fifty livres per ton on exports and seventy-five livres per ton on imports. No payment, other than tariff charges, were due the Crown. The only *quid pro quo* was that assistance be given to the proselytization of the Roman Catholic religion throughout the company's processions.

The company could acquire ownership of land, including extensive territories in which it would have powers of justice over both Frenchmen and natives. Ownership would also give rights to minerals beneath the surface of the land. The defense of trading posts came under company jurisdiction. It could garrison and fortify any posts. It could equip and arm ships for trading, and call upon the royal navy for assistance. It could nominate ambassadors in the name of the Crown to any other government, whether European or native, in the Far East. Service in the company was to be honored by the Crown. Artisans returning to France after eight years of service could be granted the title of master craftsman. Officials and officers were to receive letters of nobility.

The provisions regarding company finances were designed to enable it to conduct a profitable trade. Capitalization was set at fifteen million livres, divided into shares with a par value of one thousand livres each. The Crown immediately put up one fifth of the capital value by subscribing to three million livres worth of shares. It paid three hundred thousand livres down, the remainder was to be paid in installments of three hundred thousand livres contingent on the company raising paid-in capital amounting to four hundred thousand livres through the sale of shares to the public. The shareholders could be anyone. Aristocrats would not lose their rank through subscription to its stock or service in the company. The royal family was among the first subscribers. The queen mother, the queen and the dauphin each subscribed 60,000 livres. Leading courtiers and functionaries followed suit: the prince de Condé subscribed 30,000 livres, the prince de Conti inscribed 20,000 livres, Colbert gave 30,000 livres and chancellor Seguier promised 50,000 livres.

Colbert organized a governmental effort to promote the sale of company stock among the merchant communities throughout France. Instructions were issued to mayors of towns to set up meetings to announce the establishment of the company and proclaim the Crown's desire that merchants subscribe to the stock. Similar instructions were sent to the intendants governing the provinces of France.

The initial stock sale went well among the courtiers, but even they languished in making their payments on schedule. The response of the merchants in the port cities was not as enthusiastic as Colbert had hoped. It was even more tepid in the inland cities. As of April 1665, one million livres had been raised in Lyon; 550,000 livres in Rouen; 400,000 livres in Bordeaux; 200,000 livres in Nantes; 100,000 livres in Saint Malo; 150,000 livres in Tours; 100,000 livres in Rennes; 120,000 livres in Toulouse; 113,000 livres in Grenoble; 100,000 livres in Dijon; and smaller sums elsewhere (Weber, 1904, 132).

All private investors were to pay for their stock subscriptions in three yearly installments. In order for the company to receive full payment of the three million livres promised by the Crown, private investors had to pay in 3,600,000 livres. Then the company's paid in capital would have amounted to 6,600,000 livres, which would have been considerably below the target capitalization of fifteen million livres. Even that modest target was not attained. Investors did pay their first installments, but not their second and third. Total payments on the first installment totalled 2,468,396 livres, but payments on the second installment amounted to a lesser 704,333 livres, while the third installment brought in a paltry 24,000 livres. The company's paid up capital summed at 3,196,729 livres from private investors as of December 1666. By that time, the Crown had paid two million livres.

Notwithstanding the shakiness of the company's finances, plans went forward in establishing the company's organization. The company's chambre de direction générale was to have two types of directors. Twelve directors were to be elected by the Parisian stockholders and nine directors chosen by the chambres particulières in five other towns. They were Lyon, Rouen, Bordeaux, Nantes and Le Havre. The Lyonnais chambre chose three directors, the Rouen chambre chose two directors, and the remainder each selected one director to the chambre de direction générale.

In the interim between June 1664 and the selection of the directors, management was in the hands of the syndics chosen by the shareholders of eleven towns: Rouen, Nantes, LaRochelle, Saint Malo, Caen, Dieppe, Dunkerque, La Havre, Lyon, Marseille and Tours. The directors were to serve for periods of seven years, thereafter for staggered terms during the next five years so that eventually two would be replaced each year. A director could be re-elected. Only larger shareholders with at least six thousand livres worth of shares could belong to a chambre particulière and have the right to vote in the election of directors, who in turn had to be big shareholders with at least twenty thousand livres of stock. Directors were guaranteed against seizure of their personal property to meet the debts of the company. The Crown also guaranteed not to confiscate the shareholdings of foreign shareholders in the event of war, which was a provision that might help sales of shares to foreign buyers.

Each chambre particulière chose a cashier, a secretary and a bookkeeper, elected by the shareholders. The chambres had some degree of autonomy, and could perform the company's functions of making purchases and sales of goods, equipping, provisioning and crewing ships. Their accounts, however, had to be sent to the chambre de direction générale for verification. It incorporated such accounts into its annual preparation of the company's balance sheet.

The chambre de direction générale had three departments to handle company affairs. An internal affairs department kept the books and minutes of directors' deliberations; a provisions department made purchases, armed and built ships, and hired personnel; a sales department oversaw auctions of incoming cargoes and controlled the foreign posts.

On March 20, 1665, six months after the company's official registration, the shareholder assembly met at the palace of the Louvre under the chairmanship of Louis XIV. The syndics presented their accounts and elections were held to choose the directors. The twelve Parisian directors included Colbert who was also named the president of the company. The others were two aristocrats, sieur de Thou and sieur Louis Berryer de la Ferriere, who was also the councillor of state in the royal government. The other Parisian directors were the merchant Bachelier, the clothier Cadeau, Chanlatte, de Faye, the barber Herinx, the merchant Everard Jabach, the banker Langlois, the clothier Pocquelin, and Varennes. The nine directors from elsewhere in France were being elected by the chambres particulières.

The company was honored by the granting of a coat-of-arms. It was a round escutcheon set in a blue field full of golden fleurs de lys, enclosed in a palm and an olive branch meeting at the top and joined by another golden fleur de lys, and supported by two figures, one signifying peace and the other abundance. The coat-of-arms bore the following words: *florebo quocunque ferar.*

The one explicit obligation of the company was to establish the Roman Catholic religion in its possessions, which meant building churches and recruiting priests and other clergy. The company also had to transport colonists for free and grant land to settlers at reasonable terms. The Crown sought French emigration and granted many privileges to colonists: their children with native wives were to be considered French as long as they were Catholics, artisans received the title of master on their return to France after eight years of service. Otherwise, the French were subject to the company's laws and regulations while under its jurisdiction.

The company's articles had provided for the company's organization abroad. It was to receive possession of the island of Madagascar and could seek and obtain possession of other territories and towns in the East. Throughout its domain, it recognized the sovereignty of the Crown while having full powers of taxation and justice over all inhabitants whether French or not. It also was to possess the mineral rights in its territories. Its law courts were free and conformed to French law.

The company could appoint a governor-general to exercise overall supervision of its operations and possessions abroad. He was to have the title of lieutenant-general of the king, which was a high rank in the royal army. The first governor-general was François-Lopis, marquis de Mondevergue who held office from 1666 to 1670. The governor-general was assisted by a sovereign council of seven members who aided him in administrative and judicial matters: three members judged civil cases, and five judged criminal cases. The site of this overall authority was first at Fort Dauphin, then at Surat as of 1671 and later at Pondichéry from 1701 on. It directed the company's officialdom at headquarters and throughout the other posts where the officials were ordered in a hierarchy of merchants, submerchants and clerks who handled the commercial operations of buying goods for shipment home, warehousing them and loading the cargoes into returning ships.

The company could recruit soldiers, appoint officers, make cannons, and buy weapons and munitions for the army as well as possess warships, and crew and provision them. Its ships could capture enemy prizes in its waters and seize their cargoes. Besides its powers of waging war, the company had full diplomatic powers of sending ambassadors, in the name of the king, to local rulers and of concluding treaties of peace and alliance.

In its possessions abroad, the company appeared as a state-within-a-state under only token supervision by the Crown. The reality was different. In France, it
was only nominally a private organization with shareholder owners and elected
directorate. In fact, it was under the control of the Crown through the person of
Colbert. He immediately set the directorate to continuing the work of the syndics
on the four tasks: construction of ships, establishment of posts, selection of merchandise for trade, and recruitment of personnel. Orders for ships were placed
with shipbuilders in the French ports of Saint Malo, Havre and Rochelle, even
though Havre was to be the company's official port. Envoys were sent to the Shah
of Persia and the Grand Mogul in India in an effort to secure rights of trade. Purchases of the necessary material, armament and supplies began for a spring expedition in 1665. Most importantly, personnel were recruited and attempts made
to get experienced people, particularly those who had worked for the Dutch East
India Company. The luckiest selection was François Caron.

He had been born in Brussels early in the century of French parents. Before
the French ambassador, le comte d'Estrades, in Holland convinced him to join
Colbert's company, he had worked for twenty-two years for the Dutch East India
company in important capacities that had given him much experience in trading
in India. He proposed grand plans to his new employer: the spread of operations
beyond Surat into posts in Bengal and the Coromandel coast, and into the Dutch
preserve in the East Indies.

The weak link, however, in the company's visions were its finances. Its efforts
did not fully meet the hesitant confidence among the shareholders. By December
1665, the shareholders had paid in only 625,000 livres of the contracted second
installment of 2,726,000 livres.

Chapter 3
First Expeditions

From the very beginning, the company's ties with the Crown became its nemesis. The Crown wanted to secure a base on the island of Madagascar as a stepping stone in the plan to establish a French empire in the East. To this purpose, it envisaged that the Compagnie de la Meilleraye's post at Fort Dauphin on Madagascar would be taken over by the new company and strengthened.

A code was issued that set out the statutes, regulations and rules by which the company would organize its rule in Madagascar. It gave instructions regarding the conduct of French administrators towards the island's natives. In particular, it outlawed a slave trade (Cole, 1939, 1, 525).

The company began to arrange an expedition. It posted notices throughout France to recruit craftsmen and other colonists for the colony at Fort Dauphin. The notices listed the privileges that the Crown would give to the craftsmen. By the time the expedition left, a total of 518 men signed on as colonists, soldiers and sailors. The craftsmen included masons, carpenters and blacksmiths. The fleet consisted of four ships purchased at Havre, Rochelle and Saint Malo by the company. They were the *Saint Paul*, the *Taureau*, the *Vierge-de-Bon-Port*, each of around three to four hundred tonnage and the small *Aigle-Blanc* of between seventy to eighty tons. The cost of equipping the ships was about five hundred thousand livres.

The fleet left Brest on March 7, 1665, but did not sail in company. The fastest ship, the *Saint Paul*, sailed on ahead, and arrived at Fort Dauphin in July. The other two large ships, the *Taureau* and the *Vierge-de-Bon-Port*, arrived during the next month, while the smallest ship did not arrive until November.

They brought a very substantial contingent to strengthen a garrison of only sixty men who were having a bad time in just barely holding out against attacks from the natives. The resident commander, seigneur de Champmargou, was not pleased to hand over a command that he held in the name of old Compagnie de la Meilleraye.

Nevertheless he did, and a governing council was chosen. Sieur Pierre de Beausse was its president and Souche de Rennefort was its secretary. The other members were de Moutaubon, de Champmargou and four syndics. Although de Champmargou was the captain of the guard, he did not replace de Beausse who died at the age of seventy-seven in December 1665. The successor was de Moutaubon.

The council took an inventory of the existing assets at Fort Dauphin and re-assigned the reinforced garrison to its duties. It sent expeditions of reconnaissance into the interior, and ships into reconnoitering expeditions into neighboring waters. The latter was not particularly successful. The *Saint Paul* was supposed to explore the Red Sea and Persian Gulf, but got only as far as the northern tip of Madagascar before returning empty to France. The *Aigle-Blanc* sailed to the island of Bourbon. The *Taureau* wrecked on the coast of Madagascar. The council was more successful in collecting a return cargo of the products of Madagascar. It included leather, ebony, aloes, pepper, amber, tobacco and gold. The cargo was supposed to represent the outcome of the company's efforts at colonization. The cargo was loaded on to the *Vierge-de-Bon-Port* which set sail for France on February 20, 1666. Fate intervened. It was captured by English pirates just outside the port of Havre on July 6, 1666, and taken to England where its spoils were divided among the privateers and sold.

The expedition was a commercial failure. Nor was the colonization successful notwithstanding further provisioning which came in 1666 when a small expedition arrived. Its sole purpose was to supplement the colonies' supplies. Two ships, the *Saint Louis* and *Saint Jacques*, left Havre in July, 1665. The *Saint Louis* arrived in February 1666. Even with the additional provisions, the colony fell into sad straights during late 1666 and early 1667. Food supplies, largely from provisioning brought from France, fell to near famine conditions. The unabated hostility of the natives continued with the result that it was too dangerous for the colonists to embark on much hunting or farming. Nor had they the means of giving up and leaving for France. Only one of the French ships remained, and there were not enough officers remaining to command and navigate it.

Salvation came with the arrival of the second and larger expedition which the company's directors organized soon after their election to office. They asked the Crown to nominate the commander of the expedition. The choice was the marquis de Mondevergue who had been an army officer.

The expedition consisted of ten ships that had been purchased and built in France and Holland. The cost of the ships, the provisions, and the merchandise and specie for trade amounted to more than two million livres. The ships carried 1688 people, including the new governor Mondevergue, two directors François

Caron and François de Faye, and about a dozen other administrators and merchants. There were also four companies of soldiers and even some wives.

The convoy, escorted by four warships out of European waters, sailed from Rochelle on March 16, 1666. It picked up another ship, loaded with wine, in the Canaries. Because one ship was leaking water, the fleet took a long detour to Brazil where they lay in port for three months repairing the ship and seeking provisions. The provisioning was not a success. Their cost in Brazil was too high for the provisioning to be adequate. The detour and long lay-over meant the journey took one year from departure in France to arrival at Fort Dauphin.

Although many of the relieving force were weakened by poor food and sickness, they found the garrison in even worse straits. Mondevergue set his force to work at reviving the colony: the starving garrison was fed and brought back to health, the wooden palisades of the fort were replaced with stone walls, a quay with a stone roadway was built, outlying posts were strengthened and peace treaties were negotiated with the natives. Unfortunately, his efforts were not fully appreciated at home. Two ships of the first expedition stopped at Fort Dauphin on the way back from Surat to France, and their officers gave alarming reports to Colbert about the conditions at the fort. Nevertheless, he waited for further news before taking any actions.

In the meantime, François Caron was actively pursuing company interests. He took three ships to India. They left Madagascar on October 27, 1667 and landed at the Dutch post of Cochin before proceeding to Surat where they arrived in February 13, 1668. While in India, he succeeded in establishing posts at Vizapur, Balpatam and Masulipatam, and staffing them with company merchants and submerchants. He sent ships to the Persian Gulf where they obtained cargoes of sugar and textiles. While in India, he traded and purchased goods, and collected and loaded them for a good return cargo to France. Although Caron's mercantile efforts were a success, his mission was marred by conflict with his assistant, the Persian merchant named Marcara Avranchinz. Caron had him placed in leg irons on his ship bound for France and left him at Fort Dauphin during a short stop over.

The mission of Caron's fellow director, François de Faye, was less successful. Three ships under his command left Fort Dauphin on October 18, 1668, and arrived in Surat on March 15, 1669. The ships lost contact with each other in a storm and staggered into port in very poor condition. The commander died of dysentery soon after arrival. He and Caron had not been in agreement over shipping and trading plans.

On the whole, the French efforts were successful from the company's perspectives. A sizable fleet of French ships did come to anchor at Surat. They successfully sold and bought much merchandise, opened trading contacts with native merchants, and established trading posts in Persia and the Malabar and Coromandel coasts of southern India. The Crown, however, was not content: the colony in Madagascar was not thriving. It wreaked its disappointment on Mondevergue who was ordered home and arrested on his arrival in France on February 9, 1671. Before being convicted of the trumped-up charges, Mondevergue died in prison at Saumur. He was replaced as governor of Fort Dauphin by Blanquet de la Haye, who turned into an unmitigated disaster.

Chapter 4
Dutch Wars

Although the early expeditions had included warships, the company's operations were not much disrupted because the fighting did not directly involve France. Instead the second Dutch war was a conflict between Holland and England that lasted for two years, 1665-1667. Militarily, the Dutch won in a war that featured the stirring feat of the Dutch fleet, under Admiral de Ruyter, sailing up the Thames and destroying the English fleet at anchor off Chatham. Nevertheless, the Treaty of Breda of July 31, 1667 more favored the English.

French inaction had been due more to fate than intention. Louis XIV had been contemplating an attack on Holland as the opening move in his aspirations to dominate Europe. The moment was auspicious: Spain had been defeated and the Treaty of the Pyrenees in 1659 had ceded some Spanish strongholds in Flanders to France, and the Habsburgs were occupied in meeting the Turkish threat. Unfortunately, the Dutch war broke out prematurely for Louis XIV, and France was bound by treaty agreements to aid Holland. It did and declared war on England in January 1666, but remained inactive.

The French attack came elsewhere on May 24, 1667 when the French army, under Henri de la Tour d'Auvergne, vicomte de Turenne, invaded the Spanish Netherlands. The diplomatic excuse for the attack was that Louis XIV claimed the territory as the inheritance of wife, Maria Theresa who was the sole surviving descendant of Philip IV of Spain's first marriage. The invasion was a marked success: the French army quickly overran the southern half of the territory and captured many important cities including Lille. French successes, however, led to a diplomatic resolution between England and Holland. They mended fences and became allies, and joined with Sweden in forming the Triple Alliance designed to halt Louis XIV's aggressions. It did. The Treaty of Aix-la-Chapelle soon followed in May 1668. France was the main gainer in the treaty, although not to the extent that French government wished. France got some Flemish territory, including the city of Lille.

Aside from the risk of privateering, which forced its expeditions to sail in convoy, the company was not much harmed by the war. It was, however, indirectly affected. In the midst of the company's concerns over its trading expeditions, the Crown decided that the company needed its own ports as a convenient depot for its business. The port was to be at Lorient. Nothing much, aside from a little fishing village named Port Louis, existed there before it received the new name of Lorient and the infusion of much expenditure in the construction of facilities. The location was on the estuary of two rivers, the Scorff and Blavet, where the waters were deep and calm. The coasts had already been surveyed by a commission appointed by Colbert (Cole, 1939, 1, 507). It had recommended that an arsenal be built at the mouth of the Cherente River, but no action had been taken.

Work on the new project began in 1666. The land sites were deeded to the company in August upon being purchased from duc de Mazarin who had been a principal shareholder of the old Compagnie de la Meilleraye. Construction work began shortly afterwards and brought shipbuilding facilities into operation quickly enough for two small ships to be launched in 1667. A larger ship lay in the yards under construction.

Port facilities, to be named Port Louis, were scheduled for construction. It was to occupy a park facing the Scorff River with earthworks and wooden palisades on the other three sides enclosing a space designed for buildings for stores, workshops and houses for the chief officers. The construction and strengthening of the fortifications took some years to complete.

During the interim before readying its permanent base in Lorient, the company had stores and merchandise spread around at the ports of Havre, Saint Malo, Nantes and Bayonne. In total, they amounted to 600,000 livres in specie, 230,000 livres in merchandise, 473 millers weight of hemp, 100 anchors, 229 cannons, 72,560 aunes of cloth as well as many shipbuilding supplies. It had twelve ships built by 1667, when seven more were in the process of construction (Sottas, 1905, 34).

Ample supplies were required for trade, but their cost, when added to a yearly wage payment totaling 53,430 livres, gave the company a sizable deficit. Up to February 1666, the company's expenditure summed at 4,991,000 livres, whereas stockholders' payments on their subscriptions amounted to 3,196,730, leaving a deficit of 1,794,270 livres (Sottas, 1905, 33). The reason for the deficit was a stockholder revolt in paying their subscriptions at the prescribed times. They had good reason: no dividends had yet been paid.

The Crown came to the rescue in 1668 when it put down an additonal two million livres. The bailout did allay stockholders' fears, but additional concessions seemed expedient and stockholders were allowed to postpone on the second call until November 25, 1668 and on the third call to January 15, 1669. Unfortunately, the Crown's bounty was soon negated by the sad letters from Mondevergue requesting his replacement. More seriously, the treaty of Aix-la-Chapelle brought only a pause in French military aggression.

The groundwork for the next onslaught was carefully laid with the diplomatic success of the treaty of Dover in May 1670 which neutralized England and forestalled the possibility of a revival of the Triple Alliance. It was a secret treaty that provided for the payment of subsidies by Louis XIV to Charles II, thereby ensuring that England remained a French ally. French plans envisaged the Dutch possessions overseas being partitioned between France and England, and Holland becoming a French satellite with William of Orange, who was the son-in-law of Charles II, becoming the Stattholder as the leading political official in the Dutch republic. He had been kept out of the office through the machinations of rival factions in the Dutch republic led by the deWitt brothers. The flaw in the schemings lay in William's consent being only presumed.

In June 1672, a huge French army invaded Holland in what initially looked like a walk over. William of Orange, instead of collaborating with the French, organized a political coup that overthrew the deWitts and got himself installed as Stattholder. He led a defense that stopped the French outside of Amsterdam and left the French army marooned in a sea of flooded land when the Dutch opened the dikes and deluged the countryside.

English support of the French was minimal and consisted of a naval cooperation that featured the defeat of the Anglo-French fleet by the Dutch at the battle of Solebay. During the hostilities, English political opinion steadily veered towards sympathy for the Dutch, particularly as the consequences of a French domination of Holland became more apparent. The delta of the Rhine would have fallen under French control, and France could have emerged as a much more formidable naval power than had ever been posed by the Dutch. English naval support ceased by 1674, but Louis XIV at least retained English neutrality. Nevertheless his attack had been stalemated, and the war staggered on until ended by the Peace of Nijmegen in 1679. The peace became a series of treaties that gave some border extensions to France, but left Holland unconquered.

The war was a mishap for the company. Its involvement entailed a naval expedition of nine ships commanded by Jacob Blanquet de la Haye. It sailed from Rochefort on March 29, 1670 and arrived eight months later in Madagascar. De la Haye relieved Mondevergue of command and followed his predecessor's reconnoitering practices in that he sent two ships on a voyage exploring the African coast. Other policies, however, went into a drastic and disastrous reversal in that an attack was launched on the natives who responded with a general insurrection. Many French, including the commanding officer, La Caza, were killed in a ferocious struggle.

Having set off the hornet's nest in Madagascar, de la Haye left on a two-month cruise to the island of Bourbon, which he decided would make a better refuge for the French. He shipped all his force, except a small remaining contingent of forty men, to Bourbon. Soon afterwards, he sailed for Surat. He arrived on September 29, 1671 to find French affairs much better managed. François Caron had done yeoman work in organizing French trade. He had opened eight trading posts on the Malabar and Coromandel coasts, one of which later became memorable as the chief French fort and headquarters of Pondichéry. He had also led an expedition to Java in the Dutch East Indies. It had supplemented his efforts to accumulate commodities for a large return cargo to France.

The cargo, however, was not immediately shipped. Instead, de la Haye led his ships out of Surat and proceeded down the western coast of India with many stops before reaching its final destination in Ceylon. The plan was to conquer Ceylon and establish a French post in a better position to enter the spice trade. That objective, however, meant some fighting.

The French force consisted of thirty ships, which included four picked up on the way down the coast. It was met off Cape Comorin by a Dutch fleet of about the same size. De la Haye did not take the course of valor. He changed the route to a round-about one that brought the French to Trinquemale on March 22, 1672 after failing to seize the fort at Point de Galle. At Trinquemale, they did succeed in expelling the Dutch garrison that had been posted on each side of the bay, but did not follow up with a successful occupation. Instead de la Haye opened negotiations with the king of Ceylon for the establishment of a French post on the bay. Before the negotiations got far, a Dutch fleet, commanded by Admiral Ryckloff van Goens, arrived to sail back and forth, surveying the scene, in front of the entrance of the bay. A little isolated fighting came in time. De la Haye decided on abandonment without a fight because of widespread sickness among the troops and shortages of supplies in the ships. Upon his departure on July 9, 1672, the Dutch began cannonading the remaining French garrison left on the bay's posts, which led to the surrender of one hundred eleven remaining French soldiers.

The French fleet sailed to Tranquebar on the Coromandel coast where the crews were able to re-supply their ships. At this neutral Danish post, de la Haye found dispatches from France awaiting him. They told him the war with the Dutch had begun in Europe, and that François Caron was recalled to France.

Caron's successor was François Martin, who had been born in Paris in 1634 and worked for the Dutch East India Company before joining the French company at the time of its foundation. He had served as Caron's assistant since they came back to India. He soon negotiated a settlement with Sher Khan Lodi, the nawab of Bigapur, to cancel the ruler's debt to the French in return for obtaining possession of a region on the sea coast, near the mouth of the Jing River. The coast was low and sandy with lagoons, but the river's mouth gave access to a rich hinterland of fertile land cultivated by a sizeable population. It was Pondichéry, which became the most famous of the French posts.

In the meantime, a re-equipped French fleet proceeded to Saint Thome on a mission of revenge. The king of Golhonda had killed the native merchant dealing with the French and absconded with 27,000 rupees. The French assault came on July 25, 1672. Its success was, however, only temporary because the king immediately besieged them with an army of sixty-thousand men while a Dutch fleet later arrived in June 1673 to blockade from the sea. Martin led the garrison in a valiant defense that held the enemy at bay until the summer of 1674. By that time, the Dutch had landed enough troops to conduct a close besiegement of the fort. The native interception of supplies from the land and the Dutch interception from the sea made the French position untenable. Their capitulation on September 6, 1674 meant the loss of ships and munitions, but permitted the French garrison to march out and proceed as they willed. Martin led a body of sixty men to the newly purchased town of Pondichéry. Others went to Surat, and the Dutch repatriated the rest, but only through a long passage via Batavia and then Amsterdam that brought death through sickness to most of the prisoners.

The defeat at Saint Thome allowed the Dutch to close the French posts of Masulipatam and Balasor. The company's misfortunes did not particularly upset de la Haye whose fate was considerably more fortunate. He left India with two vessels, stopped first at the island of Bourbon and then at Fort Dauphin in Madagascar. He found the fort abandoned as the native insurrection had accomplished an evacuation of the French garrison, some to Mozambique and some to India. He proceeded to France and a hero's welcome from the Crown, which honored him with the appointment in the army of Lorraine. It was an ironical reward. His expedition had been a complete failure: his fleet annihilated, Saint Thome surrendered, and the colony at Madagascar abandoned. At least he was not responsible for a worst disaster for the company, which was the loss of its good servant, François Caron. The ship carrying him back to France was wrecked on entering the port of Lisbon, and he was drowned.

François Martin continued Caron's good work. He used the tax revenues coming from the district of Pondichéry to fortify the town, build warehouses and purchase stores and merchandise for trade. His efforts, however, could only partially revive the company's fortunes. The war had had severe repercussions on the company's trade. Annual expeditions had commenced two years before the war began, and continued during the war with all incoming and outgoing ships arriving safely in 1672 and 1673. Nevertheless, fear of privateering disrupted shipping and brought additional expenditures on the company. Coastal fortifications had to be strengthened and garrisons reinforced. Some of the expenditure was financed by the Crown, but the company also had to contribute.

The number of shippings declined, and the company met its reduced demand for ships by closing its workshops on the Manche and selling excess supplies to the Crown: 70,000 livres worth from the Manche and 43,000 livres worth from a sale at Le Havre. One very serious problem lay in organizing the company's annual auctions of merchandise. Although no cargoes were lost on the high seas, enemy privateering disrupting coastal shipping and hindered the consolidation for auction of cargoes arriving at various French ports.

Nor was everything in order in India. Caron had been replaced at Surat by three men, two of whom died within the year. The French defeats allowed the Dutch to shut down French posts. Surat remained the main French post although peace eventually restored Balasor and Masulipatam. Chandernagor on the Hooghly was founded and Pondichéry, thanks to Martin, was well-established. The expenses of founding and the trading difficulties had an unfortunate effect on the company's finances, including even a willingness to face facts. Although the company's articles specified annual shareholders' meetings, the second meeting came three years after the first meeting and the third meeting came only after a lapse of seven years. At neither meeting did the king preside over the gathering.

The balance sheet as of December 1668 shows that the Crown had paid its portion of 1,500,000 livres and that private shareholders had paid in a total of 6,207,239 livres. The funds had been used to finance constructions, stores, equipment and ships to a tune of 6,325,799 livres, which included 2,292,745 livres for ships, 500,000 livres spent on the colony of Madagascar, and 800,000 livres on the posts in India and the East. Remaining cash on hand amounted to less than a million livres (Sottas, 1905, 61).

The expenditures did permit trading. Between 1669 and 1675, fourteen ships sailed to India in ten organized expeditions. Eight ships returned to French ports with cargoes that were auctioned at 4,718,741 livres. The trading expeditions brought a return. Other expenditures could, at best, only have a pay-off in the future. In particular, the company's facilities at Lorient were expanded with warehouses for provisions and residences for officials so that the company's establishments at Havre could be closed down. The constructions also included a stone chapel and an enclosing wall on the land side. Neither added particularly to the company's trading potential.

At the height of the war, the company's trading became much diminished: only two ships were sent and two arrived from India in 1676. To some extent, the Crown came to the rescue in so far as paying for its use of company's docks, harbors and shipbuilding facilities. On the other hand, the compensation was not always equal to the full cost, including depreciation, of the use of company resources. Nor did the Crown reimburse the company for contributions to the abortive de la Haye expedition.

In 1675 , the company paid a dividend of ten percent on fully paid up shares and on shares of which at least eight thousand livres had been paid. It was the first since 1669, and amounted to a payment of 448,137 livres. The return was not high considering the degree of risk in the company's operations, and did not go far to boost shareholders' confidence in the company.

Although the war came to an end with the peace of Nijmegen, the company faced severe problems in restoring trade. Its shipping fleet had been decimated. One ship had been captured by Dutch privateers while eight had been sold, five in India and three in France. As a result, its fleet stood at nine based in Lorient, four in Havre, one in Rochefort and three in India as of the autumn of 1678.

Nevertheless, the company managed to round up cargoes for voyages in 1679 and smaller ones in 1680. The ships later returned with cargoes, although a particularly rich cargo of pepper was lost in a wreck on the return trip. The limited commercial successes were considerably negated by the Crown's failure to honor its obligations. It did not adequately compensate the company for the costs involved in de la Haye's expedition, the maintenance of the colony in Madagascar and the naval supplies at Lorient that had been provided to the royal navy. Nor did the Crown sufficiently pay the bounties, fifty livres per ton on exports and seventy five livres per ton on imports. That debt had accumulated to more than 350,000 livres by 1680 (Sottas, 1905, 70).

Chapter 5
Reorganization

An abridgement of the company's monopoly came with the Crown's proclamation on January 6, 1682 that private traders could infringe on the company's trade on condition that they shipped their goods on company ships, stored them in company warehouses and sold them at company auctions. They paid the company for these services, which meant the company was turning to a leasing out of its trading privileges. The free traders dealt mostly in diamonds, pearls and precious stones rather than bulk commodities. A number of such businesses set themselves up, one of them was run by Mathe de Vitry-la-Ville and Robert Pocquelin who were directors of the company. The concession was to last for five years, but it was extended at the time of the company's reorganization in 1685. The intruders are considered to have had some financial success although de Vitry-la-Ville retired from the business in 1686 (Sottas 1905, 72). The success was not shared by the company. Its shipping fleet had fallen to five ships by 1683, the payments from the free traders did not cover the actual costs of the services to them, and company's export cargoes were used to pay off creditors in India, rather than purchase returning cargoes.

A blow to the company came on September 6, 1683 when its great protector, Colbert, died. His son-in-law, the marquis de Seignelay succeeded him as minister of the Marine, while Le Pelletier succeeded as controller-general of finances. The marquis took an active interest in the company, and presided over a stockholders' meeting held on 1684, at which only shareholders holding stock amounting to more than 6,000 livres were permitted to attend. He presented a report that gave a balance sheet of 4.2 million livres in assets, of which 1.7 million were goods in inventory and in transit, and good debts. The rest was mainly bad debts and ships in bad, much depreciated state with an actual value that was probably much less than the recorded value.

At the shareholder meetings, some radical measures were taken. The Crown agreed to turn its loan of four million livres into a gift. Shareholders with unpaid balances were declared to have forfeited their investment. A stock buy-out, scheduled over two years without interest, was set up for shareholders who failed to pay up a quarter of their subscriptions. These measures did not succeed in restoring confidence even though four ships returned with cargoes that were sold at the autumn auction. Share prices continued to fall and reached a quarter of their par value.

At the final stockholder meeting in November, any remaining shareholders were required to deposit at least 8,000 livres or a quarter of their subscriptions with the company. The consequence was that the company's capitalization fell from 3.35 million to 839,491 livres, which actually became 729,000 livres after the company reimbursed shareholders who chose not to participate. Shortly afterwards in February 1685, the Crown declared that new shareholders could not attend stockholders' meetings if their shares amounted to less than 30,000 livres. The effect was to make the company into an enterprise controlled by a small coterie of large shareholders. The directorship was reduced to eleven men, each having shareholdings of at least 30,000 livres. They began to get paid stipends and were separated into three departments with administrative responsibilities. One set handled general administration, another kept the finances and the third dealt with trade and its related concerns of shipping and armament. The hope was that the reorganization, by putting the company in the charge of a few men, would bring more commercial success.

There was some discussion over requiring the company to attempt a reconquest of Madagascar. Fortunately that obligation was rescinded. Instead the company could attend to its main concern which was the trade that its monopoly gave with the East. At that time, the company's operations centered on four regions of India. Surat continued to be a large entrepôt where the European companies, including the French, had posts commissioned to purchase cotton goods, as well as a wide variety of goods shipped there from elsewhere in India and from the Persian Gulf and Ceylon. The cotton was purchased as raw cotton, cotton thread and cotton cloth. The favored textiles were calicos and muslins. The calicos could be bleached, colored or printed.

The Malabar coast was the source of pepper and the company had posts at Balapatam, Tellicheri and Rojapur. The Bengal posts of Chandernagor, Balasor and Cassimbazar tended to specialize in the purchase of silk goods, which included raw silk as well as finished cloths such as taffeta, damask, satin, gauze and velvet.

The principal French post had come to be Pondichéry on the Coromandel coast. It and its subsidiary post at Masulipatam handled primarily cotton goods, although Pondichéry was an entrepôt center for goods from Ceylon and other areas in southeast Asia. The two entrepôts, Pondichéry and Surat, were important sources for many goods: coffee, spices, indigo, dyes, drugs, saltpeter, hides, spices, perfume, lacquer and rare woods.

Although the hopes were not fully realized, trade did undergo a considerable expansion and fell into a rather regular routine. Ships left Lorient towards the end of winter in February and March, travelling around the Cape of Good Hope and then often split for the final destinations of either Surat or Pondichéry. Surat was the entrepôt for the trade with the Malabar coast, Persia, Arabia and the domain of the Grand Mogul in the Indian interior. Pondichéry handled the Coromandel coast and Bengal. The ships arrived in India in July or August with cargoes usually consisting of twice as much specie as French merchandise. The next six months were devoted to unloading and selling the French goods, and buying and loading return cargoes. The ships left India in January and February, returned by the same route and generally arrived back in Lorient in July and August. Their cargoes were transported and sorted for auction sales in September and October. The sales were held under the auspices of one or more of the directors from Paris. For a time, rented quarters in Rouen or Havre served as the venue for the sales. Then war drove the sales to Nantes, which intercoastal shipping from Lorient could reach more safely. In 1693, permanent quarters in Nantes were purchased and served thereafter as the place for the auctions. The sales usually produced prices at around double the cost of the merchandise in India.

The revival of company trade came with a major shift in its nature. The importation of cotton and silk textiles underwent a huge expansion. They were imported in both the bleached and printed states. They were subject to French tariffs, which meant they had to enter France through designated towns where offices for duty collection resided. The towns included Rouen, Havre, Dieppe, Calais, Rochelle, Nantes, Bordeaux, Bayonne, Lyon, Septemes, Narbonne, Dunkerque, Besancon, Metz, and Luxembourg (Sottas 1905, 91-92). Only Havre, Nantes and Rouen were near enough to be relevant since the regular port of debarkation was Lorient.

Unfortunately, the textile imports created a storm of political opposition within France from the French textile manufacturers whose business was being hurt by the foreign competition. In 1686, the Crown responded by interdicting imports of silk and colored cotton textiles. Only textiles were affected. No restrictions were put on imports other than textiles. The company complained about the quota restrictions and managed to convince the Crown to relax the prohibition in the beginning of 1687. It allowed the company to land textiles in transit to other countries and to import them into France if the annual total was not in excess of 150,000 livres of the prohibited textiles. The company reciprocated by agreeing to export a half million livres worth of French textiles. All other Indian textiles in inventory were to be destroyed under the penalty for non-compliance. The right to import for re-export was to lapse after March 1691. Sales of prohibited textiles in France were subject to confiscation of the merchandise and a fine of 3,000 livres, half to go to informers and half to the state.

Notwithstanding the infringements on the company trade, its expansion did permit, perhaps unwisely, the payment of dividends on stock. They amounted to annual dividend payments of 240,000 livres or ten percent on stock during each year between 1683 to 1692, with supplemental payments of twenty percent in 1687 and an additional ten percent in 1691. The total return for the entire period of ten years was 110% of the stock value.

The new policy of regular dividend payments may have been the result of the reorganization having concentrated ownership in the hands of the few. In 1685, eleven directors held about three quarters of the total value of 1.7 million livres. By 1687, twenty directors held about the same proportion, while the remainder was distributed among about a hundred other people. The dividend payments had, however, a more serious consequence. They were largely financed by company borrowings which reached a total of 10 million livres by 1701.

Two subsidiary expenses added to the financial drain on the company. One was a considerable enlargement of the facilities at the port of Lorient: stone buildings were constructed, warehouses enlarged, and stores and supplies accumulated. Although the improvements were useful to the company, they were an attraction to the royal navy, which increasingly imposed on the company's facilities with naval ships putting into port for repairs and supplies, and not always paying fair prices for the services. Even major expeditions proceeded partly from Lorient, including the landing in Ireland in the fruitless attempt to return James II to the English throne. Such ventures contributed nothing to the company's main business of the Eastern trade.

Another company operation was also eastern in nature, but became an even more fruitless adventure. It was an attempt to open up trade with the kingdom of Siam. The French connection with Siam had come much earlier in 1658 when three French missionaries travelled overland through Syria and Persia. One died on the way, but the other two reached Siam after a four-year trip. They obtained permission to set up a seminary and hospital. Other missionaries arrived during the following decade, and the suggestion was made that the company post of Surat send a trading mission. It did send three ships in 1679, which were well received and the Siamese agreed to send an embassy to Paris. The first embassy perished in a ship lost off the Cape of Good Hope, a second embassy arrived safely in Calais in 1685 and proceeded to Versailles where they were presented to the king.

A French expedition was soon organized. It had elements in common with contemporary academic junkets; the party included ten Jesuits, some of whom were mathematically trained and equipped with maps and instruments to study astronomy, take surveys and make maps. Their stipends were paid by the Crown, and the company supplied a cargo worth one hundred thousand livres. The two ships sailed from Brest and arrived safely in Siam in 1685. The cargo was sold, a treaty was signed that allowed the Jesuits to proselytize, and another Siamese embassy travelled back to France on the returning ships.

A larger French expedition came in the following year. It included five ships packed with forty Jesuits and twelve companies of infantry numbering more than six-hundred men. In accordance with treaty provisions, the French occupied and fortified positions at Bangkok and Merguy, and provided a guard for the king of Siam. In effect, Siam became a kind of French protectorate.

Business was done: the cargoes sold and returning cargoes purchased. On the return of the French ships in 1688, plans were laid for a third, and even larger, expedition. They were abortive. A palace revolution broke out during the last illness of the Siamese king. In the hostilities, the French agent and representative, Constance Phaulkon, was killed and the other side won. The French garrisons abandoned Bangkok and Merguy, and sailed for Pondichéry in early 1689. The French immediately launched counter- moves, and a small French expedition with three hundred soldiers returned in the same year, occupied the island of Jon-salam off Siam for a time, abandoned it shortly afterwards and sailed away. Thus ended a French connection that was not renewed until after a space of nearly two centuries.

Chapter 6
Failure at Hegemony

A much greater disaster for company trade came in July 1686 with the beginning of the War of the League of Augsburg. Peace had reigned for a decade in Europe, but it had been a troubled peace with the powers continually under tension from Louis XIV's threats. In reaction, Emperor Leopold formed an alliance, the League of Augsburg, for common defense with the Elector of Brandenburg and other German states. Although Holland was not a signatory, William of Orange strongly backed the League. In 1688, he took a step that greatly strengthened the diplomatic and military position of the League. He led an army into England, and successfully overthrew Louis' ally, James II, with the result that England was added to the support of the League. Spain and Sweden also joined the League.

Hostilities began in the autumn of 1688 when the French staged a march into Germany with raiding parties plundering as far south as Augsburg. Serious fighting, however, began in the winter of 1689 when the French army was ordered to lay waste to the Palatinate. Campaigns continued in Germany, the Netherlands and Savoy with the French winning some memorable victories of which the most famous was the battle of Fleurus in 1690. Nevertheless the war ended in stalemate with the Treaty of Ryswick in September 1697.

The war brought an immediate disaster to the company. Two ships, the *Coche* and the *Normandie*, were captured off the Cape of Good Hope by an Anglo-Dutch fleet. They carried rich cargoes, and their loss was valued at three million livres.

The succeeding expeditions were fleets of royal and company ships pursuing a mixture of commercial and military purposes, with the capture of prizes falling into both categories of objectives. The first such expedition of six ships, the *Oiseau*, the *Gaillard*, the *Florissant*, the *Ecueil*, the *Lion* and the *Dragon* was commanded by Abraham Duquesne. It left Lorient in early 1690, and returned in August 1691. Its military accomplishments were minor: it sank one English ship, captured one small Dutch ship and idly cannonaded Madras. It did, however, land cargo at Pondichéry and Balasor, and picked up a fairly large return cargo.

Before organizing another sizable expedition, the company sent a captured ship with a small cargo to Balasor. It landed its cargo, and became blockaded in harbor by a Dutch fleet. It soon had company. A French fleet of four ships, the *Fendant*, the *Florissant*, the *Lonray* and the *Ecueil*, left Lorient in January 1692, captured two English ships on route, and unloaded part of its cargo at Surat. One ship proceeded to Balasor, bypassing Pondichéry because a Dutch fleet was operating in those waters. It became blockaded, while the other ships returned, with long layovers in Brazil and Martinique which ruined their seaworthiness. Their relatively small cargoes were sold in a May auction.

Two other ships were sent in 1692. One's destination was supposed to have been Pondichéry, but found it in Dutch hands on arrival. The Dutch had besieged Pondichéry with a fleet of forty ships that landed a force of 3500 soldiers against a French garrison of two hundred men. The garrison surrendered in September 1693. The bypassing ship put in instead at Balasor where it promptly joined the other blockaded French ships. The other ship also never reached its destination. Instead of landing at Surat, it put into the Portuguese port of Goa in order to escape from pirates.

The next expedition was a complete failure. It consisted of three royal navy ships and three company ships. Their objective was to prey on Dutch and English shipping. Instead, they became the prey. The fleet left Lorient in March 1695 and arrived off the Malabar coast where it was joined by the ship idling at Goa. The fleet proceeded to Surat where two English and one Dutch ship were in port. No hostilities, however, occurred because the Grand Mogul, as overlord of Surat, enforced a strict neutrality between European powers. His governor wanted the French ships to convoy an Indian fleet to the Red Sea and protect it from pirates. On the French refusal to cooperate, he forbade the unloading of their cargoes. During the abortive negotiations, the French went on a cruise off the Malabar coast, encountered a Dutch fleet of seven ships, fought an engagement and scurried back to Surat. They were allowed to reprovision, but not to unload or pick up a return cargo. They returned, empty-handed, to France in March 1697, having neither sold an outgoing cargo nor purchased a return cargo. Their only accomplishment was the capture of a Spanish ship on their way home.

The French situation in 1697 was not good: Pondichéry had been captured, French ships were blockaded at Balasor and Surat, the French post at Cassimbazar was threatened by an Indian army and only escaped by paying a levy of 9000 livres. Worst of all, the business operation of dispatching and returning with cargoes began with some success, but ended in complete failure.

The Peace of Ryswick, signed in September 1697, rescued the company. In Europe, the peace merely restored the status quo. Louis XIV gave up all the conquests except Strasbourg and withdrew from the left bank of the Rhine. He recognized William of Orange as king of England and agreed to a prohibition on further aid to James II. The Dutch were permitted to garrison barrier forts in the Spanish Netherlands.

In India, the peace returned Pondichéry to French possession and released the blockaded French ships on the Ganges. Problems remained with the Grand Mogul who demanded compensation for losses to his subjects because of the conflicts between the European powers. A French embassy to his court managed to arrange a settlement.

The French posts reverted to Surat with sub-posts at Ponnoly and Calicut on the Malabar coast, Pondichéry on the Coromandel coast with sub posts at Masulipatam and Cabrigatnam, and three posts in Bengal at Chandernagor, Balasor and Cassimbazar. Attempts were made to restore their trade, but they were only partially successful. The settlement with the Grand Mogul permitted the ships at Surat to be loaded with Indian goods, but the ships on the Ganges had laid at anchor for so long that no efforts, except at the last moment, had been made to find cargoes.

Cargoes began being sent from France even before the peace. One small ship left in 1697 for Pondichéry, which it did not reach because it was captured and pillaged by English corsairs on route. Peace saw a bigger expedition in 1698 with two ships bound for Surat, two for Pondichéry and another for Surat with a stopover at the island of Bourbon to unload provisions and pick up specie. Only three of the ships returned in time for the autumn auction. The expeditions of 1699, 1700 and 1701 were similarly constituted: two ships for Surat and two for Pondichéry in each of the earlier voyages, and three for Pondichéry and Bengal in the later one.

There was a further expedition that had military rather than commercial purposes. Two company ships were assigned to a royal navy fleet of six ships commanded by the chevalier de Chateaumorant. The fleet sailed for India where it was supposed to suppress piracy in the waters around Siam. It captured no pirates, did not even see any, and returned to France leaving behind one damaged ship.

The Crown was an albatrose on the company in other ways. It did restore the company's shipbuilding facilities in Lorient, but kept the forests near Lorient and Brest that it had commandeered for masts and it was tardy and uncooperative in replenishing the stores and provisions that it had requisitioned.

The Crown, however, was not the main difficulty. Finances were the problem. The return cargoes had been so scanty that the company had little to sell at its auctions, and therefore lacked the means to send goods and specie in exchange for return cargoes of Indian goods. It turned to borrowing.

The company had lost its governor, the marquis de Seignelay in 1690, but his death led to the position passing to Louis Phélypeaux, comte du Pontchartrain. He lasted until 1693, when the governorship was transferred to his son Jerome Phélypeaux under whose auspices a stockholders' meeting was held in July 1697.

At the meeting, the decision was made to float a loan of 1,500,000 livres with the surety being the credit of the company directors and shareholders, which was a move that incited some of the wiser to resign their positions. The borrowing was to be used to finance commercial operations and pay off some of the indebtedness, which amounted to five million livres in 1697. Instead, the borrowing was used to service the interest payments on the company debt, and the commercial operations were financed by additional loans which brought the debt to a figure of ten million livres by 1701, in which year the borrowings were also used to pay out dividends.

The Crown tried to help. It reaffirmed the company's monopoly in 1701, raised the quota on its imports of Indian silk textiles and made a one-year, interest-free loan of 850,000 livres. Nevertheless the company's difficulties continued.

It shifted somewhat to the position of a lease holder of its monopoly powers by permitting interlopers to trade in its territories. It had already allowed prizes captured during war to be sold in competition with its own goods at its auctions, an action that did not help its own sales although it did receive a small commission on those items. That course had been a temporary measure. A more permanent infringement came with peace when rival companies were founded by merchants from Saint Malo. One was the Compagnie de la Chine founded by sieur Jourdan in 1698. Its charter was renewed for ten years in 1705 and its name changed to the Compagnie Royale de la Chine. Its main line of business was the Chinese pearl trade. The other company was the Compagnie de la Mer du Sud which was supposed to trade with the Pacific coast of South America, but in reality did little trading. Neither company directly operated in the trade with India. Each paid an annual indemnity to the Compagnie Royale des Indes Orientales.

The company was floundering: its auctions yielded modest sales, its commercial operations were being financed considerably by borrowing and its indebtedness was climbing. Disaster was looming and came to a head with the War of the Spanish Succession.

The war had been brewing for some time over the issue as to whether the Spanish and French thrones were to be combined to form a power bloc likely to dominate Europe. Philip IV of Spain had died in 1665, and his heir Charles II was a sickly four-year-old who was expected to die at any moment. He instead lasted thirty five more years, married twice, but had no children. Without a direct heir, the three claimants were Prince Joseph Ferdinand who was the son of the Elector of Bavaria, Duke Philip of Anjou who was the son of the French dauphin, and Archduke Charles who was the son of Emperor Leopold of Austria. Prince Joseph Ferdinand had the best claim, but he died in 1699. An intense diplomatic sparring ensued between the remaining two claimants. Either claimant could have joined the Spanish throne with a major power, but European fears were more directed against union with France than Austria as France was the stronger power.

The initial reaction of powers to the budding crisis was negotiations to partition the Spanish dominions, and a treaty between England, Holland and France did propose a partition mostly between the Bourbons and the Habsburgs. Charles II rejected the proposals just before his death on November 1, 1700. His will named Philip of Anjou as the heir of the entire Spanish empire, and Louis XIV announced the acceptance of Philip.

England, Holland and Austria responded with the treaty of the Hague, signed on September 7, 1701. Its goals were that Austria would obtain some of the Spanish possessions, while Dutch and English trade with Spain and its dominions would not be subject to discrimination. Louis XIV did not respond.

Nevertheless, France was not in a good diplomatic position. Each side had a slue of allies. France had Spain and Bavaria as allies, but Bavaria was a lesser power. Its enemies were England, Holland and Austria, which were major powers. The two sides began mobilizing in the spring of 1701 and fighting occurred in Italy, the Netherlands and Germany. England declared war in May 1702.

The war lasted for thirteen years and was a disaster for the French. Their armies suffered memorable defeats at Blenheim, Ramillies, Oudenarde and Malplaquet. A recurrent pattern unfolded of a French push, a French defeat, a French regrouping of its armies, another push, another defeat, another regrouping until Louis XIV finally gave up. Notwithstanding the French defeats, the Treaty of Utrecht in April 1713 left French power undiminished.

The principal accomplishment of the treaty was that Philip of Anjou renounced all claims to the French throne. Holland got some protection against further French invasions by establishing a line of barrier forts on its southern border with the Spanish Netherlands which were transferred to the Austrian crown. In substance, the Spanish dominions were somewhat partitioned and French-Spanish union denied.

The war was a fourteen-year disruption of French trade. In particular, the company drastically cut back its trading expeditions. Two ships left in 1702, one for Pondichéry and one for Bengal. None were sent for trading purposes in 1703. Instead, two company ships, under the command of marquis de Fontenay went on a raiding cruise that caught one English ship with a cargo valued at 400,000 livres. Another privateering venture came in 1704 when a fleet of two royal navy ships and two company ships, under the command of the baron de Pallieres, cruised in Indian waters and captured a small English ship off Surat, two Portuguese ships off Goa and one Dutch ship off Pondichéry. Their prizes, however, were small. No ships were dispatched in 1705, and the three in 1706 went to trade in Chile instead of India, although one returned via Pondichéry.

The company had better luck with the return cargoes. Five ships returned in 1702 and their cargoes sold for more than three million livres. The company's returns were boosted by the Crown renouncing the duties on a sizable quantity of silk imports. The Crown also released the company from its obligation to export a half million livres worth of French goods each year, which would have been an onerous task when outgoing shipping fell off so much.

The good luck ran out in 1703 when one of the returning ships was captured by the enemy off the Breton coast. The other four landed their cargoes but the goods could not be safely transhipped in French waters and the autumn auction was a small one. No further merchandise, other than prizes, came during the following years.

The commercial failure took a financial toll. The company continued its policy of borrowing to finance its expeditions, but faced increasing difficulty in raising the loans. The first wartime shareholders' meeting in early 1702 was marked with such disagreement over raising more capital that the Crown intervened and commandeered a forced loan from the stockholders. Each had to lend an amount equal to half of his shareholdings with the company recompensing him with billets paying eight percent annually and maturing in two years. The directors were somewhat more accommodating. They agreed to replace their salaries of 3,000 livres per year with a payment of 280 livres for each actual attendance at directors' meetings, which would not have reduced their compensation if they were conscientious in their attendance. They helped finance the 1702 expedition by lending more than 200,000 livres at an interest of seventy-five percent. Neither action may have been so helpful, and could be interpreted as an insider's milking of an increasingly defunct operation.

During the next years, the Crown tried to help by issuing a series of commands to shareholders to buy more shares. Few cooperated. The company turned to a radical recourse in 1706, when it embarked more actively on the policy of leasing out its trading privileges. The first contract to sieur Jourdan was not consummated due to the opposition of the Compagnie de la Chine. The next contract, with sieur Martin de la Chapelle of Saint Malo, was successfully negotiated and resulted in his leading two ships into the Persian Gulf and Red Sea where they picked up cargoes of coffee and captured four prizes. The disbursement of the prize money created a controversy among la Chapelle, the company, the Crown and the ship officers; it took a royal edict to settle.

The leasing business did in time settle into a routine. In 1708, contacts were arranged with the firm of Crozat and de la Landes-Magon and the firm of Crozat, de Beavois le Fir, Columbier-Cris and Chapdelaine. Each firm was based in Saint Malo. The first enterprise sent an expedition of three ships in 1708, and the other sent four ships in 1709. The contracts provided for commissions to be paid to the company that amounted to ten percent of incoming cargoes and five percent for prizes. The same provisions were followed in subsequent contracts and the company also continued to collect subsidies from the Crown for the export of French goods to the East. At least one expedition was made in each year of the following decade. The firms did lose some ships, but managed to obtain goods for sale either from returning cargoes or captured prizes.

Besides the leasing business, the company raised some money from the Crown which agreed to pay five thousand livres each year for the use of the company's port facilities at Lorient. The Crown also bought four ships, the *Bourbon*, the *Phélypeaux*, the *Aurore* and the *Princesse-de-Savoie* which were the best in the company's fleet and could serve as warships in the royal navy.

These measures did not, however, rescue the company from financial distress. The auction in 1702 had reduced the company's indebtedness from ten million livres to six million, but subsequent borrowings raised it. The problem, however, was not so much the level of indebtedness, but the inability to borrow more when its revenue from auctions fell so drastically. The consequence was that it could neither pay rent for its offices nor pay the salaries of its employees. Nor could it even pay for the shipment of its last returning cargo in 1709 to Nantes for auction.

By the end of the War of the Spanish Succession in 1713, the company was in trouble. Its presence in India had not been much affected by the war because little in the way of military action had occurred there. Surat had been replaced by Pondichéry as the leading French post, and Chandernagor and Masulipatam had grown in importance. The company's success in business was another matter. It had no ships, no cargoes for sale, and little business other than leasing out its monopoly privileges, which had been extended as of 1714 for another ten years.

Salvation did come. John Law suddenly burst into the French financial firmament.

Chapter 7
The Mississippi Scheme, 1718-1721

John Law of Lauriston was born in Edinburgh in 1671, and his father, a goldsmith, died in 1683. John remained in Scotland for his schooling, but left for London at the age of twenty-three.

He immediately launched on a life of a rake, which was financed out of his inheritance and gains from gambling. Pleasure, however, led to a scrape with the law. He was convicted of murder after having killed a man in a duel. Before he could be hanged, he escaped from prison and went to the continent where he travelled between Holland, France and Italy, stopping in various cities where he pursued his gambling pastimes. He is recorded as being successful enough to support a stylish life. (Murphy, 1997, 35-44).

In 1705, he returned to Scotland where he continued his gambling vocation albeit adding more serious endeavors in the form of proposals for banking reforms for Scotland. He wrote an essay in favor of a land bank that would issue bank notes and lend to landlords with their lands acting as collateral. His scheme was submitted to the Scottish parliament during the summer of 1705, but failed to be enacted. Years later, his book, *Money and Trade*, elaborated the argument, which underlaid the land bank plans, that the scarcity of specie put a crimp on the operation of the economy and the addition of bank notes to the money supply would stimulate the functioning of the economy.

A banking career in Scotland, however, turned abortive when the impending Act of Union between Scotland and England envisaged a combined legal jurisdiction that would have changed Law's legal status to a convicted murderer. He chose escape to the continent where he travelled for nine years in a fruitless search for some monarch or finance minister to act on his projects.

Finally he struck success in France where he settled in 1714. He had met Philippe, duc d'Orléans, who was the regent of France during the minority of

Louis XV. In conversations with the regent, Law recognized that his favorite ogre, an inadequate money supply, was not the only predicament facing France. It also had financial problems arising from the French government being deeply in debt at interest rates that were exceptionally high for those times. Subsequently, his scheme involved a linked solution for both issues. Nevertheless, Law's suggestions, as developed in his *Memoire sur les Banques* (1715), dealt more explicitly with monetary matters and recommended the establishment of a general bank issuing bank notes. His proposal was initially rejected at a meeting of Council of State in October 1715. Success came the next year when letters patent were granted to Law to establish a general bank. It was, however, to be a private bank and not the state bank that he wanted. It was to be capitalized at 6 million livres consisting of twelve hundred shares, and opened for business when subscriptions were complete. Law had three hundred shares, and the regent and his courtiers also subscribed.

The cash reserves of the bank were rather slight in relation to its note issue, which reached around one hundred fifty million livres by 1718. The stock subscriptions were paid one-fourth in specie and the rest in *billets d'état* which were government debts that were selling at a sixty percent discount at the time. Only one-quarter of the subscription was actually called up, with the result that the specie reserves were less than one-half million livres. Nevertheless, the bank was an instant success: its note issue increased sevenfold during 1716 and became a medium of exchange partly because the government ordered tax collectors to accept the bank notes in payment. The year ended with the bank paying a good dividend to its shareholders.

Although the expansion of the note issue continued during the next years, the focus of Law's concern shifted to debt management and he devised a way to reduce the government's debt burden. The vehicle was to be the Compagnie d'Occident which was founded in August 1717. The company had two objectives: 1) exchange its common stock for government debt through shareholders being required to sell the debts to the bank in return for its stock, and 2) develop the colonial trade. The objectives were intertwined. The anticipated profits from the colonial trade would provide the incentive for bondholders to buy the company's stock. The profit could, conceivably, become large because the field of the company's trading operations was to include the French possession of Louisiana, a vast expanse of the American interior drained by the Mississippi River and its tributaries. The company received a trading monopoly in the territory for a period of twenty-five years, and Law's dreams acquired an epithet in history: the Mississippi Scheme.

Law envisaged a sale of two hundred thousand shares at five hundred livres each. The first issue, however, was a considerable disappointment to Law. The subscriptions amounted to only about thirty million livres, of which approximately one-third came out of Law's own funds. That capital base was too small for the trading company to be much of an operation at its inception. His bank was also small: most of its note issue was regularly cancelled through redemption, and its specie reserve generally stood at about one-fourth of its note issue in circulation.

In December 1718, the government converted Law's bank into a royal bank with unlimited de facto powers to issue bank notes. It was allowed to establish branches in Amiens, Rochelle, Lyon, Orleans and Tours where the public was prohibited from using silver coins in large transactions. Only gold coin or bank notes could be used in transactions of more than 600 livres in value. The bank repaid the original shareholders in specie, while other subscriptions paid in *billets d'etat* were converted into shares in the Compagnie d'Occident. In that way, the capital base of the royal bank became part of the equity of the company.

Once the banking operation had been expanded to Law's aspirations, his attention shifted to the trading company. In May 1719, a royal edict merged the Compagnie des Indes Orientales and the Compagnie de la Chine and a little later, the Compagnie d' Afrique. The conglomerate was named the Compagnie des Indes. Although it acquired a monopoly of French foreign trade, its capitalization was too small for it to exploit its trading monopoly without the infusion of more capital. To meet the problem, the company was allowed to issue fifty thousand shares which could be purchased with *billets d'etat*. At the time, the share price was somewhat below five hundred livres and Law invested a substantial portion of his wealth in the shares in order to bring their price up to par.

Two further stock subscriptions were opened in June and August, but their purchase was restricted to the original shareholders. At the same time, Law's bank increased its note issue through loans that borrowers could use to buy shares. In late August, the French government agreed that the Compagnie des Indes would take over the tax farms which could become a lucrative source of revenue for the company. In return, the company agreed to lend to the government sums sufficient to pay off the indebtedness of the French state. Shortly afterwards, an additional stock issue was floated.

In October, Law reorganized the management of the Compagnie des Indes. It was divided into two main parts. One was to handle the mint and the trade with Louisiana, India, Senegal, Guinea and the Canadian fur trade, which involved the establishment of company agencies for buying and selling merchandise. The other part would run the tax farms that had been granted to Law's company.

The overall plan was that Law's bank would print bank notes that could be used to buy French government annuities from their holders among the public, and the erstwhile annuity holders would use the bank notes to buy the shares in Law's company. In this way, government debt would be converted into company shares and bank notes would come to constitute the bulk of the money supply.

Although the profits on the company's trading, tax and mint operations were seen as yielding sufficient profits that would incite the public to invest in Law's company, the initial success stemmed from the capital gains coming from rapid appreciation of share values. They rose from around 2500 livres per share in the summer to 10,000 livres at the end of the year (Murphy, 1997, 208) which is one of the most memorable stock market booms in history.

By 1720, France had shifted from a specie to a paper money. The transformation was abetted by government regulations that encouraged the use of bank notes and restricted the use of gold and silver coins. The export of specie was prohibited in January, the production and sale of gold and silver objects and their export were outlawed in February, specie holdings were limited to five hundred livres per person and all payments in excess of one hundred livres were to be made with bank notes, gold was demonetized in March and silver was scheduled for demonetization at the beginning of 1721.

These measures were implemented after Law had been appointed controller-general of finances, which was the chief post in the regent's government. He issued another stock subscription soon after his bureaucratic elevation. It was another success, but was soon followed by an abandonment of the bank's program of purchasing shares in order to maintain their value. Share prices fell immediately and reached eight thousand livres by the end of February. Law's reaction was to announce that he would peg the price at nine thousand livres.

In mid-May, Law decided to abandon the peg and reduce the bank's note issue and had the necessary edict decreed. Share prices started to fall, public resentment resulted in protest in the streets and in the parlement of Paris. The regent bowed to pressure and revoked the edict. He also dismissed Law from the office of controller-general.

Share prices collapsed to five thousand livres per share, but revived somewhat when Law was returned to office. During the remaining term of office, Law found himself in the sad position of dismantling his system. The government returned to borrowing through annuities and bank notes started being taken out of circulation. In June, the prohibition on holding gold and silver was revoked. In July, the Compagnie des Indes agreed to redeem six hundred million livres of bank notes over a period of a year. In August, high denomination bank notes were to be demonetized and low denomination bank notes to later follow. In October, bank notes were to cease being legal tender. Share values collapsed to 2500 livres at the end of 1720.

Notwithstanding the stock crash, Law had, ironically, accomplished the fundamental objective of a debt reduction for the French government. The public had exchanged, on a massive scale, their holdings of government debt for equity in a bankrupt company. Many were understandably furious at the losses in their wealth when the share prices began falling, and there was widespread antipathy towards John Law with vociferous demands that he be arrested and executed. Fortunately for Law, his royal friend remained true and arranged for his safe conduct out of France. He left Paris on December 13, 1720 and crossed the border into the Habsburg's Netherlands on the road to Brussels.

His legacy for the Compagnie des Indes was not particularly bad. The company was operating sixteen ships by March 1719 and thirty by the end of the year. During the year, it sent out eight million livres in specie while return cargoes worth twelve million livres returned in 1720. Furthermore, the company's capital plant was enlarged when it acquired Belle-Isle on which it subsequently built warehouses and ship-building works (Weber, 1904, 317-318).

Law's merger of the old Compagnie de la Chine and Compagnie des Indes Orientales into one entity was probably good for French trade. It was certainly better for the company, particularly when its monopoly in the eastern trade was extended to 1770. The drawbacks for the Compagnie des Indes were its continued commitment to the financial bog of Madagascar and its involvement in the expenses of the futile efforts to develop French trade and settlement in Louisiana.

On Law's departure, the company was left with its shipping and capital plant, its trained corps of employees, its monopoly in the eastern trade, and a variety of financial assets. Furthermore, it retained the tobacco monopoly and the more nebulous prospect of profits and custom revenue from its economic link with Louisiana. It lost one-quarter of the rental income from the Crown even though it had fulfilled its obligation to purchase one hundred million livres of *billets d'état*.

Notwithstanding its liabilities, John Law left a Compagnie des Indes that had a large and solid presence in the eastern trade. It was in a better position to exploit that trade than its defunct predecessor, the Compagnie des Indes Orientales.

Chapter 8
Reconstitution

The Compagnie des Indes survived the collapse of Law's system. It retained a monopoly of the French trade with India, the Mascarene Islands, China and the east African coast. A royal proclamation of August 29, 1720 reduced the company's directorship from thirty to twenty-four men selected by the Crown, but whose successors were to be elected by the shareholders. A director's remuneration was set at twenty thousand livres per year, on condition that he deposited two-hundred shares with the company's cashier.

The administration of the company was separated into two divisions, commerce and finance, each having a number of departments. Commerce had eight departments: India and the auctions, Louisiana, Senegal and Barbary, armament, purchasing, money exchange, bookkeeping, and sailings and the port of Lorient. Finance had six departments: revenue, *gabelle* taxes, other taxes, the tobacco farm, bookkeeping, and council business. Each department was usually headed by two directors who could serve more than one department.

The directorate was under the control of the Crown through a council of the Indies, which included six members from the Council of State and fourteen other commissioners of whom ten were merchants and four came from the royal navy. A proclamation of March 24, 1721 named Cardinal Guillaume Dubois as the first chief of the council and controller-general Dodun as the first president. The council was divided into two bureaux. The first exercised overall control, while the second bureau was composed of the ten merchants serving in two chambers, the chamber of commerce and the chamber of tobacco. The first chamber was divided into ten departments: India and the auctions, Louisiana, Senegal, Guinea, bookkeeping and cash, audits, purchasing, employment, Barbary, and armament and provisioning. The chamber of tobacco never got properly organized.

The life of the reorganization was short, lasting until the death of the regent, the duc d' Orléans in 1723. A new proclamation on August 30, 1723 reduced the directorate to twelve men selected by the Crown from shareholders holding at least fifty shares. Two new bodies of overseers were created. They were four inspectors, chosen by the Crown from the council of the Indies, and eight syndics who were elected each year at shareholders' meetings. The inspectors were supposed to oversee the interests of the Crown, while the syndics were to represent the shareholders. The inspectorship was abandoned in 1731 when the controller-general took over sole overall control, albeit through a commissioner that he appointed. The actual administration, with the directors heading particular departments, was little changed except the chamber of tobacco ceased when the tobacco farm became leased to the general farm in 1729.

The next major reorganization came in 1748 when the directorate was reduced to eight, and the syndicat to six members. The company's internal organization otherwise underwent little change. It consisted of a general assembly of stockholders that was supposed to meet once a year. In fact, it met annually during the early 1720s, then never met once between 1731 and 1745, and thereafter met once a year when the financial report was presented. It had a less active role in management than in the old Compagnie des Indes Orientales in that it never issued direct orders, except at the behest of the Crown, to management.

The key managerial entity was the administrative assembly of eight directors and six syndics. They met daily to handle general management. Both directors and syndics were appointed by the Crown in accordance with different procedures. The directors were appointed through decrees issued by the Council of State and confirmed through the appointees taking oaths before the parlement of Paris. Each selection was made from a list of three candidates proposed by the administrative assembly. The syndics were selected through a more elaborate procedure. Each was selected from a list of two candidates elected at the annual meeting of the general assembly out of a list of four proposed by the administrative assembly.

Besides the power of selecting management, the Crown could exercise a direct control. The controller-general could have the final say in any matter, as well as exerting a continuing direction and influence through his royal commissioners whom he could appoint at will and whose numbers could be changed at will. They attended meetings of the administrative assembly and reported the company's business to him at weekly meetings. He could command the assembly to reconsider any decision at its next meeting.

The actual daily work of management was done by the administrative assembly. It met daily to read incoming correspondence, approve outgoing correspondence, assign and recall employees to and from posts and make general decisions. Its decisions were made on the basis of a plurality of the votes of its members and were presented to the royal commissioner who joined the meeting once a week.

The controller-general presided once a month at a meeting that generally considered more important issues.

More particular managerial functions were handled by the administrative assembly divided into two general and three particular departments. One general department was headed by four directors and two syndics and dealt with commerce and armament. The other was chaired by two directors and one syndic. It attended to purchasing, finance and bookkeeping. Each particular department was led by one director. One of them dealt with the auction sales, another with the port of Lorient and the third with the archives and registers. A secret committee, later called the Indian committee, was devoted to military matters.

Notwithstanding the many changes in its organization, the company remained essentially a Crown corporation with private ownership of the company shares. The royal commissioners exercised broad control, while the directorate and syndicate managed actual company operations. The commissioners, directors and syndics were, in effect, chosen by the Crown. Only the shareholders were private. They, holding approximately fifty thousand shares in total, met, at most, in annual shareholders' meetings.

The Crown company had a run of twenty good years during the peace that reigned in Europe before the outbreak of the War of the Austrian Succession. Both its finances and trade prospered. Its financial condition was re-established after the collapse of Law's system by a proclamation of March 22, 1723. Its capital was the Crown debts in the form of promissory notes (Haudrère 1989, 1, 106-107) with the capitalization set at one hundred and twelve million livres, divided into forty eight thousand shares with a par value of two thousand livres and eighty thousand shares with a par value of two hundred livres. A share was to pay an annual dividend of a fixed amount of one hundred livres which was soon to raise to one hundred and fifty livres. It could also pay a variable amount depending on the profits from the company trade. The total dividend payment was estimated at amounting to around eight million livres per year.

The means for paying the dividends were varied. The Crown had a debt of one hundred million livres paying five percent interest that it had borrowed from Law's Compagnie d'Occident. That debt was converted to a deeding of the tobacco farm with an estimated return of two and a half million livres per year and the *domaine d' occident* yielding about three hundred thousand livres per year. The tobacco farm collected taxes on the sale of tobacco in France while the *domaine* collected import tariffs on produce coming from the French colonies in America. Both were later converted into fixed payments from the Crown, the *domaine* within two years and the farm within eight years. The farm was transferred as of September 1730 on a eight-year lease to the government's general farm with the provision of annual payments of seven and a half million livres to the company for the first four years and eight million for the second four years. The lease was subsequently renewed in 1738 for another six years at the higher payment.

The company was also excused from a state debt that Law had promised to pay off. It was converted into a debt of sixteen million livres of *rentes viagères* at four percent interest and thirty one million livres of *rentes perpétuelles* at two and a half percent interest. In return the company gave up compensation for six million livres, most of which were sums due from Law's defunct bank.

Other sources of company revenue came from its monopoly, granted in August 1723, on the sale of coffee in France and its right to run lotteries. The latter privilege was withdrawn in 1725, but the company was allowed to continue running some lotteries. The lottery business had an effect on the company's stock ownership because lottery tickets could be purchased with company shares.

The coffee sales joined the rest of the company's sales of goods which was the principal source, other than the tobacco lease, for meeting its obligations. The profits on trade climbed and more than doubled within few years. The company's trading success was reflected in the stock prices on the bourse. Initially stock prices were less than a third of par, but became somewhat above par by the beginning of the fourth decade of the eighteenth century. During the same time, shareholdings of two thousand livre shares had dropped from fifty six thousand to 51,134 shares in 1736 and 50,269 in 1743 as shareholders exchanged them for debt and lotteries (Weber 1904, 555-556).

Chapter 9
The Company's Establishment

The company's headquarters in Paris were located in a building on rue de Richelieu, which later housed the Bibliothèque Nationale. The ground floor was occupied by the various cashiers' offices, the sales offices, and the wrapping room where goods were packaged for shipment to Lorient. The second floor had the royal commissioner's office, some directors' offices, other cashiers' offices, store-rooms, and the offices for bookkeeping, purchasing and correspondence. The third floor had directors' offices, offices for the Indian bureau, the armaments bureau, a committee room and assembly hall. The attic held the archives.

The company employed a large clerical workforce to carry out management's decisions. They were organized into offices directed by one or two directors or syndics. Six offices worked on the financial business: a general office paid the company's debts, received payments on account and made temporary loans; a cashier office received and paid out the cash; a dividends office paid out dividend and interest payments and redeemed bonds at maturity; a rents office paid the annuities on the company's lotteries; a stock conversion office redeemed stock and bonds when their coupons expired; and a discounts office was the discount bank for bills of exchange.

A bookkeeping office did the accounts and audits, along with the annual statement. An additional bureau was added in 1753 when the committee of the property offices was established to determine which bills of exchange were to be discounted at the discounts office. Other offices included the purchasing office which handled requests for supplies approved by the administrative assembly and ordered agents to buy goods and provisions to be shipped to Lorient. The biggest office was the Indian bureau. It sorted incoming correspondence from foreign posts for the attention of the administrative assembly and wrote out the correspondence dispatched abroad. Much of the correspondence dealt with requests for supplies, which were sent on to the purchasing department if approved. The bureau for armament attended to naval affairs which included the construction, repair, provisioning, equipping and crewing the company's ships. The smallest bureau was the archives, although its main job was burning most of the company's papers older than a year.

The company's accounts were quite elaborate. They included a variety of journals and registers that recorded the company's holdings of real estate and fixed assets, stores of merchandise, payments and receipts into the cashier's office, records of *rentes viagères* and *rentes perpétuelles* (Barbier, 1919, 35-39).

Besides the headquarters building in Paris, the company also got other parts of John Law's company. The principal capital plant in France consisted of the port facilities at Lorient on the Breton coast. In time, they were much expanded and came to consist of docks for loading and unloading cargoes, lighters for handling cargo, a watch-tower, warehouses for storing merchandise, lodgings for senior employees, shipbuilding works, forges and workshops. Other edifices served the needs of employees and included a hospital, bakery and waterworks. The entire establishment became solidly entrenched in stone buildings behind massive walls by the mid century. The waterworks initially took its water from the Scorff River, then through piping from a spring. The port employed many tradesmen: carpenters, dockers, pilots, caulkers, coopers, surgeons, apothecaries, architects and sailors employed in building and repairing ships, loading and discharging cargoes, and performing a wide range of ancillary services connected with company's shipping. They were under the direction of a resident company director.

The director was in charge of the port's main functions, which were loading and unloading cargo and building ships. The company relied on its own ships and only chartered other ships during war time emergencies when war losses were heavy. Its shipping was divided into two categories: "first navigation" ships of 450-600 tons berth used for the Far Eastern trade and "second navigation" ships used in the African trade. Although it owned seventy-six ships in 1723, no more than eight ships returned each year with cargoes since the voyage to and from India took two years, and there could be a variety of mishaps.

The ships were mostly built in Lorient, but some were built at Saint Malo, Dieppe, Dunkerque, Nantes, Havre, and a few in Hamburg, England and Holland. The cost of construction averaged three-hundred livres per ton. Ships built elsewhere were delivered to Lorient because the company's officers were not experienced in sailing in the English Channel. A few ships were also built at Pegou in India, but the company officials abroad were not experienced in overseeing construction.

The ships had to be well gunned because they sailed in dangerous waters during war time. Peace time was good for trade in many respects, including an increase in cargo space because some of the armament, which was heavy and took space away from cargo, could be removed when there was less threat of enemy attack. The life of a ship averaged six trips to India, although many believed the maximum should be only four. The ships were examined periodically, especially in India, where they rotted more quickly in the warmer waters.

The company inherited a fleet of about a hundred ships from Law's company. The number subsequently fell, but the quality of construction improved (Barbier, 1919, 55). So did the size. It had fifteen ships of more than one thousand tons by the time of the War of the Austrian Succession as well as almost fifty ships of somewhat smaller tonnage. Each ship carried between twelve to sixty cannons and a crew ranging around two hundred sailors.

The rest of the company's capital plant was located abroad where the company's essential purpose, the purchase and sale of merchandise, was accomplished. In some places, a single post sufficed. The posts were spread throughout the giant continent, and some system of overall defense was required even though most posts had neither garrisons nor fortifications. The defense requirements contributed to the creation of an elaborate administrative system. After the abandonment of a company presence in Madagascar, the Mascarene Islands of Bourbon and Île de France in the Indian Ocean grew in importance. Both had been occupied earlier by the French, but became more firmly established with a military garrison during the era of John Law. Each had a governor until 1727, when the position was demoted to a military commander under the direction of the commandant general stationed in Pondichéry. Seven years later, in 1734, a further administrative change created one governor general in control of the civil and military matters in both islands.

In India, the French presence was extensive. The principal places were Pondichéry on the Coromandel coast and Chandernagor in Bengal. Both encompassed a territory under French jurisdiction. Elsewhere, the French had only trading posts. A post existed at Masulipatam on the Coromandel, while others were added at Yanaon in the Northern Circars in 1721, Mahé on the Malabar coast in 1725 and Karikal in Tanjore in 1739. Balasor at the mouth of the Hooghly River was less a trading post than a settlement for pilots employed in French shipping along the Hooghly River. Surat in Gujarat fell from the chief French station to a mere trading post. Although Calicut on the Malabar coast was abandoned in 1722, the remaining posts came to include Patna in Bihar which was the center for opium production, Dacca and Jougdia on the Brahmaputra River in Bengal, Cassimbazar in Bengal and Gigouria. The company also had posts outside India, at Bender Abbas and temporarily at Basra on the Persian Gulf, at Moka on the Red Sea and Canton in China. Most of the posts were only commercial places for trading, and were under native jurisdiction.

Pondichéry was the administrative center in India. It was not so much a coherent geographic entity as a grouping of enclaves ceded to the French by the nawab of Arcot. The area under French control eventually reached fourteen enclaves totalling twenty nine thousand hectares in area. The concessions gave the French the rights to levy taxes and custom duties, mint coins, provide policing and justice over all inhabitants, and fly the French flag.

The town was unfortified until a fort was built in 1702-1704 by the engineer Danyon. Only a hedge surrounded the site until walls were built two decades later, first on the north side, then the south side and later on the land side. The walls had bastions, redoubts, artillery platforms and moats. Much later, in 1747, a sea wall was built to make the post into a solidly constructed fort containing the company's headquarters. Buildings included the governor's residence, an administrative building, a customs house, a warehouse with sales rooms, a mint, a hospital, workshops for finishing cloths and churches. Some of the buildings stood within the fort; others were outside. The town had no wharves or docks because the port was an open roadside and relied on lighters for loading and unloading ships. The French and natives lived in separate neighborhoods, and the housing for the French consisted of comfortable abodes on lots with many trees.

Pondichéry lay in one of the main Indian centers for textile manufacture, and the company operated other posts, Karikal, Masulipatam and Yanaon in the region where the French could buy textiles from Indian suppliers. Masulipatam and Yanaon were located in the Northern Circars, which was somewhat distant and over which the company did not possess jurisdiction. Karikal was only twenty miles south of Pondichéry, and served as a source of food supplies as well as textiles. It was a French possession, purchased over the years until it reached 13,515 hectares in area by the mid century. At that time it was garrisoned and fortified.

Chandernagor was the second most important French possession. It was smaller in area than Pondichéry, but handled a larger and more varied trade because its location on the banks of the Hooghly River permitted the company to tap the trade of Bengal which was the most populous region of India. It was protected by a fort, called Fort d'Orléans, which was shaped in a square with bastions at each corner for cannons and surrounded by a glassis and dry moat. Besides trading, the French concern at Chandernagor was to keep navigation open on the Hooghly River which was plagued by shifting sand banks. Four pilots were regularly employed for shipping between Balasor at the river's mouth and posts upstream. Patna had a lodge for buying saltpeter and some opium, while Dacca and Jougdia had small lodges for the purchase of fine cotton cloth. None of these posts was fortified; nor were the posts at Mahé, devoted to pepper purchases; nor Moka, for the coffee trade; nor Bender Abbas, for trade with Persia; nor Canton, which became the source of tea. By the mid-century, Calicut and Basra had been abandoned and Surat had shrunk to insignificance as a place for French purchases or sales.

The entire company operation, both administrative and judicial, was under the direction of the governor-general. He was responsible for the care of the company's affairs in India and carrying out the company's mission and orders. He commanded the civil, military and naval services in India. He was assisted by a superior council, but he usually made the important decisions which were rubber-stamped by the council. His sense of independence came partly from a pattern of longevity in service. Benoit Dumas served for twelve years and Dupleix for twenty years. The slowness of communication also weakened any central control from Paris.

Both the governor and the councilors were appointed by the administrative assembly in Paris although the patronage of important people in the French government and the company was a significant factor in making these appointments (Manning, 1996, 57-65). The governor was in charge of all French posts in India, including his seat at Pondichéry. He was in command of all inhabitants in the towns and the forts at French posts and was the president of all councils whether superior or provincial. Over the years, the powers of the governor tended to enlarge, and included an authority over the sea captains of the company ships while in Indian waters.

The division of labor between the governor and the superior council was that the governor concentrated on major decisions, while ordinary administration was split among the councilors. Together, they received and carried out instructions from the headquarters in Paris, issued instructions to the provincial councils at the lesser posts, handled diplomatic relations with other powers in India, oversaw shipping and cargoes, arranged financial matters, and commanded the military forces. Council meetings were presided over by the governor or his deputy. At their meetings, all correspondence from the company's directors in Paris had to be opened in the presence of all councilors, and all of them had to sign any correspondence to the directors. The superior council was obliged to send annual reports on trade, shipping, local commerce, fortifications, military forces and operations, employees and diplomatic affairs.

Although council decisions could be vetoed by the directors in Paris, the guiding principle in the company's organization was to allow local authorities to adapt to circumstances, and most of their administrative actions were condoned. Particular administrative functions were divided among the individual councilors who administered the stores and cash, hospitals, schools, parks, sanitation system, water supply, police and military.

The superior council was also the highest judicial court in India. It dealt with both criminal and civil law. Its right to administer justice to Frenchmen rested on decrees of the Crown, while the same rights over Indians came from treaties with native rulers. Inferior courts existed at the other posts, each of which had three judges, a president and two assistants whose decisions were by majority vote. They had authority to punish with fines, confiscations, whipping, imprisonment, banishment, branding, mutilation, enslavement and death. In the case of imprisonment, separate quarters existed for Christians and Hindus. The judicial decisions of the lower courts could be appealed to the superior council.

Although the superior council exercised a control over and issued orders to the provincial councils in charge of the posts, those councils had quite a fair degree of local authority in the management of commerce and personnel. They were in direct communication with the Paris headquarters and handled their own administration insofar as assigning duties to the employees, negotiating salaries, and making promotions. Each provincial council had a director, but the number of other councilors depended on the size and importance of the post.

The councils had large crews of employees under their direction. Administrative and commercial personnel were recruited for lifetime employment. Some entered employment as copyists and clerks without pay, most worked in Paris before being sent, at company expense, to India. They could look forward, as long as their work was satisfactory, to more or less automatic promotion on the basis of seniority through the ranks from supernumerary, sub-commissioned clerk, commissioned clerk, sub-merchant, and principal merchant. Sometimes they were allowed to supplement their salaries through trading on the side. Typically, they received bonuses from time to time, but could be shifted at will from job to job and post to post without care about their families.

Although administrative personnel constituted most of the French civil employees, other professional people were employed. Most of the posts had at least one surgeon to provide medical care, while Pondichéry had a couple of engineers employed in the construction of civil and military works. It also had a port master as did Chandernagor at which a few river pilots were also stationed. The company fulfilled its religious obligations under its article of incorporation by subsidizing chaplains at its posts. They belonged to the Capuchin, Carmelite and Jesuit orders and included a convent of Ursuline sisters. The clergy, who were under the jurisdiction of the Archbishop of Paris, devoted themselves mainly to the spiritual needs of the French which suited company purposes for it felt that proselytization hurt commerce.

Craftsmen, such as carpenters, blacksmiths, coopers, millers, locksmiths, and cannoners, were hired on a contract basis, usually for three, five or six years. No French unskilled labor was hired for service in India because the company relied on large numbers of Indians to do the menial work. Not all Indians were servile. Some Indian craftsmen and clerks were hired, and more importantly, the company relied on Indian brokers to interpret and draw up contracts and on Indian merchants to supply goods.

The navy did rely on unskilled French labor even to the extent that the sailors were sometimes conscripted, upon authorization by the Minister of the Marine, out of the pool liable for service in the royal navy. They were paid by the voyage, with some of the remuneration paid to their families while the men were at sea and the remainder paid in a lump sum at end of voyage. Most of the company's seamen were Bretons. Officers were recruited on the same basis as administrative personnel and were mostly the sons of company employees, merchants and gentlemen from the lower ranks of the nobility. Upon recruitment at an earlier age, they received instruction in navigation and seamanship at the company's school at Lorient. When they passed into service, they were classified into two grades of officers depending on their navigational competence which much affected their chances of promotion through the ranks of second ensign, first ensign, second lieutenant, first lieutenant, and captain (Barbier, 1919, 58-60). The purser, master, pilot, surgeon and almoner were numbered among the officers. Captains and some other officers could be put on half pay, waiting for another ship assignment. Officers' salaries were supplemented with port permits, which allowed them to bring a certain value of goods back for sale at the company's auctions in France. The value of the permit depended on rank, and the company followed the practice of lending money to the officers so that they could fill their permits.

On the whole, the navy did not hire natives. The army did. Most of the natives were sepoys who were Indians, topas who were half-breed Portuguese and cafres who were slaves from Madagascar. Their officers were mostly French aristocrats, although the non-commissioned officers could be native. The company's troops were not part of the royal army, although the Crown issued the commissions and sometimes assigned royal officers to the duty of training company troops, and less frequently, to serve with the company's army in India.

The ranks in the company's army were mostly natives, trained in the European style of battle by French officers. Their earlier service was at garrison posts and as the marine guard on ships. That service became much less significant as the company entered more into power politics in India, at which point service in field armies employed most of the French forces. Europeans were also recruited as soldiers, with the regiments of Europeans and natives being separate.

The size of the army varied with circumstances. At the eve of the War of the Austrian Succession, it consisted of twenty two regiments, each having about twelve officers and three hundred soldiers. An infantry regiment had two captains, two lieutenants, one sub-lieutenant, six ensigns, fourteen sergeants, fourteen corporals and eight fifers and drummers. The pay of the captain was about a thousand livres per year. A lieutenant received about seven hundred, an ensign around six hundred, a sergeant about two hundred, a corporal below two hundred and a soldier one hundred livres (Barbier, 1919, 48).

The total number of French in India was quite small. The company's servants engaged in trade rose from seventy in 1727 to one hundred seven in 1750, while the total civilian workforce increased from ninety in 1727 to one hundred sixty-four in 1747 (Manning, 1996, 51-52). The army was the biggest employer of French and other Europeans. Its ranks increased from about seven hundred fifty in 1727 to around fourteen hundred in 1747 (Manning, 1996, 54). The total French population in India was about one thousand in 1727 and became approximately two thousand by 1747 (Manning, 1996, 69).

Chapter 10
Commerce

The essence of the company's trade between France and India was the exchange of specie for cloth. The specie exports were estimated at about twenty five million livres worth each year during the twenty years of peace prior to the War of the Austrian Succession (Dalgliesh, 1933, 63).

French law prohibited the export of specie from France. Although the Crown did, on occasion, rescind the prohibition, the company usually obtained the specie from elsewhere. The main source was Cadiz. It was the point of arrival of Spain's annual convoy of treasure from America. The French company bought mostly silver coin, piastres of Peru and Mexico, which was a Spanish coin stamped at 916 2/3 purity and containing twenty four grams of pure silver. The specie purchases were made through brokers who were mainly French bankers based in Saint Malo, Bayonne and Paris. If France was at war with Spain, the silver purchases were mostly made at Amsterdam. Some purchases were also made from smugglers during wartime.

Some gold coins were also purchased and shipped to India. Most of the gold purchases were from Portugal. The total company shipments of silver and gold to India amounted to around five million livres tournois per year in the second decade of the eighteenth century, rising to double that figure in the third decade, and reaching around thirteen million livres in the fifth decade. The specie exports, however, fell off very considerably during wartimes (Haudrère, 1989, 1, 404).

Although specie amounted to more than half the total value of company exports to India, many other goods were exported. Foods stuffs, such as flour and salted meat, and beverages, such as wine and brandy, totalled around one-quarter of the merchandise exported. They were, however, mostly consumed in passage or sold to Frenchmen at company posts. The rest of the exports were somewhat minor. They included the metals of copper, lead, tin and iron; they were shipped in plate and ingot forms and were the major components of weapons and navy equipment. These items were much used by the French employees rather than sold to natives. Woolen textiles and luxury goods were, on the other hand, salable commodities. The principal luxury goods were coral and gold thread, along with ginseng which was used as an aphrodisiac in the East. The market, however, for these commodities was rather limited.

Return cargoes were equally varied in nature. Not all came from India. The company inherited the trade with north and west Africa from John Law's company. The north African trade was a small one in grain and hides, and the company surrendered its monopoly rights to import in 1730. The west African trade was the slave trade centered on Senegal and Guinea. The slaves were transported to the Caribbean islands, and some other imports, such as gum, were shipped to France. The company's transportation of slaves was somewhat large in the mid-years of the third decade of the eighteenth century and then dropped off to next to nothing.

The big trade was with Asia. Some of the goods were obtained at place of origin. Coffee came from the Mascarene Islands and Moka on the Red Sea. Tea, porcelain, copper, camphor, lacquer, sugar, raw silk and silk textiles came from China. Indian goods included saltpeter, drugs, dyes, lacquer, rare metals and shells. The main Indian products were, however, textiles. They came in varied form: thread, yarn, and unbleached, bleached and colored cloth. The material could be cotton, wool, silk or linen. Textile imports greatly complicated the company's handling of cargoes because textiles were subject to many government regulations, restrictions and controls.

The company's trading operation meant that cargoes had to be loaded into and out of ships. Out-cargoes included a wide range of provisions, some used on the voyages and some to supply the needs of overseas posts. Much of the cargoes were goods and perishables including medical supplies. The rest were mostly military and naval stores. The port director had responsibility only for the purchase of naval stores, although some could be purchased by ship captains at ports on route. Most of both the provisions and sale goods were purchased by the Paris office either directly in Paris or through agents throughout Europe. Payment was usually in cash, although big purchases could be on credit. On the whole, the Paris office responded to requisition lists drawn up by officials at the overseas posts or at Lorient.

Unloading was a more complicated procedure. The return cargoes had been purchased abroad in accordance largely to requisitioning set by the company officialdom in Paris and Lorient. Most of the goods were purchased through Indian merchants, but some were manufactured on contract and some purchased directly from Indian producers. The goods were sometimes loaded directly into waiting ships, but more frequently were stored in warehouses until time of loading. Although the more perishable goods had to be loaded nearer to sailing, most of the returning cargo consisted of textiles, which were kept for some time before being shipped out in returning ships.

The principal French ports of transhipment in India were Pondichéry and Surat. Pondichéry specialized in cloth, some of which came from Bengal which produced the best of some kinds of cloth. Surat also provided cloth, but of poorer quality. On the other hand, it was a better source for the various other products including drugs and spices which were purchased from the Dutch company. On the Malabar coast, Mahé replaced Calicut as the principal French trading post whence pepper was obtained. From each of its ports, the company shipped a wide range of goods. Most of them sold well in France, and sometimes yielded a profit of two hundred percent. The cargoes were carefully inspected before being shipped home. At Pondichéry, a day was set aside for the inspection, and the inspectors graded the textile goods as acceptable or not. Those deemed acceptable were washed and graded, first by Indian employees and then by Frenchmen.

On arrival in France, the ship and its cargo was inspected by government customs officials, guarded by a detachment of soldiers. They stayed on the ship day and night until the ship was unloaded. They took an account of the goods, inspected the crews' and passengers' baggage and confiscated any contraband. Unloaded cargo went into company warehouses until the auction sales were held, although some more slow-moving goods were sometimes sold on contract. The goods were divided into three categories: cotton and silk textiles subject to the mark, prohibited textiles and other goods. The mark was the company's lead seal attached to the cloth by commissioned agents in the presence of a subdelegate. In the case of such goods coming from a foreign shipper, a second seal had to be attached. The placing of the first seal became mandatory in 1711, while the second seal only became required in 1727. Textiles so marked could be sold to French consumers. Prohibited goods, which were mostly silk and cheap cotton textiles, were placed in storage after the auctions and had to be re-exported within six months. They were not subject to tariffs whereas most permitted goods paid a tariff of three percent on value although some goods, such as porcelain, were charged by weight and some permitted goods were not liable to import duties. The tariffs were appraised on values realized at the company auctions, and the sums collected by the company were paid to the Crown's general tax farm.

The auction sales were held in Nantes during the first decade of the new company's existence. The warehouses were old wood constructions in such poor condition that the company's goods were much exposed to theft and the risk of loss through fire. Although the Nantes officials agitated for reconstruction, the company decided in 1733 to build new facilities at Lorient. It had the advantage of not requiring a coastal transhipment exposed to wartime privateering, but Lorient was not as accessible and convenient for merchants coming to the auctions. On completion of the new buildings, the auctions shifted to Lorient in 1734. The favorite month for the auction was October, but war could delay the date and large inventories led to more than one auction per year. The auction could last for a week, with the sessions being held twice daily.

Handbills of the prospective sales were distributed well before the auction dates and updated editions were issued a few days before the auction. These handbills gave the quantities of each item to be sold as well as the names of the ships that had brought the goods to France. Buyers, who were mainly merchants, could inspect the merchandise before the auction; the grading done abroad meant the inspection could be done by sample. The auctioned goods included goods from seizures, prizes and contraband, as well as officer and crew allotments. The auctions were well attended, with the bidders mostly from Paris and Breton towns, but also from the rest of France and Europe. The auctions were conducted in an auditorium under the auspices of two directors, assisted by a cashier and clerks. They sat on a raised platform along with government agents including the customs inspectors and the director of the tax farm. The merchants sat on benches facing the dais.

Discounts existed and were subject to negotiation between the traders and the company prior to sale. The most important discount was a ten-percent discount for cash payments. Nevertheless, most purchases were made by bills of exchange, those payable in a month gave a discount of nine percent. Payment in installments could last from three months until March of the following year, although goods had to be removed from the company's premises by the end of the year of the auction. The merchants were subject to a township tax, ten sols per lot in the case of Nantes, and a company tax, one tenth of one percent, for charitable purposes.

Goods could be examined in the presence of sale officials before withdrawn from company storerooms, but no claims were allowed once the goods had left the storerooms. To prevent contraband, most merchandise had to be labelled and sealed by the company before delivery to the purchaser. This was done, in the case of cloth, with little parchment labels attached to each bundle. Goods lacking the seal were subject to confiscation. When the goods were later sold at retail, they were often to be marked by the local government and considered fraudulent if the second mark was not present. Government officials periodically checked the goods in shops.

Nevertheless, a contraband trade was a problem. The company itself did not break the law, but its employees could bring in more goods than their limit per person. Government officials could also sneak goods into the country. An elaborate system of inspection tried to prevent the contraband trade at four points: on leaving Lorient, arriving in India, leaving India and returning to Lorient. Nevertheless, some contraband got through the net even with the provision of an additional safeguard of rewarding informers with a portion of the seizures.

On the whole, the company's commerce made a vital contribution to the French economy. It brought many commodities that were unattainable in France or Europe. Cotton textiles were an exception as they were also manufactured in

France. They were the biggest import, and their contribution to the French standard of living must been critical during the warm months of the year.

Chapter 11
War

The two good decades for company commerce came to an end with the War of the Austrian Succession. It imposed major expenditures for military campaigns while severely disrupting the company's trade. French ships were captured in European waters off Lorient and even richer cargoes seized on the Indian and Chinese routes.

The war was not so much over the succession as brought on by it. In 1703, Leopold I had ruled that female heirs could inherit the Austrian throne in default of male heirs. The issue was initially moot because male heirs lived, but it became relevant and Emperor Charles VI arranged in 1713 a family compact, known as the Pragmatic Sanction, by which his daughter Maria Theresa was to inherit the entire Habsburg dominion. He devoted his remaining years to negotiating with other states into recognition of the Sanction, and many did. He died on October 20, 1740 and was succeeded by his young daughter. It was a signal that the Austrian empire was ripe for the plucking.

Frederick II of Prussia saw an opportunity for aggrandizing his state, and his army invaded Silesia in December 1740. It quickly conquered the province, and turned back an Austrian counterattack at the battle of Mollwitz. The other vulture, France, concluded a Franco-Prussian alliance and sent two French armies into action. One entered Westphalia and the other crossed the Rhine in support of Elector Charles Albert of Bavaria whose army had invaded Austria in September and threatened Vienna before being sidetracked into Bohemia where it captured Prague. The French reaped little from the campaign other than securing the election of their candidate, the Elector of Bavaria, as Holy Roman Emperor.

Then the house fell in on the French. Instead of the Habsburg Empire disintegrating, the Austrian army counterattacked in Bavaria, and English diplomacy obtained the neutrality of Prussia at the price of keeping Silesia. England entered the war against the French in March, although it was not militarily involved in the war in Europe until it sent troops into Belgium in May 1742. The English force remained inactive until 1743 when it helped parry a French invasion with a victory at the battle of Dettingen. The French tried again with an abortive attack on Holland in 1744.

Frederick the Great re-entered the fighting in 1744, then withdrew in 1745. The war continued for another three years of desultory and aimless campaigning for the French although one of the most famous of French victories, at Fontenoy, occurred in 1745. Peace came with the treaty of Aix-la-Chapelle in 1748. Prussia was the chief gainer and Austria the chief loser, with Silesia passing permanently to Prussia.

For the French and English, the significant fighting during the war occurred abroad in wide-ranging conflicts throughout their colonial empires. In India, the French took the initiative in intervening in Indian power politics. The opportunities for intervention arose out of a shifting political scene. The Mogul empire still existed in the north, where it extended from the Punjab, Sindh and Kashmir to the Gujarat and down the valley of the Ganges River, although Bengal had become semi-independent under Aliverdi Khan. Central India was the site of the Maratha confederacy which was a loosely linked grouping extending from Peishwa on the west through central India. The Maratha's mode of operation consisted of swift raids into neighboring territories, plundering and quick withdrawals, although they sometimes established more permanent jurisdictions such as Tanjore far in the southern tip of India. The Marathas surrounded the largest state in the south of India, the Nizam of Hyderabad, on three sides. Its southern border abutted on the plateau of the Deccan, where the other large Muslim state of Golconda existed. An array of smaller principalities, ruled mostly by Hindu nawabs lay between and to the south of the Muslim states. The consequence was that much of India, particularly in the south, was in a state of political flux into which the European companies soon entered.

The French governor, Benoit Dumas, had successfully sought the favor of the nawab of the Carnatic, Dost Ali, since his appointment in 1735. Five years later, Dost Ali hoped to gain more independence from the Nizam and instigated attacks on Trichinopoly, Medura and Tanjore. The Marathas invaded the Carnatic, defeated and killed Dost Ali and pillaged the country. They half-heartedly besieged the French at Pondichéry and Mahé on the Malabar coast but failed to assault the fortifications. Both sieges were raised when a French fleet arrived, under the command of Bertrand Francis Mahé de la Bourdonnais, governor of the Mascarene Islands. The Marathas retreated from the Carnatic after capturing Trichinopoly and taking Chanda Sahib, the son-in-law of Dost Ali, prisoner.

The French company had done well in the conflict with the Marathas, repulsing the attack and securing the appointment by the Nizam of their ally, Anwar-ud-din Khan, as nawab of the Carnatic. Dumas requested retirement, which the company granted. It appointed Joseph-François Dupleix as his successor.

Dupleix was born in Flanders in 1697 and entered the service of the Compagnie des Indes Orientales in 1715. He served first on company ships before obtaining the position of first councilor of the superior council at Pondichéry in 1721. His appointment came partly from the influence of his father who was a tax-farmer and company director. In 1730, he was appointed intendant in charge of Chandernagor where he soon instigated a much more thriving country trade. He invested his own funds in the trade and encouraged his subordinates to do the same by making loans to them. Although his efforts were successful in promoting the town's trade, they subsequently laid him open to charges of corruption.

His time in history came in 1740 when he succeeded as governor in Pondichéry. He soon found that he inherited a delicate situation from his predecessor, who had given refuge to the widow of Dost Ali during a Maratha invasion. The French had been in some danger, and their act of mercy had increased the eagerness of the Marathas to capture the town. Fortunately, the French weathered the threat, and Dupleix was able to capitalize on the nawab's goodwill when the War of the Austrian Succession broke out and an English fleet, cruising in Indian waters, could have threatened attacks on French posts in South India. Dupleix appealed to Anwar-ud-din Khan to keep the peace between the English and French. He did, and warned Morse, the governor of Madras, that he would not permit the Europeans to attack each other.

Dupleix effectively used the peace to French advantage. He was well supplied with money because the company had just sent the funds to finance bigger purchases of goods for the return cargoes. Instead, Dupleix used the money to finance the construction of the sea walls at Pondichéry and thereby provide a secure base for military operations. His overall objective was to supplement the company's sources of revenue by obtaining from allied Indian princes the possession and right to tax the inhabitants in territory deeded to the French.

The peace gave time for the French to mobilize for the attack as well as defense. In January 1746, Bourdonnais arrived with a small fleet of five ships: one was a ship of war of seventy guns, while the others were merchantmen armed with small eight- and twelve-pounder cannons. The fleet had met a tempest in passage and put into port for repairs which Dupleix arranged to be done quickly. The fleet, reinforced to nine ships, sailed out of port and headed south where it confronted the English fleet, commanded by Commodore Peyton, off Negapatam. The English turned tail and sailed for Hooghly far in the north, thereby removing the threat to Pondichéry.

Once armed with a well-gunned and provisioned fleet, Dupleix was eager to use it on an attack of the English center at Madras. The stumbling block was Bourdonnais, whom he kept pestering until he got action. The fleet sailed out on a reconnaisance mission in August and then returned to action in September when two thousand troops were landed at Madras. A siege began and shore batteries were erected. The ships and batteries opened fire on September 18, and brought an English capitulation within three days. The English soldiers became prisoners, the civil servants were allowed to leave and the rival company's stores and provisions were confiscated.

The problem stopped being the English and became themselves. Dupleix and Bourdonnais were diametrically opposed over the articles of capitulation to be negotiated with the English. Dupleix had a plan. He wanted to placate Anwar-ud-din Khan for having broken the peace, and thought that the grant of Madras would have sufficed. The difficulty was that the town had to be surrendered to the French in order for them to make the offer, and its fortifications had to be destroyed before the offer was made. Then his plans could be realized: the English could be effectively expelled from the south of India, for an unfortified Madras would have meant a very vulnerable position for the English even if the nawab ever sold or gave it back to them.

Bourdonnais refused to cooperate. He wanted to ransom the town back to the English with a large side payment to himself. He got his way in that he and the English signed articles of capitulation that provided for French military evacuation by the beginning of 1747, restitution of half the captured munitions and the payment of the ransom. Unfortunately for him, the council at Pondichéry was under the sway of Dupleix, and refused to ratify the articles.

The denouement came in the autumn with a storm that so damaged the French fleet that it returned to Pondichéry for repairs. On being outfitted, it sailed on an abortive mission to Achin before sailing to the Mascarenes where Bourdonnais found that he had been replaced as governor of the islands and ordered home. He got as far as Martinique where he boarded a Dutch ship that was captured by the English. They released him. When he arrived in France, the king threw him into the Bastille where he languished for five years. He died shortly after his release.

The departure of Bourdonnais did not end the problems that his obstinacy had created for Dupleix. The month wasted between the capitulation and the departure of Bourdonnais meant there was not enough time to demolish the fortifications before handing the town over to the nawab. He became suspicious of Dupleix's willingness to honor the promise, turned hostile and sent an army of ten thousand men to encamp under the walls of Madras, which caused Dupleix to feel that the razing of the walls had become inexpedient. Instead, Dupleix ordered the commanding officer, Jean-Jacques Duval d'Eprémesnil, to defend Madras with the garrison of about one thousand European and Indian troops. The defense initially followed Dupleix's instructions of committing as few acts of hostility as possible until the enemy cut the garrison's only source of good water. D'Eprémesnil ordered a sortie, which met an enemy cavalry charge with cannon fire that decimated so many horsemen that the charge turned into headlong flight.

In the meantime, Dupleix toiled at organizing a relief column of about one thousand troops, mostly Indian. Near Saint Thomé, the column confronted an Indian force posted on the far bank of a small river, the Adiyar. The commander, Captain Louis Paradise, led a dash into the river, up the bank, halting for a volley and then a charge. The enemy fled. The two engagements transformed French military calculations in India. They revealed the superiority of European discipline and training, and caused the French to be more willing to intervene militarily in Indian politics.

Dupleix decided to renege on the commitment to the nawab and keep Madras. He appointed Paradise as its governor, and ordered him to annul the ransom treaty. He did, expelled the English and confiscated all their property except their personal effects. Some, including Robert Clive, escaped to Fort St. David which became the English seat of government even though it was only twelve miles from Pondichéry. Dupleix laid plans to also conquer it. Paradise led a detachment of three hundred men from Madras while another force of fifteen hundred men with cannon came from Pondichéry. The quarry, a town garrisoned by only two hundred English soldiers, looked like easy pickings. Unfortunately, Dupleix felt obliged to appoint his senior officer, general de Bury, to command the besieging force. He dithered to such a degree that the nawab launched a surprise attack that just missed complete success. The French retreated but rallied. Nevertheless, de Bury raised the siege and retreated to the offshore river island of Ariakupum.

Notwithstanding French military failures, their position was strengthened by a treaty with the nawab that left them in possession of all their conquests, including Madras. They tried another attack in the spring on Fort St. David when Paradise marched a force to a renewed siege. It was soon aborted because an English fleet arrived to reinforce the garrison with a force of two thousand men. The English position became too strong to be successfully assaulted and the French retreated to Pondichéry.

In mid-1748, more English ships arrived. It was a large fleet, commanded by Admiral Boscawen, of nineteen ships carrying fourteen hundred troops. The admiral first considered an assault on a Mascarene island, but reconnoitering revealed its strength and the fleet sailed on to Fort St. David. Enough troops were landed to begin besieging the derelict French force on Ariakupum, forcing an evacuation. The English next moved on to a siege of Pondichéry, met vigorous French sorties and gave up the attempt in October.

Madras was evacuated by the French by a treaty signed in August 1749. French troops marched out under their colors to waiting ships, and English marched into the town. The treaty provided that English commissioners take an inventory of goods and provisions left in the town. Compensation subsequently became a bone of contention (British Library, London: 1/1/1/452).

Desultory fighting continued elsewhere. The war had revealed two key elements in the conflict between the French and English in India. European led forces could defeat much larger Indian armies, and sea power was crucial in giving one side a military advantage over the other.

Although the Treaty of Aix-la-Chapelle had ended the war in Europe, military operations of the French and English companies continued in India because their policies had become closely intertwined in Indian power politics. They mounted attacks on Indian rulers, parried assaults on their posts and lent their troops to allied Indian rulers.

The warring unfolded in a kaleidoscope of marches and counter-marches, sieges and reliefs. In 1749, Raja Sahuji appealed for English help to recover a throne taken by the French candidate, Partab Singh. Two English expeditions came. One, consisting of a force of four hundred Europeans and a thousand sepoys led by Captain Cope, proved futile. The other, consisting of eight hundred Europeans and one thousand sepoys led by Captain Lawrence, was more successful and stormed the town of Divicotta.

The French had the same experience of success and failure. In 1748, the Nizam of Hyderabad died and was succeeded by Nasir Jang, but the succession was contested by Muzaffer Jang. At the same time, Chanda Sahib was released from captivity by the Marathas, and arrived in the Carnatic with Marathas' support. Both received French help. In mid-1749, a small French force of sixteen hundred men under the command of Louis-Hubert de Combaud, comte d'Auteuil, defeated Anwar-ud-din Khan at Ambur, from whence it passed to occupy Arcot which became the capital of Chanda Sahib. Anwar-ud-din Khan had been killed in battle, and his succession was disputed between the French candidate, Chanda Sahib, and the English choice Muhammed Ali who was ensconced in Trichinopoly where the French attempted to help Chanda Sahib conduct a siege that began in May 1751. A French expedition, led by Duquesne arrived and marched to Tanjore which was ruled by a raja allied to the English. It failed to capture the city and instead retreated to Pondichéry, where the officers promptly mutinied.

Dupleix suppressed the mutiny by arresting the disaffected officers and using more pacific means to restore morale. The revived French army went out to do battle as part of the army of Chanda Sahib. They surprised the camp of Muhammed Ali, defeated the bigger army of twenty thousand men and captured the stronghold of Gingi which was a crucial fortress, perched atop a summit and considered impregnable, in the Carnatic.

In the meantime, the French scored a success in the Deccan where they won an overwhelming victory at Velimdonpat in December 1750 over Nasir Jang. It was an important victory, because it enabled the French to replace Nasir Jang by Muzaffer Jang as Subader of the Deccan. A grateful Muzaffer Jang repaid with a grant of a half million rupees for the use of French troops and territorial accessions which increased the company's tax revenue by an estimated four hundred thousand rupees per annum (Malleson, 1909, 275).

The victories left Dupleix as the master of southeastern India. Direct French rule, with Dupleix nominated as nawab nominally under the Mogul emperor, extended from the Vindhaye mountains to Cape Comorin while an ally ruled in the Deccan. The latter was Muzaffer Jang who was killed in battle and succeeded by another French ally, Salabat Jang.

The year of 1750 was a time of heady success for the French. They had boxed the English into the two posts at Madras and Fort St. David. The success, however, did not last. In 1750, the English decided on a more active support for Muhammed Ali, and sent a column of six hundred Europeans and sepoys commanded by Captain Cope to help in the defense of Trichinopoly, and another column of sixteen hundred men to serve with Muhammed Ali's army in the field. The field army marched on Verdachelen which commanded the communications between Fort St. David and Trichinopoly. Their assault was repulsed, but they were not pursued in retreat and were able to march back to Trichinopoly. Although the siege continued, the French pre-occupation with it allowed a small English force, under Robert Clive, to take the opportunity to invade the territory of Chanda Sahib and seize his capital, Arcot, in a surprise attack. Chanda Sahib immediately reacted to pull some of his troops out of the siege, but his attempt to regain his capital failed after repeated assaults.

In March 1752, Major Stringer Lawrence led a relief column of fifteen hundred men. On route, the French tried to ambush the English force, but their numbers were too small to break the English advance. Instead, the French commander, Jean Law, abandoned the siege and retreated to the neighboring island of Shirangam where he held out against an English siege until June when he surrendered his entire army and all its supplies. Quoting from Major Lawrence's dispatches:

We took under convoy a large quantity of stores and ammunition for Trichinopoly and proceeding without molestation till we came near Giladdy on the 28th. When the enemy strove to take advantage of our incumbrence, for a strong detachment of French from Chanda Sahib's army having thrown up an entrenchment in the way we were to march. Cannonaded us from it, and endeavoured to interrupt our passage, which induced us on the Nabob's part to return the compliment, on occasion of loss of some men on both sides, but they did not advance, and we went on the next day. I was determined to reach Trichinopoly, which was about sixteen miles distant, and as the road lay in sight of the enemy's camp, they came out to oppose us with their whole force and I to receive the baggage went to meet them that it might be safe to camp in the meantime, which was effected. This brought on a cannonading which did us but little damage, but our guns galled the enemy very much, and forced them to retreat into a hollow way, on which I thought proper to draw off my men who were very much fatigued with their long march and joined the army that night. The enemy lost in this action above three hundred horse besides Allumin Caron, a man of great industry in the country.

We soon obliged Chandra to raise the siege of Trichinopoly and collect his forces in Syringham a pagoda on an island which was near, and by possessing ourselves of all the strong posts quite round it, we so effectually prevented provisions from joining them that Chandra's great army of above thirty thousand men was disposed or destroyed in less than two months, and himself with the French and a few black horse and sepoys that held out were in a miserable condition from want of sustenance.

This induced the Nabob to summon them to surrender prisoners, and after they had sent Chandra in the night time to Monaeje, our tanjore ally begging his protection, they delivered up the pagoda on the 3 June on condition that the French officers should have leave to go to Pondichéry on their parole never to serve against the nabob or his allies, and the soldiers to be sent to Europe. As the allies could not who should keep Chandra, to end the dispute his head was cut off. (British Library, London: I/1/2/72-73).

The French defeats in the Carnatic did not, however, mean that they ceased to be the paramount power in the south. In fact, their possessions increased appreciably through grants by Chanda Sahib, and Muzaffer and Salabat Jang of the jurisdiction and taxation powers over towns and hinterlands of surrounding villages. Karikal was the most important acquisition (British Library, London: I/1/1/125).

North in the Deccan, they had more military success thanks to the diplomatic shrewdness of Dupleix's agent, Charles-Joseph Patissier, marquis de Bussy-Castelnau.

Bussy was born in 1718 to a noble family living near Soissons. He came east to the Île de France and joined Bourdonnais afterwards in 1746. He later remained with the army at Pondichéry and came under Dupleix's command. He was placed in command of a French force that was marched to Aurangabad where Salabat Jang was crowned on June 20, 1751. Bussy's troops were concentrated at Aurangabad where he acted as protector and councilor to Salabat Jang. When a Maratha host threatened, Bussy countered with a march on Bider and decisively defeated them. Unfortunately for the French cause, Bussy became sick and retired for health reasons. His successor, Goupil, did not maintain discipline among the French troops and their misbehavior antagonized the population. The discontent was further fomented by Saiyid Lashhar, the hypocritical advisor to Salabat Jang, who secretly opposed the French while pretending to collaborate.

Bussy was recalled to duty and quickly brought the troops to order. He marched on Hyderabad and promptly signed an advantageous treaty for the French. The company got the concession to the four provinces of Mustafanagar, Ellur, Rajamahandri and Srikakolam, which later became known as the Northern Circars. The provinces yielded estimated rent payments of about 400,000 pounds (Malleson, 1909, 380) coming from an economic base that included teak forests, rice fields and cloth manufacturing. The treaty also specified a French guard for the Subadar and the requirement that state decisions in the Subadar's realm receive Bussy's consent.

Thanks to the stalemate in the south and Bussy's successes further north, Dupleix felt the French position was secure enough for him to sue for peace. The stumbling block was the English insistence that the French enemy, Muhammed Ali, remain as the ruler in the Carnatic.

A worse denouement, however, was in store for Dupleix than the petering out of peace negotiation. He had lost the support of the company directors in Paris. His warlike policies had depleted the company's exchequer and hurt the company's trade. He had devoted company funds, designed to buy return cargoes, to military purposes. Share prices for company stock held up, but dividends were cut to half from 1746 onwards and shareholders' discontent mounted. Notwithstanding the lack of support from Paris, Dupleix maintained his authority in Pondichéry more from the force of his character than formal powers, although they were somewhat strengthened when the governor regained, in 1750, sole authority in designating promotions in the company's ranks.

Dupleix was recalled in August 1754. The messenger was a company director, Charles-Robert Godeheu, who had nominally been commissioned to conduct an audit of the company's finances in India. He had earlier served under Dupleix who considered him a friend. Instead, he was an intriguer who subsequently took legal action against Dupleix and succeeded in financially ruining him.

More significantly, Godeheu succeeded Dupleix as governor, and promptly reversed Dupleix's policies of supporting Bussy's efforts to keep the Deccan in the French camp, maintaining the French occupation of the Northern Circars and keeping up the siege of Trichinopoly. In his concern for making peace with the English, his approach was to unilaterally make concessions. He freed the Swiss soldiers captured by the French with the consequence that the English could promptly re-employ them. Although reinforcements of two thousand French troops arrived, he refused to reinforce and adequately supply Mainville in the siege of Trichinopoly. Instead, he soon replaced Mainville with the more lackadaisical commander Jacques de Maissin who neglected to take vigorous counter measures against an English convoy, led by Major Lawrence, that entered the town, and re-provisioned and reinforced the garrison with twelve hundred English troops and three thousand sepoys. The siege became a lost cause and the French abandoned the besieging posts.

A truce was declared on January 11, 1755. It was preceded by prolonged but abortive negotiations in London between the duc de Mirepoix and the secret committee of the English East India Company, acting in concert with a secretary of state, Robert Darcy, the Earl of Holderness. The issues of contention were the garrisoning and division of the company's territories and the recognition of Muhammed Ali as the legitimate ruler of Arcot. (British Library, London: 1/1/1/162-169). There was an inherent problem for the negotiations. Some garrisoning of each company's posts was required if the posts were to have protection against attack from warring Indian potentates, but the presence of soldiery provided the companies with the wherewithal to field armies and engage in the play of Indian power politics. Although nothing was resolved at the London negotiations, they may have eased the way for agreement between Godeheu and Thomas Saunders, the governor of Madras. The truce was soon followed by a peace treaty that required each company to renounce the titles and powers obtained from the Mogul rulers. The French were to keep Pondichéry and Karikal with limited settlement elsewhere while the English were to possess Fort St. George, Fort St. David and Divicotta. The French abandoned claims to Masulipatam and Divicotta but were allowed to keep trading posts guarded by soldiers. Both agreed to construct no more ports. An indemnification plan was set up. Nevertheless, the peace was more apparent than real. In the spring of 1755, the British government reinforced the English company by sending a squadron of three warships, commanded by Admiral Charles Watson to India. They carried soldiers of the 39th regiment and an artillery detachment from the regular army.

The worse repercussions from the phony peace were the effects on the allies. The English kept their ally, Muhammed Ali, while the French had to forsake their allies to such an extent that they came to doubt the value of a French alliance. Godeheu's pusillanimity also had consequences for the French position in the Deccan. Palace intrigues, instigated by the chief minister Shah Nawaz Khan, led to Bussy's dismissal as advisor to Salabat Jang in May 1756. Bussy reacted promptly and led a force of about six thousand men, mostly sepoys, to the capital of Hyderabad where he set up an entrenched position in a northern suburb of the city. Most of sepoys soon deserted, but Law brought a relieving column of around one thousand men, and the combined force was sufficient to induce Salabat Jang to reinstall Bussy.

In the meantime, Godeheu had been replaced on March 25, 1755 by Duval de Leyrit who tried to preserve the accomplishments of Dupleix. He mildly acquiesced to the English breaking the treaty when they sent a column to help Muhammed Ali. In April 1757, de Leyrit roused himself to send a force, under d'Auteuil, to attack Trichinopoly. The French siege was, however, raised when the English succeeded in relieving the town.

Chapter 12
Debacle

The unofficial fighting between the French and English was more wide ranging than India and also included North America and the Caribbean. In late 1755 it came to a head when the British government ordered its navy to seize all French ships wherever they were on the high seas. The French government replied with an ultimatum, and the countries were officially at war by January 1756. In the same month, Britain concluded the Convention of Westminister with Prussia. It provided that Prussia would protect George II's possession, the electorate of Hanover.

In the meantime, factional infighting within the French government resulted in the French signing of the Treaty of Versailles in May with Austria. It was a drastic reversal of French alliances that gave little advantage to France, but brought French support and protection of the Austrian Netherlands during an Austrian attempt to regain Silesia. Frederick the Great read the signs correctly, and promptly invaded and occupied Saxony on August 29, 1756.

The French army won the initial victory at the battle of Hastenbeck when the beaten English army surrendered and disbanded in accordance with the Convention of Kloster-Seven. The French proceeded to occupy and pillage Hanover, but was otherwise inactive while the Prussian army went from victory to victory in 1757: it parried a Russian advance into East Prussia at the battle of Zorndorf in August, put an allied army to flight in Saxony at the battle of Rossbach in November, and defeated the Austrian army in Silesia at the battle of Leuthen in December. Soon afterwards, an Anglo-Hanoverian army drove the French out of Hanover and Westphalia. The French renewed the attack in 1759, but their invasion of Germany met defeat at the battle of Minden.

The last years of the Seven Years War looked bleak for Prussia. It was a small country with a small economic and manpower base. Its advantage was a well-disciplined and well-led army that won the battles but it was threatened by being ground between the armies of Austria and Russia. Fortunately for Prussia, salvation came when Tsarina Elizabeth died on January 5, 1762 and her successor Peter III promptly signed a peace with Prussia on May 22, 1762. Peace came with Austria on February 15, 1763. It brought a return to the status quo: Prussia kept Silesia and gave up Saxony. No peace treaty was needed with France. Prussia and France had not officially been at war, even though French armies fought with allies against the Prussian armies. Nevertheless peace treaties were required between Britain, France and Spain.

The victories of Frederick the Great were disastrous for France. So much French resources in manpower and treasure were wasted on fruitless campaigns in Germany that the British were able to pick off the French colonies abroad. In Canada, British forces captured Louisburg, Fort Duquesne, Fort Frontenac, Quebec and Montreal. In the West Indies, they seized the French islands of Guadeloupe, Martinique, Grenada, Saint Vincent and Saint Lucia. The losses were subsequently confirmed by the Treaty of Paris signed on February 10, 1763. Canada and some of the Caribbean islands passed to British possession, while Louisiana was ceded to Spain, which had entered the war late in 1762 as a French ally, and got nothing for its pains aside from getting Louisiana in place of giving up a more valuable colony, Florida, to the British.

India, however, was the scene of the worse French disaster. It was sealed where it began, far in the north in Bengal which had long been little involved in the warring between the rival European companies. The local Indian ruler was the nawab Aliverdi Khan who had inherited the governorship of the three provinces of Bengal, Bihar and Orissa, and exercised an independent rule with only nominal obeisance to the Mogul emperor. He had come to view the European trade privileges as an infringement on the sovereignty of his state, but took no overt actions. He died in April 1756 and his successor, Suraj-ud-Dowlah, shared the same feelings but was much less judicious. When he threatened the English, they proposed to the Dutch and the French that the three unite in opposition. Both refused although the French offered safe haven for the English in Chandernagor. They refused. In June, the nawab attacked Calcutta and quickly overwhelmed it. One hundred forty-five English men, women and children were imprisoned overnight in the infamous Black Hole of Calcutta. Only twenty-three survived to emerge next morning and be marched in chains to Murshidabad.

The English promptly retaliated by sending a fleet of five warships with transports under Admiral Watson. The transports carried a force of twenty four hundred men under the command of Robert Clive. The troops disembarked at Fulta at the end of 1757, marched on Calcutta, re-occupied Fort William almost without any fighting, recaptured Hooghly and fought a victorious battle at Baj Baj.

Although an awareness of the outbreak of war in Europe existed, the English were prepared to treat with the French through fear of the nawab's main army which their force had not yet encountered. Renault de St. Germain, the French commander at Chandernagor sent delegates to Calcutta with a proposal of a local neutrality. The English were initially interested and almost signed a treaty before procrastinating to await the military outcome. They dispatched a column of around two thousand men who marched on Chandernagor and began investing the land side, while the newly arrived fleet sailed up the river and bombarded the town from the shore side. The French garrison consisted of only five hundred troops, who surrendered within a couple of weeks. The soldiers became prisoners of war, while the civil servants and priests were allowed to leave from Chandernagor and the nearby French post of Cassimbazar. The French presence in the north of India was wiped out.

The English faced a more serious threat in the nawab's army which they met in June at the battle of Plassy. It was a memorable English victory in which about three thousand English troops beat and routed an army of fifty thousand men. Clive's report sets out a battle that was mostly a cannonading.

The Subject of this Address is an event of much higher Importance no less than the entire overthrow of Nabob Surajah Dowlah and the placing of Jaffir Ally Khan on the Throne. I intimated in my last how dilatory Surajah Dowlah appeared in fulfilling the Articles of the Treaty. This Disposition not only continued, but We discovered that he was designing our Ruin by a Conjunction with the French; To this end Monsr. Bussy was pressingly invited to come into the Province, & Monsr. Laws of Cossimbuzar (who before had been privately entertained in his Service) was ordered to return from Patna, about this time some of his principal Officers made Overtures to us for dethroning him, at the Head of these was Jaffir Ally Khan then Buxey to the Army, a Man as generally esteemed as the other was detested, as we had reason to believe the disaffection pretty general, We soon entered into engagements with Jaffir Ally Khan, to put the Crown on his head, all necessary preparations being completed with the utmost Secrecy the Army consisting of about 1000 Europeans and 2000 Seapoys with 8 pieces of Cannon marched from Chandernagore the 13th June and arrived the 18th at Cutiva Fort, which was taken without Opposition, the 22nd in the evening we crossed the River and landing on the Island of Cossimbuzar marched Straight for Placis Grove where we arrived by one in the Morning, at day break we discovered the Nabobs Army moving towards us consisting as we since found of about 15000 Horse and 35000 Foot with upwards of 40 Pieces of Cannon. They approached apace and by Six began the attack with as great number of heavy Cannon supported by their whole Army and continued to play on us very briskly for several Hours, during which our Situation was of the utmost Service to us, being lodged in a large Grove surrounded with good Mud Banks. To Succeed in an attempt on their Cannons was next to impossible as they were planted in a manner round us and at a considerable distance from each other. We therefore remained quiet in our Post, in expectation of a successful attack upon their Camp at night, about noon the Enemy drew off their artillery, and retired into their Camp, being the Same which Roy Dulob, had left but few days before and which he had Fortified with a good Ditch and Breastwork; We immediately sent a Detachment accompanied with two Field Pieces to take Possession of a Tank on the high Banks which was advanced about 300 yards beyond our Grove, and from whence the Enemy had considerably annoyed us with some Cannon managed by Frenchmen, this Motion brought them out a Second time, but on finding them make no great effort to dislodge us, we proceeded to take Possession of one or two more Eminencies lying very near an angle of their Camp, from whence and an adjacent Eminence still in their Possession they kept a smart Fire of Musketry upon us. They made Several attempts to bring out their Cannon, but our advanced Field Pieces played so warmly and well upon them that they were always drove back. The Horse exposing themselves a good deal on this occasion many of them were killed and among the rest Four or Five Officers of the first Distinction by which the whole army being visibly dispirited and thrown into some confusion, we were encouraged to storm both the Eminence and the Angle of their Camp, which were carried at the same instant with little or no loss, though the latter was defended (exclusive of Blacks) by 40 French and 2 Pieces of Cannon and the former by a large body of Blacks both Foot & Horse; On this a general Rout ensued and we pursued the Enemy Six Miles passing upwards of 40 Pieces of Cannon they had abandoned with an infinite number of Hackaries & Carriages filled with Baggage of all kind, Surajah Dowlah escaped on a Camel and reaching Muxadavad early the next morning dispatched away what Jewels and Treasure he conveniently could and he himself followed at midnight with only two or three attendants.

It's computed there were killed of the Enemy about 500. Our loss amounted to only 22 killed and 50 wounded and those chiefly Blacks during the warmest part of the Action we observed a large body of Troops hovering on our Right who proved to be our Friends, but as they never discovered themselves by any Signal whatever, we frequently fired on them to make them keep their distance; When the Battle was over, they send a Congratulatory Message and Encamped on our Neighbourhood that night. The next morning Jaffir Ally Khan paid me a Visit and expressed much Gratitude for the Service done him assuring me in the most Solemn manner that he would faithfully perform his Engagements with the English. He then proceeded to the City which he reached some hours before Surajah Dowlah left it.

As immediately on Surajah Dowlah's Flight, Jaffir Ally Khan found himself in peaceable possession of the palace and City. I encamped without to prevent the Inhabitants from being plundered or disturbed, first at Maudapoor, and afterwards at the French Factory at Sydabad; however, I sent forward Mers. Watts and Walsh to enquire into the State of the Treasury and inform me what was transacting at the palace. By their Representations, I soon found it necessary for me to be present on many Accounts. Accordingly the 29th, I entered the City with a Guard of 200 Europeans and 300 Seapoys and took up my Quarters in a Spacious House and Garden near this palace. The Same Evening I waited on Jaffir Ally Khan who refused Seating himself on the Musnund till placed on it by me, which done he received Homage as Nabob from all his Courtiers. The next morning he returned my Visit, when after a good deal of discourse on the Situation of his affairs, I recommended to him to consult Jaggaseat on all occasions who as a Man of Sense and by far the greatest property among all his Subjects would give the best Advice for Settling the Kingdom in Peace and Security; On this He proposed that we should immediately set out together to Visit him which being complied with Solemn Engagements were entered into by the three Parties for a strict Union and mutual support of each other's Interest. Jaggaseat then undertook to use his whole Interest at Delhi (which is certainly very considerable) to get the Nabob acknowledged by the Mogul and our late Grants confirmed likewise procure for us any other Phirm-maunds we might have occasion for. (British Library, London: I/1/2/341-344).

Plassy was a signal victory that gave the English control of Bengal, which was the most populous and richest territory in India. The British suzerainty was not immediately apparent. The nawab's treacherous general, Mir Jafer, became the official ruler of Bengal even before Suraj-ud-Dowlah was captured and executed. Mir Jafer signed a treaty that gave a large indemnity to the English and extended their territory and taxing powers in the vicinity of Calcutta. French posts and property were transferred to the English company.

During the remainder of the Seven Years War, the military action moved south where the French had an initial advantage of a larger army (British Library, London: I/1/2/388-389). The French government had planned an expedition of three thousand men drawn from the regiments of Lorraine, Berry and Lally along with artillery under the command of Thomas Arthur, comte de Lally-Tollendal. Before sailing from Lorient in May 1757, one-third of the troops were redirected to Canada. The fleet's admiral, the comte d'Aché, was an incompetent who insisted on a round-about route to India, via Brazil, that took twelve months to complete. The fleet only arrived at Pondichéry on April 28, 1758 at which point Lally replaced Duval de Leyrit as governor-general.

Lally found nothing in readiness to supply his army. The Pondichéry council was uncooperative, the admiral refused to give the appropriate naval support, and Lally was limited to land campaigns. He immediately led a small column against Gudalur but broke off the siege following an indecisive action between the French fleet and the newly arrived English fleet under Admiral Pocock. Lally reacted by leading his army on Fort Saint David which capitulated on June 2. It was the last French success.

In order to strengthen his army, Lally ordered Bussy to join him in Pondichéry. The withdrawal of the French troops from the Deccan resulted in Salabat Jang treating with the English company. He ceded Masulipatam, which an English force, under the command of Colonel Forde, took by assault in April 1759. The French commander, the marquis de Conflans, surrendered with his garrison of about 500 soldiers. (British Library, London: I/1/2/533-534).

A diversionary assault on Janjur failed and a later expedition in November of around seven thousand men failed in an attack on Madras because provisions ran out and the French ships had departed to the Mascarenes by the time an English fleet arrived in February to relieve the town. Lally retreated to Pondichéry, where d'Aché soon afterwards arrived with his fleet, but sailed away rather than encountering the English fleet. In October, the French troops mutinied over arrears in pay and were only brought to duty through payment of their wages. Lally led the French army out of Pondichéry and engaged the enemy at the battle of Wandiwash on January 22, 1760. Although the two sides were fairly equally matched, each having around five thousand soldiers, the French were beaten. Quoting from a narrative of the action:

> A body of about 2000 Moorattes, commanded by Innis Cawn joined the enemy at Ascot on January 9 and their whole army invested on Wandiwash on January 15. Our army marched to the relief of the place on January 21, arrived in evening at Isembore which is 8 miles north of it. Next morning, about day break, the whole army moved from Isembore, towards Wandiwash between 7 and 8 o'clock. Enemy cavalry appeared whereupon our Horse, and some companys of seapoys, with two pieces of Cannon, were ordered to advance upon them, which did some execution. Our army then inclined to the right, for about two miles, still continuing skirmishing with the enemy, after o'clock the two armies cannonaded each other very briskly, for about an hour. The enemy's line of infantry then marching up. Our army advances to attack them, and Colonel Cooke perceiving a tumbal of ammunication, to blow up on their left. Major Breeton with Colonel Draperc's regiment was ordered to wheel, and flank them upon which occasion they behaved with remarkable gallantry. Then two armies continued to advance upon each other, the whole lines made the action general which lasted till two o'clock, when the enemy were put to the rout, and fled under cover of their cavalry, in which they had a great superiority, and left us masters of the field of battle. Brigadier General Bussy, Colonel Murphy, the Chevalier de Godville, Quarter Master General and fourteen inferior officers are taken prisoners. The enemy had six hundred men killed and wounded, of which two hundred were killed on the spot. We are the masters of their whole camp, baggage and artillery, consisting of twenty one pieces of cannon, of which six are twenty four and eighteen are ten pounders. Our loss in the action is as follows. Ensign Stewart, Collins, and Evans killed, and ten officers wounded. Major Breeton amongst the latter, and it is feared dangerously, and one hundred and ninety non-commissioned and private killed and wounded. M. Lally with the remains of the French army retired to their garrison of Chelleput and Gingey. (British Library, London: I/1/1/488-489).

The battle at Wandiwash was decisive. It put the French on the defensive. Their army became isolated at Pondichéry where it was besieged. Lally capitulated after a long siege in January 1761. The English also mopped up the other French positions in the south of India.

The French empire in India was extinguished. Its last defender, Lally, suffered the same fate. He was transported as a prisoner to England where he was released and allowed to return to France. There he was tried for treason on the basis of the testimony of the Pondichéry councilors, convicted and beheaded on May 9, 1766. It was their treachery and the admiral's incompetence that had contributed to the French defeat. Not that they were principal cause. It was the victories of Frederick the Great. They set forth the salient weakness of a French maritime empire. French military commitments in Europe meant the French government had to scrimp on its navy, which was kept too weak to protect overseas routes for French shipping. As a result, the French could neither sufficiently reinforce their forces in either India or North America, nor carry on an adequate trade with India during wartime.

Chapter 13
Aftermath

The Treaty of Paris returned Pondichéry, Chandernagor, Mahé, Karikal and Yanaon to France on condition that fortifications be razed and military garrisons be limited to numbers needed for police protection. The company was also allowed to keep trading posts at Surat, Calicut, Balasor, Dacca, Cassimbazar, Patna, Jougdia and Masulipatam. The French presence in India became a few trading stations in a sea of British ruled and controlled territory.

The disaster of the Seven Years War led to another company reorganization as of August 1764, but not registered until June 28, 1768. It ended Crown control. The company was renamed the Compagnie Commercante des Indes. Its debts were liquidated and its administration changed to six directors elected by the shareholders for life and receiving salaries of fifteen thousand livres per year. They were assisted by six syndics also elected by the shareholders, but for terms of only six years. The departmental organization of two general departments and three particular departments was retained. Shareholders would meet twice a year, once in January when the directors were to present the annual report and in July when auditors, elected at the January meeting, reported.

Although the company's trading and financial condition was abysmal, similar conditions had existed after previous wars. Nevertheless, the Seven Years War was different. It had driven French power out of India, and the re-establishment of that power would have required a major commitment of monies and arms by the French state. The will did not exist. France had too many other more pressing obligations in Europe.

The climate of opinion had also changed. The company had been founded in the heyday of mercantilist thought by Colbert who is renowned as a great, if not the greatest, practicing mercantilist. A new school of economic thought, the Physiocrats, had appeared in the mid-eighteenth century. They came to formulate the leading system of economic thought in terms of intellectual and governmental influence. They launched a concerted attack on the company. It commenced with a report by Jean-Claude Vincent, seigneur de Gournay while he held the position of intendant general of commerce. His report in 1755 was addressed to his superior, Moreau de Séchelles, who was controller-general. It began with a discussion of the alleged faults of the company: a poor entrepreneurial spirit, finances resting too much on debt rather than equity, a personnel too concerned with private trade over attendance to company duties. The conclusion was that the company should be liquidated with its trade ceasing and its assets sold to reimburse its creditors. The report recognized that the assets were insufficient, and it recommended that the government make up the difference through a dispersal of very long-term debt obligations of the state. No action was taken, and the company continued in existence. It used a loan raised in 1767 to pay off much of its debt, but that repayment left it with few resources to re-equip its ships for trade. It tried to borrow again from the Crown. Its request was rejected.

The literary attack on the company continued and featured an essay by Abbé André Morellet (1769). He was a physiocrat who came to a physiocratic conclusion: government support of the company should be abandoned. He painted a dismal picture that helped mobilize opposition to the company. Notwithstanding the chorus of antagonism to the company, it had some defenders. In particular, Jacques Necker spoke out from his position as finance minister in the company's defense (Necker, 1769).

The culminating blow came on August 13, 1769, when the Council of State issued a declaration that took away the company's monopoly. Negotiations between the company and the Crown continued until 1770 when two declarations of February 17 and April 8 settled the financial affairs. The company ceded its rights and real estate to the Crown which obligated itself to pay an annual rent of 1.2 million livres so that the company could continue to pay the pensions to its personnel (Weber 1904, 614-615). The company was allowed to try to improve its finances by opening a lottery for twelve million livres.

Although the company lost its monopoly privileges, it retained an existence as a licensing bureau. Private traders were allowed to trade with the East, but had to get permission through the issue of passports at the company's office in Paris. Although the passports were free, they entailed awkward restrictions: ships had to be provisioned at one of twenty-one French ports of Bayonne, Bordeaux, Brest, Caen, Calais, Cette, Cherbourg, Dieppe, Dunkerque, Granville, Havre, Honfleur, Libourne, Marseille, Morlaix, Nantes, Rochelle, Rouen, Saint Malo, Saint Valery and Vannes. On their return, they had to put into Lorient even though they could later be unloaded at Nantes. During the next seven years, the private trade flourished and grew four-fold. In particular, the China trade grew to being worth about two-thirds of the Indian trade. (Weber, 1904, 616-620).

War again intervened when France became involved in the American revolution. It featured major French successes that were too belated to be significant. A French fleet of twelve ships under Admiral Pierre André de Suffren beat the English in four battles that gave the French a freedom of movement along the eastern coast of India. The French, however, were operating out of unfortified posts and were unable to capitalize on their naval successes to consolidate and extend their territorial possessions. Peace returned with the Treaty of Versailles in September 1783, and the French posts reverted to a continued unfortified state.

French trade went into its usual hiatus during the war. In an effort to reopen trade, the Crown decided to equip an expedition of two ships. No passports were to be issued to private traders until the expedition's return. Although the expedition did bring rich cargoes, the Crown reconsidered its plans and embarked on a different course of action. It reconstituted the company.

The newly appointed controller-general of finance, Charles Alexander de Calonne, was so instrumental in the company's rebirth that the new creation has gone down in history under the appellation of the Compagnie de Calonne. An edict of April 14, 1785 established it. The company was given a monopoly of the trade with the eastern coast of Africa, Madagascar, the Maldive Islands, the Red Sea, India, Siam, Indochina, China and Japan. The monopoly did not cover the Mascarene Islands, which were open to private traders subject to obtaining passports from the company. The islands' residents could trade with India. The company's charter was to run for a short period limited to seven years of peace, which supposedly would limit its exposition to war damages. The company was to be strictly a trading enterprise without any powers of territorial sovereignty. Nor was it to be involved in the financial operations, such as the tobacco farm, of the state.

The physical plant, including the port and facilities at Lorient, were returned to the company, and the government also presented some ships to it. The company looked like its old self, but was much diminished and even more dependent on the Crown. It had no means of defense other than protection of its shipping and trade by the royal navy. It had a promise of defense from the Crown, but a promise is not equivalent to the actual means of defense. The company's internal organization was not much changed: stock was floated, Lorient remained in its port, the bureaucratic organization to handle its shipping, provisioning, trading and selling was only slightly altered. A major change was that its overall direction was put in the hands of twelve administrators appointed by the Crown.

Hostility revived and escalated as disappointed private traders added their voices to those of physiocratic theorists. Notwithstanding its burgeoning choir of domestic enemies, the company flourished during the next few years. Its capital, its shipping and its trade steadily grew between 1786 and 1789. Then the roof caved in. The French revolution broke out in May 1789. The Estates General issued a call for complaints about the condition of the country, and many towns and localities answered with memorials, called the cahiers des Etats-Généraux. On the whole, the company did not fare well in the pages of the memorials. Some of the attacks were specific, more were quite general regurgitations of the benefits of free trade (Weber, 1904, 645-648). A committee was appointed to investigate the issue. Its report led to a vociferous discussion that terminated in a vote that was decisively against the company. It lost its monopoly while remaining in existence as a corporate entity with some elements of the past still in place. It and its competitors had to import goods through designated ports that included Toulon, along with Lorient, and the imports continued to be subject to import taxes.

The revolution continued on its path and the company's fortunes turned even worse under Jacobin rule. An edict on October 8, 1793 definitely suppressed the company. Many of its officers landed in prison and some ended on the guillotine. The shareholders had a better fate: they only lost their money.

The liquidation of the old Compagnie des Indes had proceeded slowly under the auspices of the Council of State during the years between 1770 and 1785. Its creditors were mostly paid off through the collection of debts owed to it. The new company of Calonne encountered an even more prolonged process of liquidation. It had received the capital plant and real assets of the old company, and its shareholders had been mostly the ones of the old company. Its liquidation was handled by the government's treasury office. Its pension obligations to company personnel were honored, and its creditors were paid off if they presented their claims by the end of 1794.

Shareholders were left in the lurch. Involved and unending legal proceedings continued until 1875 through many courts as governments and regimes changed. The legal battles yielded little satisfaction to the shareholders, and the only definite result is that the end of French East India Company can be set in 1875.

Part Two:

Trade

Chapter 14
Trade Routes

The trade between France and India can be divided into three periods under the aegis of three companies: the Compagnie Royale des Indes Orientales (1664-1719), John Law's Compagnie des Indes (1719 - 1721), and the Compagnie Française des Indes (1721 -1770). The period extends for about one hundred years although the ending is rather indistinct. The company's power was destroyed by French defeats in the Seven Years War, but the company staggered on for years. It retained its monopoly against much opposition and launched some expeditions within a couple of years after the war. The next decades saw abortive efforts at reorganization in the face of the eventual loss of monopoly rights.

Notwithstanding the checkered fate of French trade, its essential nature remained unchanged. Its purpose was to import goods from the Far East, most particularly India and China. Initially the Indian trade was much the more important, but the Chinese trade grew substantially during the eighteenth century.

The trade routes fell into a pattern that was much governed by the seasonality of the prevailing winds. The ships usually left France in the winter or early spring depending on the destination, with the ships for China leaving earlier than those for India.

On departure, the ships skirted along, but far out, the Atlantic coasts of Europe and Africa until they reached the Cape Verde islands, then proceeded south to Brazil where they caught the southeast trade wind driving them past the Cape of Good Hope. Ships for China continued on nearly the same latitude eastward before heading north through the passages of Java, Malacca or Bali, and sometimes as far out as the Philippines. Their usual destination was Canton which was the entrepôt for the tea trade.

Ships heading for India had a choice of two northern passages after passing the Cape of Good Hope. One was through the Mozambique Channel between

Africa and the west coast of Madagascar, up towards the Red Sea, and then cutting across the Arabian Sea for the south of India and Ceylon. The more common route was east of Madagascar to the Mascarene Islands of which Bourbon was a favorite provisioning station for the French. The ships left in the summer, proceeded north and then east to India. On reaching Cape Comorin or Ceylon, the ships turned north towards Pondichéry or Chandernagor which were the common destinations during the eighteenth century. Pondichéry was an open roadstand, and faced violent weather in the winter. Chandernagor was located up the Ganges River which had dangerous currents that required navigation by experienced pilots.

The return trip generally started in late autumn or the winter in order to take advantage of the prevailing winds towards the west. On passing the Cape of Good Hope, the ships travelled in the mid-Atlantic past St. Helena Island and the Azores before turning in towards the home ports in France. The entire voyage took between a year and a half to two years depending on the destination, the winds, the stayovers for provisioning on route and the unloading and loading of cargoes in the East. Side trips, such as to get specie at Cadiz in Spain, sometimes lengthened the voyage.

An eighteenth century account gives a fuller description of the usual routes. The narrator recorded longitude measurements by the Tenerife meridian which is about 18 degrees west of the Greenwich meridian, and he referred to the Mascarene Islands as the islands of France and Bourbon.

Abridged Instruction Concerning the Navigation from Europe to India and the
Return to India

The departure of ships from Europe to India is determined by the distance that is necessary for them to travel over the seas and the monsoons or weather conditions for reaching the destinations. That is why the time for departure is usually fixed between the beginning of October and the end of March.

When one sails from the harbor of Lorient, or any other harbor in France on the Atlantic Ocean, it is first necessary to go past the Cape Finistere, at 50 or 60 leagues off the cape and make for the island of Madeira. Although the sighting of that island is not absolutely necessary, it is well, however, to know its location in order to navigate with care, either to stay between the Canaries or east of the Canaries, depending on weather conditions. The winds usually blowing between France and the Canaries are variable, and therefore the passage of the ships is uncertain. Many ships do the trip in 12 days with favorable winds while others take 15 days.

It is around these islands that one finds the east-north-east to north trade winds blowing up to the limit of the 4 or 5 degree parallel in the northern latitude. This general rule, however, is prone to some variation: sometimes violent winds from south-west to west-north-west blow over the Canaries. To tell the truth, they are not frequent and do not last long. The area covered by these trade winds is not always the same at all times or seasons.

From the sighting of the Canaries, when one wants to go to Senegal or the island of Goree, one must steer towards the coast of Africa and reach 15 or 20 leagues north of the mouth of the Senegal River in order not to miss either place. If one wants instead to put into the port on the isle of Tiago, one of the islands off Cape Verde, one would have to sail further off the coast of Africa, and go towards the islands of Boa Vista or Maio, where one usually goes into the harbor of Praia on the bay located on the southeastern side of Tiago.

Ships with no intention of putting into port, either on the isles of Cape Verde or the coast of Africa, have to sail from the Canaries past, at 36 or 40 degree leagues off, Cape Blanc and steer south until reaching about 7 degrees latitude north, then to the south-southeast as close as possible in order to cut the Equator around the prime Tenerife meridian. Steering this way, one goes at about the same distance off the isles at Cape Verde and the continent, and one goes along the 35 degree longitude until the 7 degree latitude. When one sails from Goree, one has to steer to the south-southwest to reach the same area, but when one casts off from Tiago, the course is south, southeast until the equator. As said above, the trade winds from the Canaries reign at 4 degrees or 5 degrees latitude north. This rule holds during the months of January, February and March. But it is different at other times of the year. Here is what experience has taught us. In the months of April and May, the extent of the trade winds does not go beyond the 6 degree or 7 degree parallel during the month of June until the 8th of June. Although the winds blowing during the first six months between these parallels and the equator are very fickle, one can however observe that they more often come from the south and southeast than any other quarter. On the contrary, it is during the months of July, August and September that lulls and storms are very frequent in these areas. These winds come more from the south and west than from the east, and the winds only drive ships to the 11 degree to 10 degree latitude, and it is therefore at this time that their strength is the least.

As the sun moves off the equator towards the Tropic of Capricorn, the trade winds seem to approach the equator so that during the month of October, they are found up to the 8 degree latitude. In November and December, they blow between the 6 degree and 8 degree latitudes.

When one leaves the region of the trade winds, success does not allow making for the south-southeast. The best maneuver is to tack more to south than any other direction, without attempting to cut the equator at any particular point; it is the only way to shorten the crossing and avoid the delays experienced by navigators who acted differently.

The trip from the Canaries to the equator can usually be made in 25 days.

In fact, it depends on the duration of the lulls and other annoyances that come up around the equator. Many ships did the trip in 16 or 18 days, others could only get there in 48 days.

South of the equator along 12 degree latitude south, the winds generally blow from the southeast to the east during the whole year; they are called the general winds because they reign throughout the southern seas up to the Tropic of Capricorn, except in places close to the land where the wind sometimes changes. As these winds are contrary whatever their strength to the route that one should take from the equator to the Cape of Good Hope, ships have to sail with the wind as close as possible and take a course to the island of Trinidade and Rio de Janeiro on the coast of Brazil. One continues to navigate in that way until one reaches variable winds which can be used to steer across to the Cape of Good Hope. One usually meets these winds beyond the Tropic of Capricorn: they blow from the northwest to the southwest during almost the whole year, except in the months of December, January, February and March when winds frequently come from the opposite direction. Therefore, the crossings of the ships navigating in these waters at this season are often longer than any other time. According to a close examination of logbooks, it seems that the shortest crossing from the equator to the Cape of Good Hope to about 36 days, the average crossing took 50, and the longest ones took 64 days.

When the need for provisions, sickness or other eventualities force ships to land on the coast of Brazil at either Isle Grande or Rio de Janeiro, they have to steer from the latitude of Trinidade to sight Cape Frio where one can follow along the coast to one's destination.

When leaving from the Cape of Good Hope or the banks of the Aiguilles, one can go to India by three different routes. The first is through the Mozambique Channel, the second is by the islands of Bourbon and France, and the third is called the main route which is to pass clear of all the islands east of Madagascar. Each will be examined separately to give a sufficiently clear idea of the winds blowing over the seas. In the Indian Ocean, south of the 28 degree parallel, the winds follow the same pattern as in the Atlantic Ocean. They blow from the west throughout the year, except as has already been said, in January, February and March when the winds are frequently from the northeast to the southeast. There follows two consequences in relation to navigation. The first is that ships can at all times pass the Cape of Good Hope by going further down in the Atlantic Ocean and the second is that there is only one season when it is possible to go back towards the west. Here are particular instructions that experience gives. The months of June, July and August are always the most favorable months for ships to go past the Cape of Good Hope because the western winds are at their greatest strength and are much more constant. For the same reason, those who want to pass the Cape and return west cannot succeed and all attempts have failed. In the months of September, October and November, the winds are more moderate, are accompanied with lulls and are very fickle.

Although the western winds are particularly strong in June, July and August, it happens however that in April and May these winds are so strong that they are often like the winds at the end of autumn when one meets furious gale winds in this area. In the interval, they blow from the east so that ships can also go past the Cape of Good Hope during these two months and go back and forth.

At about 150 leagues east of the Cape, thunderstorms are frequent. The sky is almost always full of lightning and thunder, followed by heavy rains, so much so that one can hardly enjoy two days in a row of clear skies. This bad weather extends for more than 300 leagues. People who have travelled on these seas have noticed that the stormy area extends to the meridian that goes through the eastern side of Madagascar. From the 35 degree to the 25 degree parallel, the winds are variable, but beyond as far as the 10 degree to 11 degree latitude south, the general winds are blowing throughout the year from the south-east to the east. From that point to the equator, the year has two different seasons or monsoons during which the winds blow for about six months from one direction and six months from the other direction. It is the same in the Indian Ocean north of the equator except the winds come in the opposite direction at the same time of the year, while one enjoys the monsoon from the east in the northern hemisphere, the monsoon from the west reigns in the southern hemisphere. The monsoon from the east starts in April and continues until November, whereas the monsoon from the west follows and lasts until April. April and November are the months of change when the winds are prone to be variable because each changeover in the monsoons does not occur suddenly.

With this abbreviated description of the winds, the different routes of ships going to different destinations can now be described.

Crossing from the Cape of Good Hope to Pondichéry through the Mozambique Channel

When one leaves the Cape of Good Hope or by sounding at the banks of Aiguilles, one sails along the 37 degree to 38 degree latitude to take advantage of the western winds that are more frequent there than those at a lesser latitude, and can go east to the 65 degree longitude which passes north and south through the eastern side of Madagascar, and one has to steer north to meet it. The reason why one does not take a more direct route is because one sometimes meets variable winds around the 32 degree to 33 degree latitude. These same winds often blow from the northeast to the east, so strongly that if ships do not take the precaution of going to the east coast, they face the danger of falling towards the coast of Africa where it would be difficult to correct the course. After having sighted the southwestern side of Madagascar, one sails along the coast to St. Augustine bay located on the island below the Tropic of Capricorn. This place is a good place to stop for good provisions at a very cheap price. The crossing from the Cape of Good Hope to St. Augustine bay usually takes 22 to 24 days.

On leaving the bay, one must sail along the coast until reaching the 22 degree latitude and then skirt between the coast of Africa and a small island named Juan de Nova where one heads towards the isles of Anjouan and Mayotte. Some navigators prefer to stop at the isle of Anjouan than at Madagascar because one is sure to find an abundance of provisions, but it appears unhealthier than St. Augustine bay. From this isle, one first makes north and north quarter north east until reaching the 5 degree latitude: then to the north-east to go past the equator at the 71 to 72 degree longitude by the Tenerife meridian.

The trip from the isle of Anjouan to the equator takes about 12 days and from St. Augustine bay about 24 to 25 days.

As the monsoon, favorable in going to India, starts north of the equator, only about the 15th of April, it is pointless to reach this point before these weather conditions occur. There would be lulls and variable winds that would make the crossing long and painful and far from making it shorter.

The latest time limit when one can cut the equator on the same trip is the 8th or 10th of September, after which time one runs the risk of meeting the contrary monsoon before reaching one's destination and therefore not reaching it. These two

conditions do not solely concern the route from the Cape of Good Hope through
the Mozambique Channel, but also for crossings made via the islands of France
and Bourbon and by the main route once the equator has been cut at the 71 degree
to 72 degree longitude.

If one plans to go north of the islands of Laccadive, which are off the coast of Malabar, one has to continue the route making for north-east and northeast quarter east
until reaching the 14 degree north latitude and then steer east up to the sight of the
coast. But to make the trip shorter, one can pass between the islands of Laccadive
through the channel of Mamale. Then one must set off from the equator and make
north-east quarter east and east-north-east until reaching 4 degrees south latitude
while sailing east and one goes through the channel towards the Malabar coast.

Bad weather conditions over this area of India from May to the end of September
make it impossible for ships to land on the coast at this time of year. That is why
as soon as they come close to land either by sighting or sounding, they must move
away from the land and sail off the coast at a distance of 19 or 20 leagues until
Cape Comorin and then sail in order to land at the Cape of Galle on the southern
coast of the island of Ceylon.

From a sighting of this spot, one follows along the coast until opposite the bay of
Trincomalee, located on the north eastern side of the island. One must cross to the
coast of Coromandel and sail close to the land up to the harbor of Pondichéry.

Voyage from the Cape of Good Hope to India through the islands of France and Bourbon

As a precaution, it is also very important to sail east before entering the area of
variable winds. If not, one always risks missing the places where one wishes to
land. Therefore, after having gone past the Cape of Good Hope, and reaching the
37 degree latitude, one has to keep along it up to the meridian of the island of
France and from this position make north-east quarter north.

Steering to reach the 30 degree latitude, it is advisable to run north to the 36 degree
latitude and then go west to land on the island of France. Although these different
routes lead ships 800 leagues beyond the meridian of this island, they are necessary in order to avoid mistakes in reckoning. These mistakes have been the reason
why several ships have encountered the wind of the island of France and sometimes the wind of Bourbon. This eventuality is all the worse because these islands
are located within the general winds blowing from the same direction. Therefore,
it is very difficult to land because the wind blows one away from the islands. The
safest harbor on the island of France is situated on its northwest side. It is there that
ships usually stop. As for the island of Bourbon, there is no harbor sheltered from
the winds. Before 1723, the route going via the islands of France and Bourbon to
India was unknown to us. Ships leaving from these islands sailed back to the south
to reach variable winds, so that stopping at the islands was a detour that made the
crossing to India longer than the one made through the Mozambique Channel or
by the main route. To find a solution to this problem a new route had to be found.
The ships, the Lys and the Union, guided by two pirate pilots, refugees on the
island of Bourbon, were the first to make this discovery.

Setting off from this island, the two ships steered to and sighted the northern part of the island of Madagascar and saw it five days later. From this position, they made north straight up the equator and passed it on the 8th day through the 75 degree longitude by the Tenerife meridian without even knowing of the existence of the isles of Juan de Nova and Amirante which can be found on English and Dutch maps. From the equator, the ships, the Lys and the Union made for the north of the Laccadive islands, sighted the Malabar coast and arrived in Pondichéry on the 6th of October, eleven days after their departure from the island of Bourbon.

The success of this trip has led to navigators preferring this route to the one they formerly used. The trip is even more shortened when going through the channel of Mamale. The voyage from the island of France to Pondichéry is made in eight to ten days at present....

This crossing would be still much shorter if one knows of the existence and location of the isles that are north of these islands of Rodrigue, France and Bourbon, as well as the location of those isles that are to the south- south-east of the Maldives. Ships would not then be obliged to sight Madagascar nor pass by the channel of Mamale. They would go by a straight route on leaving the island of France, passing south of the Maldives, sight the island of Ceylon which would much shorten the trip and lessen the risk....

The trip of the ships, the Lys and the Union, has also been used to improve the maps describing this part of the Indian Ocean by finding several mistakes that seem to have been made by all geographers. The first is locating the northern part of Madagascar which is 50 leagues more to the west than as usually shown on their old maps; the other mistake concerns the number, size and position of isles and dangers that exist north and east of this island.

What has been said about the crossing to India via the Mozambique Channel is enough to determine the time of departure of ships from the islands of France and Bourbon. That is why one can avoid talking about it here.

On leaving the island of France around the end of September or during the months of October, November and December, one must sail with the general winds towards the south, at the rhumb line, as close to the wind as possible, hold it and continue holding the course until finding favorable winds for heading east so one can then turn towards the north reaching a point to the north-west of the island of Sumatra. Then the success of the trip becomes sure and one can go across to the Coromandel coast or the island of Ceylon if one wants to go for the Malabar coast.

Crossing from the Cape of Good Hope to India by the main route

Ships stopping at the Cape of Good Hope and not heading for any specific point on the islands of France and Bourbon will prefer to choose this last route as being shorter and less dangerous than the other route. After leaving the cape, one sails as if going east, except instead of following the route to east, one should sail roughly 12 degrees beyond the meridian of the island of France, then one sails to the north in order to sight and then sail for the eastern coast of the island of Ceylon and up the coast of Coromandel to Pondichéry.

This last route requires a lot of care not to unexpectedly sail towards the Maldives or the gulf of Mannara, which has happened to many ships. One must also avoid sailing too far east of the island of Ceylon because it is very difficult to reach the Coromandel coast with the winds of the western monsoon.

I have elsewhere sufficiently explained the navigation between points in India such as Bengal.

Return from India to France

In the Indian Ocean, north of the equator, the monsoon from the east follows the western one and determines the departure of ships going back to Europe. Those that sail from Pondichéry or any other place on the Coromandel coast need to be warned that this change means bad weather conditions. Ships that cannot be sent back by October, must winter at Merguy or Achem until the end of December as there is no harbor on the Coromandel coast where they would be sheltered from storms prevailing during this period of time; that is why one must consider two periods of time for departure from this coast. The first one is from the end of September until the 26th of October and the second is when winter comes during January and February.

When north of Pondichéry or anywhere on the coast like Madras or Pulicat or Masulipatam, one must wait as late before leaving the coast. From the end of September or the beginning of October, one must leave, if not one runs the risk of hurricanes which is what happened to the fleet of Monsieur de la Bourdonnais on the 14th of October, 1746 after the siege and capture of the city of Madras.

Ships leaving from Pondichéry in October can take advantage of winds coming sometimes from the north in order to round the island of Ceylon and pass the equator at 83 or 84 degrees longitude by the Tenerife meridian. They sail towards the south down to the latitude of the islands of Candu and Addu, which lie to the south, south-east of the Maldives archipelago. In the region of this parallel, one can get the general winds which help one sail south-west one-quarter of west to west-south-west. In order to next reach the latitude of the island of France, one takes the route to the west in order to land there. The crossing from Pondichéry to this island usually takes 40 to 45 days.

Ships sailing from Pondichéry in January follow the same path but after the 8th of February, the stop-over at the islands of France and Bourbon would make them miss the best season to pass the Cape of Good Hope, and they would have to go back and winter on those islands until the following November. To avoid such a delay, one must pass the equator, go around the Cape of Good Hope and stop at the island of St. Helena. This case also applies to ships leaving from Bengal or the Malabar coast via the islands of France and Bourbon. They must begin between the 15th of November and the end of January. When leaving from the mouth of the Ganges, one makes a course towards the south in order to pass the equator at about the same longitude as if one left from Pondichéry.

The same season is the best for ships leaving from Surat, Goa, Mahe and all other places south on the west coast of India. First they must skirt along the coast without changing course, up to Cape Comorin. Second, they must sight the headland of Galle on the island of Ceylon. Third, they sail south-east one-quarter south and pass the equator on the 82 or 83 degree longitude by the Tenerife meridian. On this last route, it is necessary to steer far from the Maldive Islands where the currents are often strong. At the equator, ships take the same route as those leaving from Pondichéry or Bengal.

Crossing from the Islands of Bourbon and France to Europe

As I have described, the winds prevailing in the Indian Ocean means that one must sail from these islands sometime between the beginning of November and the end of March.

One first makes south-west by the 33 or 34 degree latitude, then navigate to cross the banks of Aiguilles and round the Cape of Good Hope. It is always good to do it by sounding and sighting the land, keeping a close but safe distance from the Cape, in order to avoid accidents that mistakes in reckoning can cause. The voyage from the islands of France and Bourbon to the Cape of Good Hope usually takes 25 to 30 days.

After having rounded the Cape, ships take a route north-west and the general winds that are contrary when going to India are always favorable for the return. If one wants to stop at the islands of St. Helena or Ascension, one can when one reaches the latitude of these islands, and one must make for the west in order to land there. Leaving either place, one sails northwest up to the equator and from there goes north-north-west, passing about 50 or 60 leagues off the islands at Cape Verde. As the winds that one meets north of the equator are contrary to the direct path, ships are obliged to steer as close to the wind as possible up to the area of variable winds which they will use to make for the Azores islands. One can sail between these islands or leave them and skirt the east coast, but one must avoid sailing between these islands and the island of Madeira especially in May, June, July and August because one very often finds in these passages the winds from north east that are directly contrary to the route that must be taken in order to arrive in Europe.

The crossing from the Cape of Good Hope to the equator takes from 30 to 35 days, including the time resting at the island of Ascension. The crossing from the equator to France takes about 45 to 50 days.

Voyage to China

It is necessary, when possible, that ships going to China use the winds running from December or at the very beginning of that month when making the passage by the islands of France and Bourbon, because the crossing by these islands is much longer than that from the Cape of Good Hope to the Straits of Sonde. So it is better, other things begin equal, to stop at the Cape than at the island of France.

On leaving Europe, ships take the same route to the Cape of Good Hope as those going to India. But after rounding the Cape, here is what must be done. When reaching 37 degrees latitude, one maintains a course east for about 1100 leagues or the same thing until one is south on the meridian that is 70 degrees more east than that at the Cape of Good Hope. It is not absolutely necessary, however, to sight the islands of St. Paul and Amsterdam. Their sighting helps a lot in the crossing to correct any reckonings. These islands are situated 56 degrees east of the Cape on the 37.50 degree latitude.

At 70 degrees longitude east of the Cape, one slowly shifts to the north so that one can cross the Tropic of Capricorn at 15 degree south latitude in order to reach 83 degrees longitude. Having taken the course north, one can use the variation or declination of the compass to make more certain one's position and one sees in this part of the eastern seas the variations of the compass reach such magnitudes that going eastward or westward, one can encounter great errors with different estimates of the longitude. But to get benefit from it, one has to take observations with good instruments and at times when the ship's motion does not interfere with the readings of the compass.

From the Tropic of Capricorn, one makes a course north-north-east going 60 leagues west of the rocks named the Triads and after passing them, sailing in the same way until sighting the island of Java, and by this means, one can land at about 40 leagues east of the Straits of Sonde, taking precautions necessary to avoid mistakes made by guesses. The coast of Java, being sighted, one has to sail along it at a distance of 4 or 5 leagues until reaching the Straits of the Sonde.

As I have elsewhere written, different routes can be taken from the Straits of Sonde to China....

Regarding ships sailing from the islands of France and Bourbon to China, they have, on leaving those islands, to sail for the south coast close to the wind as possible by the 37 degree latitude and then steer as mentioned above.

The average crossing from the Cape of Good Hope to the Straits of the Sonde takes two months and the crossing from the straits to China takes about 24 to 25 days.

The crossing from the island of France to the straits usually takes 40 days. If one adds the 35 days for the average crossing from the Cape of Good Hope to this island, it can be seen that ships usually need 15 extra days to go from the Cape to China when stopping at the island of France. One can still go to China through the Straits of Malacca when leaving from these islands if one knows the way. The passage is not more dangerous than the one going through the Straits of the Sonde and does not require more time. One must first follow the same course as going to Pondichéry. With a sighting of the island of Ceylon, and from there, one sails to land on the northwest headland of the island of Sumatra and take the Straits of Malacca. (Bibliothèque Nationale, Paris: NAF 9228/178-186. Translated by the author.).

These routes are illustrated with a map in another reference (Bibliothèque Nationale, Paris: Fr 9555/224).

The voyage could be dangerous, and the experience of the French company was unlikely to be much different than that of the English company. Disaster could occur anywhere on the route, including near the homeport.

The tale of disaster to the Company's ships is a long one. Between the years 1700 and 1818, no less than 160 Indiamen were lost by wreck, burning or capture. A high proportion of the first was due to foundering; but fire was another peril of the sea....

Two of the wrecks have become classic. The *Grosvenor*, an Indiaman of 729 tons under the command of Captain John Coxon, called at Madras in April 1782, on her way to Europe from Calcutta. All went well until 4 August, when the ship ran ashore on the coast of Africa, some five hundred miles from the Cape. One hundred and thirty-five persons, of whom several were women and children, reached the land: but none were ever heard of again except three seamen and a cabin boy who made their way by land to Cape Town....

The wreck of the *Halsewell* on the island of Purbeck off the Dorset coast on 6 January 1786, created no less sensation. In an engraving by Pollard from a painting by Robert Smirke, R.A., which was published in the same year, the commander, Richard Pierce, is represented on the poop with his two daughters, his two nieces, and three other young women who all perished with him. Of the officers, the second mate (Henry Meriton), the third and sixth mates, and two midshipmen were alone saved. Seventy Lascars were drowned, and more than thirty others among the passengers and crew. (Cotton and Fawcett, 1949, 126-128).

French ships had similar, albeit less renowned, experiences. One such tragedy occurred early in the seventeenth century to ships from Saint Malo.

All the sails clapped in the wind of a clear morning light in May: two ships from St. Malo making for the route towards India and the southern seas.

They were the *Croissant* and the *Corbin*. The first was commanded by Michel Frottet, seigneur de la Bardelière; François Crou, seigneur du Clos Neuf, commanded the second. The purpose of the voyage was to again follow the old route to the Indies, which had been followed by navigators since the beginning of the sixteenth century. That famous route had become the obligatory route.

According to the custom of the times, each captain had a writer on board. One of the two, Léon Guérin, survived the expedition and left an account of what happened.

The *Croissant* and the *Corbin* reached the high seas and crossed path with several Dutch ships. Peace existed between the countries, and the French were surprised when a cannon shot brusquely ripped the sail of the *Corbin*. While the French rapidly prepared for the offense, the Dutch admiral hastily sent his excuses and an explanation of the accident: believing he was firing a blank, the cannonier responsible for paying honors to friendly ships was drunk and fired a cannon ball. The mistake was forgiven by the French. After exchanging salutes, each continued on route.

Everything went well for the French until the Cape of Good Hope. They doubled it during the night and tried for a route that became fatal for the expedition. After passing through the channel of Mozambique, a violent storm struck them so suddenly that they did not have time to shorten sails. They were struck by wild winds. The rain fell with such violence that the sailors were hurt in their faces and hands, which made their movements slow and fumbling. Water swamped the casks and ruined the provisions and merchandise. The *Croissant* had several leaks in the hull, and the rudder of the *Corbin* was damaged.

The storm raged for four days and nights, and the crew faced unceasing danger.

Worn out with fatigue and hunger, they nevertheless reached Madagascar. Obliged to remain there several weeks to repair the damage, most of the crew contracted a pernicious fever that was ravaging the country.

Jean Crou was among the gravely ill. In hope of saving his friend, Bardelière was hard at work and hastily gave the order to depart. The ships sailed towards India and north of the Maldives. Despite the gravity of his state, Jean Crou maintained command of his ship and discharged his duties with surprising energy. At the end of the third day, he was so exhausted that he lay down and slept soundly. The sailors were without surveillance, the sea was calm, they drank too much and fell asleep.

Suddenly a brutal jolt woke them with a start. Each hurried to this post. Too late, the *Corbin* had hit a rock. Then a second more violent jolt set the ship on its side. Sinister crackings were heard. With superhuman energy, Jean Crou, while almost dead, took over the direction of the ship. During the night, the *Croissant* was so far ahead that the cannon alarm was at first not heard, and when the distress was finally noticed, Bardelière tried to return as fast as possible, but the wind was contrary and the ship was obliged to tack about.

In the meantime, Jean Crou had the life boats put out. Loaded with equipment, the boats landed on the coast where the sailors were attacked and captured by savages. Almost all, including the captain, were tortured. Only two succeeded in escaping.

The crew of the *Croissant* was distressed by being unable to prevent the capture of their friends. They continued on their route. Then Bardelière also fell sick. He continued command until his last breath and died in the twilight of December 1, 1602. La Villeschar, the second in command, succeeded him. Bad fate continued to plague the expedition: violent storms continued without abatement. More and more men became sick, the provisions were insufficient. Starving, they had to live on dogs and rats.

Finally, they met a Flemish ship that took them aboard. A new storm suddenly came, and the foresail mast split. The hull was already gravely damaged. In an instant, the *Croissant* disappeared into the sea.

Most of the sailors died during the return trip. A brilliant expedition returned to St. Malo with a few dying sailors, weakened by fatigue and sickness (*Le Lingot*, January 1952, 7. Translated by the author.).

Chapter 15
Patterns of Trade

The voyages were long and dangerous. Their overall objective was to arrive back in France so that the cargoes could be sold at auction. In time, the sale of incoming cargoes became quite routinized into auctions usually held once a year in the autumn. Earlier auctions were held in a variety of ports, but eventually they became established in Nantes at the beginning of the eighteenth century and later were transferred to Lorient. The transfer stirred considerable controversy. The company claimed that the construction of much enlarged facilities in Lorient would permit the consolidation of the company's operations in holding the auction sales and accumulating provisions, cargoes and munitions for the voyages. It would also save on the trouble and cost of transshipments from Lorient to Nantes. Understandably, the merchant community in Nantes was much upset about the proposed move. They argued that a purely company establishment could never offer the same full range of suppliers, shipping, dockers, carters, living quarters for visiting merchants, credit facilities and all the conveniences of mercantile operations, and many buyers at the auctions would still have their purchases transshipped to Nantes for shipment abroad and elsewhere in France (Archives Municipales de Nantes: HH 218/9/1-8).

Notwithstanding the opposition from Nantes, the company undertook a large expansion of its capital plant in Lorient and built warehouses, an auditorium for the auction sales, living quarters for its personnel and shipbuilding facilities. The first auction in Lorient came in 1734. The company was able to exercise a more detailed and stringent control, particularly with regard to cottons because of a concern for competition with the domestic French industry. The sales were otherwise little changed and continued to be divided into four main categories: drugs, dyes and groceries; silk and silk goods; cotton and cotton goods; and a mixture of commodities including metals, wood, porcelain and tea.

The history of the trade of the Compagnie Royale des Indes Orientales and the Compagnie Française des Indes have some close parallels. Both trades were subject to wide fluctuations about a rough trend, except during war when the trade plummeted.

The pattern holds for both companies. The import and export data are much worse for Compagnie des Indes Orientales. Statistics on the annual value of trade do not exist, and reliance rests on shipping statistics. They give yearly lists of company ships leaving and returning to France (Kaeppelin, 1967, 653-661). When those data are combined with the record of the ships' tonnages (Estienne, 1996, 67-131), an estimate of the annual tonnage of importation and exportation can be formed for the period between 1665 and 1709. These estimates are given in Table 1.

The picture of both imports and exports reveals much variation from year to year, but little indication that the trade was either gradually increasing or decreasing. War, however, had dramatic effects. Four wars occurred during the period: the War of Devolution, 1667 - 1668; the Dutch War, 1672 - 1678; the War of the League of Augsburg, 1688 - 1697; and the War of the Spanish Succession, 1701 - 1713. Each war brought a collapse in the trade, with exports declining sooner than imports.

The lagged pattern of imports is not surprising. The coming of war would be expected to affect exports quickly, and plans for collecting and dispatching cargoes were probably soon abandoned or much curtailed at the outbreak of war. In contrast, news of war would have taken approximately seven to nine months to reach India if they travelled by the usual passage. The news would then have arrived long after plans for collecting return cargoes had been made and acted upon, and the laden ships sent home even when the risks were great.

Another contrast between imports and exports is that the peaks seem more elevated for exports and immediately proceed the outbreak of war. The pattern is understandable: outgoing cargoes would be expected to be more quickly collected and dispatched as the prospect of war loomed.

A statistical analysis bears out this picture. The regression equation is the same for either imports or exports.

$Y = k + a t + b w$
Where y is the tonnage of imports or exports
k is the constant
a is the coefficient for variable time which is t
b is the coefficient for variable wartime which is w

The best statistical fit for imports is lagged one year for the trend, and two years for war. Even that fit is not good. The adjusted R- square is only 0.22. The equation is:

```
Imports   =    783.54  +  24.07t  -  693.04w
S.E.          (245.11)    (9.83)    (254.24)
t-values       (3.20)     (2.45)    (-2.73)
```

For exports, the best fit is lagged one year for both trend and war. The fit is poor, with the adjusted R- square being 0.25.

```
Exports   =   1146.71  +  19.38t  -  727.23w
S.E.          (223.81)    (1.00)    (204.18)
t-values       (5.12)     (2.15)    (-3.56)
```

The statistical record is considerably better for the Compagnie des Indes. The annual values of the company's imports and exports are available from 1725 to 1770. Table 2 gives the figures for importation and exportation. One column gives the value of sales of imports from India and China (Raynal, 185). The other column gives the data for merchandise exports (Haudrère, 1989, 14, 1198).

The picture is similar to the earlier company: much fluctuation from year to year with little in the way of trend, but trade collapsing during the wars. Only two wars, the War of the Austrian Succession, 1741 - 1748, and the Seven Years War, 1756 - 1763, plagued the later company. Imports appear to lag behind exports.

The statistical analysis is similar to that for the Compagnie des Indes Oriental-es. The regression equation is the same and is used for either imports or exports. The differences are in the lags. The best fit for imports is lagged by one year, and gives an adjusted R- square of 0.48.

```
Imports   =    15.46  -   0.01 t  -   5.47 w
S.E.          (4.66)     (0.16)     (2.55)
t-values      (3.32)    (–0.08)    (–2.14)
```

The best fit for exports is not lagged. Its fit is also good with an adjusted R-square being higher at 0.62.

```
Exports   =    14.11  -   0.07t  -   7.80 w
S.E.          (4.27)     (0.14)     (1.82)
t-values      (3.30)    (–0.47)    (–4.28)
```

Both regressions give the same story: no trend and abrupt falls during war, although the wartime effects appear lagged for imports. The lag seems to have been shorter for the Compagnie des Indes compared to the Compagnie des Indes Orientales.

Chapter 16
Structure of Trade

I

The impetus behind European trade with the Far East was the European demand for certain products that were not grown nor much produced in Europe. These goods provided the principal imports and noticeably predominated over other imports. They also overshone exports, which tended to be a mixed and varied bag of goods for which the eastern demand was so slight that specie was usually the principal export.

The statistical data on imports come from notices of the company's auction sales. The company's monopoly is presumed as effective which implies that the auctions provide a reasonably good measure of the quantities of imports. They are not perfect measures. Although the companies usually had only an autumn auction, they may have held other auctions in any particular year. No more than one auction notice was, however, located for any one year.

The imports were not all consumed and used in France. Some were re-exported. There may also have been a smuggling trade with the result that both imports and re-exports can have been enlarged, however, to an indeterminate degree.

The contents of the auction sales are laid out in Tables 3 and 4. The sources are printed handbills except for the first two years in Table 3.

Most of the commodities were measured in livres. The exceptions are porcelain, textile cloths and rattan. Porcelain was recorded in either pieces or caisses or rouleaux, cloth in pieces and rattan in pacquets. For any commodity, other measures were occasionally used. The commodities are usually listed in the English words except for textile cloth, which are listed in French words because many of the fabrics may have been particular to the French market. Drugs and dyes are also listed in the French. Table 3 gives a few auction sales for the Compagnie des

Indes Orientales: the first year being twenty-three years after its founding, and most of the remaining years are during the last two decades of its existence. The scarcity of auction notices for the Compagnie des Indes Orientales gives way to a plenitude for the Compagnie des Indes. Table 4 shows them being available for most years between 1720 and 1741, which was a period of prolonged peace for France. Few auction notices appear during the years of war except for two years, 1749 and 1750, during the War of the Austrian Succession, and three years, 1756, 1761 and 1764 during and immediately after the Seven Years War. The last years of 1766, 1767 and 1769 come after a return to peace. The auctions were held in Nantes until 1733, thereafter at Lorient. Almost all years of record are based on auction notices. The exception is 1750, for which notices of the cargoes of incoming ships are used.

Although an earlier European trade had been in spices, the Compagnie des Indes Orientales became established too late in history for spices to predominate in its trade. That was certainly the case towards the end of its existence, for which the auction notices exist.

The years show common features. In terms of quantities, the big imports are pepper, saltpeter and textiles. All came from India. Besides cloths, textiles included cotton thread and raw silk, of which some of the latter came from China although probably obtained through Indian middlemen. Other, albeit lesser, imports of significance were cowry, drugs, dyes, gum, lacquer, rice and wood. Their quantities varied quite markedly from year to year. Little coffee was imported, and the quantities of porcelain and tea were minuscule.

The trade changed considerably during the early years of the Compagnie des Indes, although pepper and textiles consistently remained as the big imports. The radical change was for coffee, porcelain and tea. Coffee again becomes imported in the mid-1720s and steadily grows into a sizeable trade in the 1730s. Initially, most came from Moka, but shifted in the late 1730s to coming predominantly from Bourbon. Tea was the great success story with its imports rising to huge figures. Porcelain became a steady import, but fluctuated considerably: sometimes imported and sometimes not. Typically, only the number of caisses and rouleaux are recorded, but sometimes the number of pieces of different kinds of porcelain is recorded, and includes all the dishes that might appear on a well-set table. The commonplace, however, predominates and the biggest imports were cups, plates and saucers.

The other imports have a much more varied record. Cowry, drugs, dyes, gum, lacquer were sometimes large, sometimes non-existent and sometimes moderate in quantities. Drugs and dyes were quite varied. Their classification is based on Savary (1723). Most of these imports appeared only occasionally. Esquine and galange were drugs that were regularly imported while curcuma was the only dye that was much of a regular import. The other dyes later become negligible.

Gum and lacquer were regular imports. Gum came from different sources and in different forms, and varied from zero to occasionally large figures. Lacquer had a more regular pattern. The principal varieties were *en bois* and *en feuille*, with the latter usually being much the larger during the times of the Compagnie des Indes. Metals were sizeable in one year in the first decade of the Compagnie des Indes and later became a regular import that varied widely in quantities. The metals sometimes included tin and usually were exclusively tutenag.

Wood and wood products fluctuated considerably and were sometimes large. Wood was primarily sapan wood or red wood with the importation of the latter being greater. Wood products included a variety of commodities, each appearing now and then. Rattan, however, was a regular import.

A variety of other products have an episodic character of importation: sometimes small imports occurred, occasionally the importation could be large, and most typically none were imported. They include the remnants of the spice trade, as well as hemp, hides, ink, ivory, mother of pearl, paper, sugar and varnish. Rice and tobacco were never appreciable imports and ceased being imported altogether, while saltpeter was occasionally imported in relatively large quantities. Sugar was sometimes imported in the early 1720s, but stopped being imported after 1731, probably because of competition from closer sources at the plantations in the West Indies (Higman, 2000).

Similar characterizations of auction sales held for the wartime and post-war periods. Coffee, pepper, porcelain, tea and textile cloths continue to be largest in quantities. There is a considerable drop in the quantity and variety of sales during the two wartime periods, and a noticeable recovery in the post-war years when most of the other commodities cease being episodic. Dyes, gum, lacquer and saltpeter seldom appear.

Textiles constituted the key import of both the Compagnie des Indes Orientales and the Compagnie des Indes. They were regularly a large import in terms of volume and had the greatest variety of product. Most were finished cloth, although there was an import of raw material, principally raw silk, and intermediate products, principally cotton thread.

Cloth sales are arranged in a classification of muslin, ordinary cottons, coarse cottons, mixtures of cotton and silk, and silk. The ordinary cottons are divided into the sub-categories of finished and finer, unfinished and finer, finished and coarser, and unfinished and coarser. The placing of particular cloths in a particular category rests on their descriptions in Savary (1723), Weigert (1964), Irwin and Schwartz (1966), Hobson-Jobson (1986), Chaudhuri (1978), Wingate (1979), and Murphy (1997).

Muslins exclude muslins particularly identified as made of silk. Ordinary cottons could have been placed in three broad categories with a middling category put between finer and coarser. The descriptions, however, are better in classifying between better and worse. Finished fabrics are more worked upon fabrics described as striped, checked, plaided or figured. Unfinished fabrics are less worked upon fabrics, *i.e.* unbleached, bleached and/or dyed. The category unfinished and coarser includes fabrics without a definition. They were: Balnat, Calbats or Chalbats, Gilmilis, Godcellet, Habassis, Halabe, Haliaffy, Halibannis, Nensougues, and Vansouques.

Coarse was the last category of cotton fabrics. It included some fabrics that may have sometimes been mixtures with linen, hemp or wool. The next category included cotton and silk mixtures irrespective of which thread was used for the weft or warp. It also included atarasoye and salasoye for which there were no definitions, but include the word for silk in their names. The final category included all kinds of silk cloth irrespective of quality. It also includes coaneuries.

Most cloths have similar descriptions in the different reference sources. Some have different descriptions. The descriptions can be found in the textile glossary which gives alternative spellings for a particular cloth. When the descriptions differed but were equally specific, the choice favored the French over the English and the older over the newer source. In other words, Savary was the preferred source. The fabrics are listed in their French names as English translations are seldom obvious.

Although there was considerable variation in the quantities of sales in any category, all categories tended to have sales throughout the entire period from 1687 to 1769. Muslin had sales in every year. There was no particular kind of muslin that predominated. The more important kinds tended to be adatis, betilles, casses, chavonis, mallemolles, tangebs, tarnetannes, terindannes and toques.

Finer kinds of ordinary cottons tended to have smaller sale; among these fabrics, the sale of chites, organdies and percales predominated. Cravates were placed in this category. The coarser kinds of ordinary cottons had much larger sales. Their principal types were guineas, battas, basins, guingans, salempores, and sanas.

Coarse cottons tended to be much smaller in the sales. Their principal fabric was garas. The sales of silk fabrics and cotton and silk mixtures were also small. Both had a varied range of fabrics with none particularly predominating.

Such is a characterization of the French trade as revealed by the auction sales. Another document exists for a shorter period of the decade between 1735 and 1743. It gives a report of estimated averages of imports by four ships during that decade (Centre des Archives d'Outre-mer, Aix-en-Provence: C/2/34/131). The figures are given in Table 5. One column gives imports from Pondichéry and the other column gives sales. Although some other goods are noted, the principal emphasis of the data in Table 5 appears to have been textile imports. There is not much agreement between the data in Table 5 and the data for corresponding years in Table 4. For textile cloths, muslin and coarser fabrics also predominate. No silk goods are reported, which suggests that the report is mostly based on the trade with Pondichéry.

II

No theoretical explanation of the imports and their relative quantities is given. It is rather presumed that they responded to the company's judgments as to the nature and size of the market demands in France and Europe.

Nevertheless, a synoptic view of the imports can be germane. Textile cloth was the one continuously significant import, and Table 6 gives the textile imports of the Compagnie des Indes Orientales and Table 7 gives the same data for the Compagnie des Indes. These tables clearly present their relative importance. Muslin and unfinished coarser cottons regularly predominate throughout the record of both companies. The unfinished coarser category includes fabrics that are definitely classified as coarse as well as some cloths that could not be clearly identified as better quality fabrics. Most of the other categories were typically imported, but in smaller quantities. Silk and mixtures of cotton and silk were quite irregular in their importations.

All other imports, as summarized in Tables 8 and 9, have a much more varied record. Coffee and tea were imported in negligible quantities by the Compagnie des Indes Orientales, but grew to large quantities under the Compagnie des Indes. Pepper and saltpeter had a reverse history: relatively large during the earlier company and eventually falling off quite markedly during the later company.

A statistical analysis bears out the above characterizations of textile and major imports. The totals for Tables 6 and 7 are straightforward sums of the yearly columns. Similarly, albeit with less justification, Tables 8 and 9 give the totals of the major imports. Textile cloth was regularly quoted in pieces as was occasionally porcelain. However porcelain was more usually quoted in caisses and rouleux, which are sometimes quoted interchangeably (Centre des Archives d'Outre-mer, Aix-en-Provence, Aix-en-Provence: C/2/50/198 and C/2/53/295) and consequently presumed to have the same content equalling 300 pieces. (Service Historique de la Marine, Lorient: C/2/49/162). Drugs and dyes were sometimes quoted in caisses, which were converted to livres on the basis of one caisse equaling 96 livres (Centre des Archives d'Outre-mer, Aix-en-Provence: C/2/6/57). The same conversion was used for metals.

Tea was sometimes quoted in ballots, barces or boetes. They are converted to livres on the basis of one ballot equaling 240 livres (Doursther, 1965, 42-44). Balles of raw cotton and silk were converted to livres on the grounds of one balle equaling 57 pieces, as in the case of muslin (Archives Municipales de Nantes: HH 222). For thread, the equivalence was one balle equaling 220 livres (Centre des Archives d' Outre-mer, Aix-en-Provence: C/2/6/57). Rattan was quoted in either pacquets or livres, but entered into Tables 8 and 9 as livres with the conversion being one pacquet equaling 29.55 livres (Centre des Archives d' Outre-mer, Aix-en-Provence: C/2/53/295).

The point of conversions is to have the figures in Tables 8 and 9 to be in pieces for textile cloth and porcelain and in livres for all the other commodities. The totals are consequently meaningless in themselves, but are nevertheless of some use in highlighting any significant contrasts in the distribution of the imported quantities by the two companies.

Not all the years for which data are quoted in Table 4 are included in Tables 7 and 9. The year 1717 is excluded because the sale in Paris appears as a limited one held after the beginnings of John Law's schemes. The year 1764 is also excluded, but for a different reason: textile cloths were quoted in aunes, which do not appear to have a common conversion into pieces (Archives Municipales de Nantes: HH 200, and Archives Departementales de Loire-Atlantique, Nantes: C.750/35). The rest of the years are from regular auction sales, except for the year of 1750 which includes only figures from cargo listings of particular ships.

Notwithstanding the data's limitations, the statistical analysis below can supplement the broad view of textile and major imports. It indicates considerable variation in the experience of each company. Not only are averages of the categories of the goods much different between the companies. Their standard deviations are also different, which indicates that much variation in yearly importations did occur.

Textile Imports

	Compagnie des Indes Orientales		Compagnie des Indes	
	Mean	Standard Deviation	Mean	Standard Deviation
Muslin	23568.4	15726.7	52943.5	40025.0
Finer finished	14130.9	20321.8	4432.4	3636.8
Finer Unfinished	4947.4	4873.5	4046.0	3382.3
Coarser Finished	8406.0	6483.2	29636.9	27534.8
Coarser Unfinished	28789.9	15099.4	76828.2	48957.2
Coarse	10679.9	15318.8	21226.7	22302.0
Mixture	4275.1	4202.8	9292.8	7790.9
Silk	3227.9	4449.9	2584.2	2154.5
Total	98007.6	53239.6	200990.5	135776.9

Major Imports

	Compagnie des Indes Orientales		Compagnie des Indes	
	Means	Standard Deviation	Means	Standard Deviation
Coffee	772.1	1836.6	966218.2	830009.1
Cowry	7244.4	10911.0	160560.3	173728.8
Drugs	9120.9	14692.0	45554.8	67157.3
Dyes	12155.1	22858.7	5330.2	7476.1
Gum	358.3	717.2	9797.4	45893.6
Lacquer	5305.9	13812.4	24547.2	36686.9
Metals	19252.9	38653.8	56164.7	85663.9
Pepper	239025.1	217514.0	435708.7	308229.6
Porcelain	5966.7	15721.7	116831.7	142813.5
Saltpeter	127032.2	170082.1	65678.9	153657.5
Sugar	311.1	993.3	18572.2	65573.7
Tea	4186.9	8816.1	598567.2	709827.7
TextileCloth	96812.6	51662.3	193252.9	130136.8
Thread	13588.9	21433.6	4099.5	6813.4
RawMaterial	8032.8	8874.6	41387.5	30388.4
Wood	73702.2	70317.2	365035.0	283533.0
Rattan	7170.8	20942.1	43519.2	46995.6
Total	628927.8	359129.2	3150837.0	1830444.6

Chapter 17
Value of Trade

The quantities of goods traded need not give an indication of their value. Some bulk items could take much cargo space and yet have little value, while valuable items might come in small quantities.

Table 10 gives the value of imports for several years spread over almost a century of trading. Only two years occur during the era of the Compagnie des Indes Orientales, and their figures come from the same reports that gave the quantities in the auction sales (Centre des Archives d'Outre-mer, Aix-en-Provence: C/2/6/57 and C/2/16/187). The high value imports were pepper, saltpeter and textiles. They overwhelmingly outweighed all other imports in terms of value. Somewhat sizeable imports were cowry, drugs and wood. Negligible imports were coffee, gum, perfume, porcelain and tea.

Textiles were, by far, the most valuable import. In total, textiles had a value that was about twenty times that of either pepper or saltpeter. Although the finished product, cloth, was much more valuable than either the raw materials or intermediate products, raw silk was still a valuable import. Its value was comparable to that of either pepper or saltpeter. Thread was a relatively minor import, being only about a fifth of the value of the raw material. In contrast to the raw material, thread was mostly cotton rather than silk thread.

Imports of the finished cloth show many differences between the two years. In 1687, the more common cloth was much more valuable in total than the finer cloth of muslin or silk. In the other year, 1691, the main categories of cloth were more comparable in value. There is also much variation between the years in the relative magnitude, by value of importation, of particular fabrics. No mallemolles were imported in the earlier year, which may account for muslins having much less value in that year. There is otherwise not so much difference. In the mixed category, salempores and sanas make up much of the imports in both years.

Among twill, coutis is the biggest import. Silk cloth has much less value, ranging from ten to twenty percent of the value of cotton cloth.

The record for the Compagnie des Indes comes from reports that are not closely connected to the printed notices of auction sales. The earlier reports are limited to much fewer commodities, whereas the later reports give figures for a wider assortment of commodities. Nevertheless, the reports give a view that has much in common with those of the Compagnie des Indes Orientales. In particular, textile cloth remained the most valuable import.

Table 10 gives the value of imports in 1721, 1725, 1758 and some years in the 1760s. The figures for 1721 and 1725 are not comprehensive and those for 1725 are mostly, albeit detailed, for textiles, while those for 1758 include many other commodities, but do not give the value of imports of particular fabrics. The statistics for the 1760s are more comprehensive, but come towards the end of the company's existence as a viable enterprise.

The statistical picture in 1725 appears much like that of the Compagnie des Indes Orientales: muslin, cottons and coarse fabrics are somewhat close in value. A major change occurs towards the end of the era of the Compagnie des Indes. Muslin falls to about one-third of the value of each of the other categories although betilles, mallemolles and terindannes stand out as the major muslin imports. Similarly salempores are the biggest among the cottons. Among the coarse fabrics, garas remain the largest import in terms of value. There is, however, much variation from year to year with respect to particular fabrics. Some items, such as handkerchiefs, have values of importation which become quite enlarged.

Silk cloth drops quite markedly in relative value, and becomes surpassed by raw silk. Among the other commodities, the most notable shift is in the growth of coffee and tea imports, with tea being about twice as valuable. The coffee comes mostly from the island of Bourbon and the tea is mostly bouy tea.

Cowry and wood remain appreciable imports, while pepper and saltpeter vary in magnitude greatly from year to year. Both are much less important than in the era of the Compagnie des Indes Orientales. Other imports, drugs, lacquer, paper and varnish are quite small. Porcelain remains an item of some importance, but much less than tea.

In summary, the value statistics give the same story as the quantity statistics. The French import trade shifts from pepper and saltpeter to coffee and tea in relative importance. Textile cloth remains the principal import.

The sparsity of records for the value of trade may warrant a look at times immediately subsequent to the ending of the company's monopoly in 1770, although the company continued in existence as a corporate entity. Its altered circumstances may not have had much effect on French trade, but it did have a profound significance for the statistical recording of French trade. No longer can the company's auctions be assumed to give a reasonably accurate measure of the volume of French trade with the East.

Fortunately, the statistical deficiency was only temporary. The French government began reporting on the French trade with the East along with other areas of the world trade. Table 11 gives a summary of the value of French imports from India and China between 1775 and 1780, which is a period that can be divided between three years of peace and three years of war. The trade drops considerably in 1777 even though the actual alliance with the Americans came in February 1778. It remains small during the rest of the decade.

Nevertheless, the pattern of trade remains much the same as in the last decade of the company's monopoly. Coffee, tea and textiles are consistently the biggest imports in terms of value. Textile cloths are overwhelmingly the largest. They run to about ten-fold the value of the next biggest import. Raw silk is also a somewhat large import, but seldom surpasses either coffee or tea. Porcelain is rather small, and so is pepper except for one year. Saltpeter and tutenag stage a recovery in the early years as a result, perhaps, of the threat of war.

The statistical reports (Archives Nationales, Paris: F/12/242-248) also give data on French exports to the East. They are much more varied in nature than imports and consist of such a range of commodities that they are harder to characterize in a consistently significant pattern, even within a short time period of six years. Nor may these statistics give much indication of the nature of exports during the prior times of company monopoly when the largest export is reported as being not a regular commodity but specie. The specie consisted mostly of Spanish coin (Dalgliesh, 1933, 62-63). Summaries of the value of exports for 1775 to 1780 are nevertheless recorded in Table 12. The commodity exports were not likely to be simple exports. Most may have been used in provisioning and arming the French posts and the French ships. Armament, equipment, provisions and supplies would likely fit in that category, as well as a good portion of drugs, hemp (for ropes), metal, tobacco, wine and liquor. Some of the other exports may have been used in the production of Indian exports to France. Dyes, gilding and textiles may have been so used. Textiles are a fairly large French export and even some thread was exported. Armament, equipment, metals, supplies, textiles, wine and liquor tend to constitute the exports with the most value.

The statistical information for the decade of the 1770s comes from reports that brought together data and presented it in summary form. The same information exists from time to time for earlier years, but is strewn through a number of archives and mostly gives the provisioning and cargoing of particular ships. Although this summary picture comes after the ending of the company's monopoly, it serves to indicate the nature of French exports to the East. The principal export was specie, while many of the other exports were only exports in the nominal sense and were actually part of the provisioning and supplying of French trading expeditions.

Chapter 18
Conclusion

Chartered companies handled the French trade with the East for more than one hundred years. The trade had some regular features: the chief import was textile cloth. War drastically reduced the volume of the trade.

Every commodity was subject to considerable fluctuation. Some ceased being imported; some appeared only in later years. Coffee and tea were negligible imports by the Compagnie des Indes Orientales, but became huge imports in the later years of the Compagnie des Indes. Pepper and saltpeter had a varied record. They were sometimes large and sometimes small. Other imports also varied much in magnitude and could be, at times, large. They were cowry, porcelain, tutenag and wood.

The companies can be considered successes insofar as their contribution to the French economy. Both brought large quantities of commodities that would have been either unobtainable or obtainable only at much higher prices.

The financial success of the companies is another issue. Their underlying problem was, ironically, the essential factor in their success. It was their association with the French State.

The State placed impositions on the companies. Some were recurrent, such as the import duties, and some were episodic, such as the royal navy's use of the companies' facilities and stores. Their effects were reduced company profits.

Nevertheless, the support of the French State was crucial for the very existence of the companies. It provided protection for the companies at home, along the trade routes and in India. Its royal navy guarded the company ships that often travelled in convoy with royal navy vessels. Its financial support enabled the later company to recruit, train and field the large armies so necessary for playing a part in Indian power politics.

The eventual tragedy for the Compagnie des Indes was that France's part in European power politics drained financial resources away from the Indian sphere. The result was that the company fell victim to the ambitions of the English East India Company.

Appendices

I. Tables

Units of measure used in the tables:

Pièce: usual unit of measure of textiles and porcelains

Livre: (1) usual unit of measure for other commodities

(2) usual measure of value for any commodity

Pacquet: usual unit of measure for rattin

Aune (aun)

Balle

Ballot

Barce (ba)

Baril

Boëte (bo)
Boîte (bo)
Caisse
Jarre
Millier (mill)
Partie
Rouleau

II. Glossary of Textile Terms

Notes on the Tables and Glossary

Commodity imports are listed in Tables 3 – 5 and 10. The more straight- forward names of commodities are listed in English. Others are left in French. This is particularly the case for the textile cloths which often do not seem to have a common English equivalent.

The French words in the tables are the more usual spelling found in the archival sources, whether they be manuscripts or printed handbills. In both the written and printed primary source materials, the spellings were quite haphazard and varied tremendously.

The spellings in the glossary are also varied. Their definitions come from a variety of French and English sources and many textile cloths are given with a number of variant spellings. The sources for the glossary, except for Savary, are much more modern than the eighteenth century.

The purpose of the glossary is not to give definitive spellings. It was to help the author put the textile cloths into categories for the purpose of analysis.

Table 1: Tonnage of Importation and Exportation, 1665-1709

Year	Importation	Exportation
1665		1040
1666		2630
1667		
1668	70	1000
1669	600	850
1670	30	1900
1671	250	1800
1672	1500	1090
1673	600	70
1674	1000	600
1675		700
1676	1300	690
1677		
1678		
1679	90	1300
1680	300	700
1681	700	900
1682	600	1500
1683	1500	860
1684	1040	770
1685	1760	3160
1686	2300	1250
1687	2110	700
1688	550	2100
1689	600	400
1690		1700
1691	2950	70
1692		1380
1693		600
1694	1450	250
1695		1350
1696		
1697	1100	150
1698	70	2260
1699	1690	2600
1700	1900	1400
1701	1350	2180
1702	2180	1250
1703	900	500
1704	500	1440

Table 1: Tonnage of Importation and Exportation, 1665-1709

Year	Importation	Exportation
1705	1300	
1706		1400
1707		
1708	1000	
1709	400	

Year	Importation	Exportation
1725/26	4537649	2058448
1726/27	8767443	3787744
1727/28	9202831	5596166
1728/29	7992395	5730411
1729/30	8128439	5838524
1730/31	7285641	9789244
1731/32	13542129	10459285
1732/33	12487504	11939990
1733/34	17530659	8248177
1734/35	16877450	6313750
1735/36	16160406	11364209
1736/37	10199659	10057743
1737/38	14492938	13773611
1738/39	18767216	15305815
1739/40	14551749	14772840
1740/41	18289937	13957908
1741/42	18600011	7157124
1742/43	18142273	10049618
1743/44	19869380	11582288
1744/45	16534696	6266734
1745/46	7282915	4064069
1746/47	5102263	2489310
1747/48		2703946
1748/49	3529870	15818566
1749/50	6473712	16767277
1750/51	15104747	18062899
1751/52	25235723	18773432
1752/53	19938871	14985034
1753/54	19025390	16954101
1754/55	26126780	20334421
1755/56	17579954	4483534
1756/57	5243625	8611301
1757/58	13015935	6718784
1758/59	9742042	2443179
1759/60	1846455	1401453
1760/61	4551262	3161731
1761/62	4762572	2463345
1762/63	607068	603856
1763/64	1200163	4055338
1764/65	6857938	9062640

Table 2: Value of Importation and Exportation, 1725-1771

Year	Importation	Exportation
1765/66	4746586	14267158
1766/67	14179385	8938348
1767/68	16410999	9498634
1768/69	23691551	7751280
1769/70	15904843	
1770/71	17863426	

	1687	1691	1699	1704	1710	1712	1714	1715	1716
Coffee	5500	1449							
Moka									
Bourbon									
Cowry	20500		24000			20700			
Drugs & Spices									
Agaric	200								
Aloe		370							
Beaume									
Benzoin							5015		
Borax				13 ca isse		500			
Camphre				36 caisse					
Canelle		3800							
Cardamore									
Chiampy									
Chincon									
Cornaline	100								
Ensens	4800		15600						
Esquine									
Galange									
Galbanum									
Gelee de Cerf									
Gerofle									
Grena									
Icquinquin									
Ikin									
Mastaqui									
Mirabolan									
Mongistere									
Muscade									
Muse			16	11					
Myrrhe									
Opium									204
Oreille de Juda									
Orpiment									
Pefouline									
Poismou									
Rhubard									

	1687	1691	1699	1704	1710	1712	1714	1715	1716
Sagou									
Sang de Dragon									
Santal									
Senne	900								
Syricanardy									
Tanfao									
Turbit									
Vif-argent				428 caisse					
Vitriol	2200	2200				380			
Other									
Dyes									
Alum									
Amidon									
Ammoniacum									
Cinnabar									
Cochineal									
Curcuma									
Ecorce Jaune									
Houboua									
Indigo						68300			
Kankou									
Kouankan									
Tumeric	19000		22000						
Vermilion				1 caisse					
Other									
Gum									
Arabique									
Lacque									
Senegal									
Gutte	1800		1425						
Other									
Ink									
Ivory									
Lacquer									
en bois			40000				476		

	1687	1691	1699	1704	1710	1712	1714	1715	1716
en feuille			1850				153		5274
sans bois									
Marble									
Metals									
Copper				1025 caise					
Tin									
Tutenag									
Lead					74876				
Mother of Pearl									
Paper									
Pepper	130000	90000	214000	14000	215000	566000	611126	284500	26600
Porcelain			1partie					divers	
Caisse				159					15
Rouleau									
Bowl									
Covered									
Mustard									
Shaving									
Sugar									
Assorted									
Bucket									
Candlestick									
Cheese mold									
Compote Dish									
Cup	1500								
Saucer									
Cup and Saucer									
Decanter									
Flagstone									
Fount									
Goblet									
Goblet and Saucer									
Handle									

136   Table 3: Contents of Auction Sales of Compagnie des Indes Orientales

	1687	1691	1699	1704	1710	1712	1714	1715	1716
Knife									
Salads									
Terrine									
Assorted									
Morter									
Oil Lamp									
Pagoda									
Plate									
Platter									
Pot									
Butter									
Chamber									
Flower									
Ink									
Jam									
Ointment									
Tea									
Tobacco									
Water									
Other									
Salad Dish									
Salad & Nest									
Sauce Boat									
Service									
Coffee									
Tea									
Other									
Shaker									
Pepper									
Salt									
Terrines									
Urn									
Wash Basin									
Other									
Rice			14500						
Saltpeter	110000	90000	540000		50290	173000	180000		
Shells									

	1687	1691	1699	1704	1710	1712	1714	1715	1716
Sugar						2800			
Cane									
White									
Chrystals									
Tea	3620			4 ballot	2382	71bo; 43ba			2bo; 12ba
Bouy									
Green									
Hayfven									
Imperial									
Kamphou									
Pekeau									
Sactchaon									
Sonlo									
Other									
Textiles									
Raw Cotton									
Raw Silk	16240	19279	11877	213 caise	451	4000			
Raw Wool			1balle						
Cotton Thread	21000	19300	16900			65100			
Silk Thread									
Cloth									
Muslin									
Adatis			300			594	560		
Alliballies									
Betilles	7540	790		6386	9580	5897	22000	13310	8454
Casses	200	3426	1839	268	449	4440	9181	447	4614
Chavonis					4800	1960		3600	1800
Doussoutis									
Jamdanis							138		
" brodez									
Mallemolles		4805	4636	1179	4473	20857	14724	2536	8907
" brodez						417	390	3	
Mamandis				108					
Mouselline						1195			
" brodez									

Table 3: Contents of Auction Sales of Compagnie des Indes Orientales

	1687	1691	1699	1704	1710	1712	1714	1715	1716
Serbatis							350		101
Tangeb	600	2442	3539	778	427	1292	1938		1920
" brodez			150	91			200		1
Tarnetanne			896	1296		920		3840	
Terindanne				89	817	1908	3079		741
" brodez									
" rayee									
Toque				421	220	739	2022	63	2584
Other									849
Finished, finer									
Allegies	100								160
Broderies									
Chite	59453		32324			10767	7276	191	206
Cravate	130		2325	772	408	2183	1556	2585	1777
" brodez		3965	900						80
Darin									
Limace									
Other									18
Unfinished, finer									
Ambertes									
Organdis					6100	4364	12885	6725	2833
Percale	4048	732		446	640	263	2400	2120	960
Toile, superfine									
Touvis	11								
Other									
Finished, coarser									
Baramete									
Caladoris						1164	1672	4	377
Calarides									
Chaperconne									
Chelas	325								
Chillies								2	60
Chuckeree									
Fottamoura									
Fottes			775			1020	960		
Guinee			1070			4800	13725		
" white	4598	808		3689	4605	4670		13295	6168

	1687	1691	1699	1704	1710	1712	1714	1715	1716
" blue	300			240	600	360	930	1290	690
Neganepaux						600			
Nekanias						2440			
Tapsel				60	695	2882			
Toile carreaux			780						
Other									
Unfinished, coarser									
Aman	580				160				
Annabas									
Bafta		2499	3300			6720	139		
" white	4830								50
" blue						600			
Basin		150	494	380	200	3	115		105
Begagis									
Boelan									
Camelot									
Chalbat									
Chander									
Chazelas									
Cirsakes									
Contelinea		2430	8880	300					
Couvevrives	1330								
Deriband						1120			
Dissouchaye									
Grisette									
Guingans	90		1709		621	64	540		187
Habassis									
Halibannis			86			540		203	
Hamans			2539	477		481	2322		
Kateguis									
Kichorkay									
Lohoria									
Manchette									
Mouchoirs	2963		3794	909	1861	3457	3061	4741	5135
Nankin									
Nensougues									
" brodez									
Platille									
Salempore		3844					31094		

	1687	1691	1699	1704	1710	1712	1714	1715	1716
" white	29960			4970	7850	14687		24236	10563
" blue				180	1760	960	2320	1760	880
Salgarn									
Sana	1080	7797	3605				2919		
" white				343		2592			1720
" blue			972		400	400			280
Sauvaguzee			4100	440		6340			
Socrotes					610	248	1860	1500	720
Stinquerke									
" brodez							100		29
" rayee									
Tapchila									
Toile divers	4661			40					11
Toile montee				45					
Other					355	4710; 104b	70		20
Coarse									
Bajutapaux						1600			
Beram			1280			2200			
Cotonine						270			
Coupis				178	298	250	199	20	276
Doutis	45113	17042	19698	1236					
Gara		575	1384			3000	400		
" white									400
" blue									300
Koratte									
Rasta				400					
Other									
Cotton and Silk									
Agabanee									
Allibannee							920		547
Atarasoye									
Balacor							44		
Charconnee			264		310				771
Chuqueles	400		230						
Dorea		1666	1374	120	2456	2109	2862	380	1653
" brodez									
Elatche									
Fatouye									

	1687	1691	1699	1704	1710	1712	1714	1715	1716
Montichour			120						
Nillas	3290		1917			98	465		400
Pinasse			1145				254		
Salasoye									
Sirsaca			380			5			
Siskrissoy									
Souci	340		385	80					120
Tepay			350						
Toile avec soye		110	134						13
Other						129	77		
Silk									
en caisse									
Armoisin	910	627	1118		280				196
Attlas			1471						
Bas en soye									
Ceintures			513						
Challis									
Coanevrive	60								
Cotonis						1400			
Damas			96						
" rayee									
Etoffe de Chine		400							
Etoffe ecorce		1193							
Gaz		350							
Gilmilis									
Gingeras			120						
Gourgouras									
" brodez									
" rayee									
Jamawar									124
Jarretierre			150						
Katequin									
Kencas	170								
Lampas									
Line									
Longuis	50								
Mandarines									
Moguys									
Mouchoir de soye		1621							

	1687	1691	1699	1704	1710	1712	1714	1715	1716
Mousseline de soye									
Nakin									
Pacotile									
Patissoie									
Pekin									
" brodez									
" rayee									
Satin	4594	168	1432			11200			
" broche			70						
" rayee			325						
Serge de soye									
Taffeta	300	1000	293			450			
" rayee									
Velour									
Other									13
Other									
Hair									
Hemp									
Hides									
Jute									
Linen									
Rugs	6013		6033						
Other [wool]						32145			
Tobacco									
Varnish				20caisse					
Wood									
Ebony									
Sapan	60000	18900	20000						81600
Red			13300	9000	30000	35000	105220	207700	82600
Wood Products									
Box									
Cabinet						4		5	2
Cane			4400	340pa-quet					3100
Chest									

	1687	1691	1699	1704	1710	1712	1714	1715	1716
Commode									
Cup									
Desk						1			
Fan				9caisse					
Flower									
Folding Screen								2	
Picture				3caisse					
Rattan			2132					52	
Rottings-Long					4220				
Table									
Tray									

Table 4: Contents of Auction Sales of Compagnie des Indes

	1717	1720	1721	1722	1723	1724	1725	1726	1728
Coffee									
Moka							944500		309540
Bourbon							7600		124000
Cowry		111343	100000				27737	135500	90000
Drugs & Spices									
Agaric									
Aloe				321		6072	20280	2124	435
Beaume					5 jarre				
Benzoin				627					
Borax		840				10990		7980	
Camphre									
Canelle		100				6480			
Cardamore				1212			9180	3780	
Chiampy				607	583				
Chincon				773	646				
Cornaline									
Ensens							1290	2165	
Esquine				5954				316293	
Galange				43644					
Galbanum									
Gelee de Cerf				637	612				
Gerofle		100						1 jarre	
Grena									
Icquinquin				2810	2601				
Ikin				123	118				
Mastaqui									
Mirabolan				2455					
Mongistere									
Muscade		100							
Muse									
Myrrhe									
Opium									
Oreille de Juda				23					
Orpiment									
Pefouline				2530	2428				
Poismou				122	121				
Rhubard					2 caisse			5241	
Sagou									

	1717	1720	1721	1722	1723	1724	1725	1726	1728
Sang de Dragon									133
Santal				615	590				
Senne						454	378		
Syricanardy									
Tanfao					211				
Turbit						2010			
Vif-argent				5777					
Vitriol									
Other						68			
Dyes									
Alum									
Amidon									
Ammoniacum									
Cinnabar				3668					
Cochineal									
Curcuma				1670					
Ecorce Jaune				2425					
Houboua				17499	13900				
Indigo				2077	5 baril	6738			
Kankou				126	121				
Kouankan					120				
Tumeric			7600						
Vermilion				3700					
Other									
Gum									
Arabique									
Lacque				999					
Senegal					230000				
Gutte						3120	4560		
Other									160
Ink				15					148
Ivory					18140				
Lacquer									
en bois		6337	19450			1736		13856	1987
en feuille		22762	18375			6037		21412	3112

146   Table 4: Contents of Auction Sales of Compagnie des Indes

	1717	1720	1721	1722	1723	1724	1725	1726	1728
sans bois									
Marble									
Metals									
Copper									
Tin									
Tutenag				249873					
Lead									
Mother of Pearl									
Paper								5000	
Pepper		289878	220000	88000		471400	238382	468884	366900
Porcelain									
Caisse							5		80
Rouleau									
							1725	1726	1728
Bowl									
Covered				163	327				
Mustard				595	141				
Shaving				325	358				
Sugar				4482	2945			467	
Assorted				21615	23042			5510	
Bucket				1268	152				
Candlestick				182	55				
Cheese mold				30					
Compote Dish				8978	16189			4624	
Cup				93093	123978				
Saucer				87584	105663				
Cup and Saucer					1365			23727	
Decanter				178	82				
Flagstone									
Fount				302	239				
Goblet				24829	15803			5320	
Goblet and Saucer									
Handle									
Knife				8750	4389				

	1717	1720	1721	1722	1723	1724	1725	1726	1728
Salads									
Terrine									
Assorted									
Morter				391	74				
Oil Lamp				65	11				
Pagoda					2				
Plate				32400	36033			19579	
Platter									
Pot									
Butter									
Chamber				419	241				
Flower									
Ink									
Jam									
Ointment									
Tea				7162	1721			410	
Tobacco				607	308				
Water				951	356				
Other				2014	1068				
Salad Dish				6014	8311				
Salad & Nest					393				
Sauce Boat				134	15				
Service									
Coffee									
Tea									
Other									
Shaker									
Pepper				90	43				
Salt				247	64				
Terrines				299	44				
Urn									
Wash Basin				504	467				
Other					400				
Rice									
Saltpeter			39670					109752	344700
Shells									

Table 4: Contents of Auction Sales of Compagnie des Indes

	1717	1720	1721	1722	1723	1724	1725	1726	1728
Sugar									
Cane									
White					225000				
Chrystals				27665	82000				
Tea									60360
Bouy				145690	64100			56861	
Green				73783	40000			43417	
Hayfven								595	
Imperial								2391	
Kamphou								6155	
Pekeau								2898	
Sactchaon									
Sonlo									
Other									
Textiles									
Raw Cotton									
Raw Silk			16856	67800	3000	15432	10440	97309	48600
Raw Wool									
Cotton Thread									4579
Silk Thread									
Cloth									
Muslin									
Adatis	29	415				500	100	574	210
Alliballies									
Betilles	862	8270	5430	2800	621	8818	7384	11310	5240
Casses	819	9809	12210			13185	5311	17105	11179
Chavonis		2000	3200			2800	3800	3600	
Doussoutis									
Jamdanis	2							640	
" brodez		90							
Mallemolles	660	12718	14105			10271	4399	8065	9424
" brodez		395	160			237		231	
Mamandis									
Mouselline				398	178		45		1167
" brodez					806				
Serbatis	85	145	80			570		240	
Tangeb	315	6148	4690			4228	1451	3600	1659

	1717	1720	1721	1722	1723	1724	1725	1726	1728
" brodez		413	320			788		377	
Tarnetanne			2160			3520	5840	3420	1300
Terindanne	83	1060	870			2230	960	5616	5245
" brodez		308	240			1398		549	
" rayee			140						
Toque	100	1100	4700			5772	3355	2300	1746
Other									
Finished, finer									
Allegies			600				415		
Broderies					2 ballot				
Chite		1080			1072	242	3769		
Cravate	158	3935	3680		130	6928	3641	5230	847
" brodez		2833			262	5212		2000	
Darin						340	231		
Limace								1620	4082
Other									
Unfinished, finer									
Ambertes									
Organdis	830	1270	5080	1020	75	6380	4553	4240	780
Percale	57	2560	80			1040	800	960	800
Toile, superfine									
Touvis									
Other									
Finished, coarser									
Baramete						150			
Caladoris		192	3600			385	1106	780	
Calarides						50			
Chaperconne									
Chelas						597	235		
Chillies			1500			460	1000	600	
Chuckeree									
Fottamoura			420			280	280	800	721
Fottes		3200	1550			2980	2980	2160	3895
Guinee	57								
" white		15879	6070	690		12427	7394	19820	18370
" blue		3120					1050	2730	7098
Neganepaux									

Table 4: Contents of Auction Sales of Compagnie des Indes

	1717	1720	1721	1722	1723	1724	1725	1726	1728
Nekanias									
Tapsel			3800					560	
Toile carreaux									
Other									
Unfinished, coarser									
Aman									
Annabas									
Bafta	293								
" white			700			100		1362	2710
" blue									1570
Basin		1666	400			2504	890	1800	2963
Begagis									
Boelan									
Camelot									
Chalbat			500				300	200	
Chander									
Chazelas									
Cirsakes									
Contelinea									
Couvevrives									
Deriband									
Dissouchaye									
Grisette									
Guingans		1260	1880		247	4280	2575	2596	235
Habassis									
Halibannis		960	2240				320	480	642
Hamans	443	1096	1900			4350	1560	4420	4082
Kateguis						5420	4780		
Kichorkay									
Lohoria									
Manchette									
Mouchoirs		5990	7200		248	12848	20816	13942	23484
Nankin									
Nensougues			160					416	100
" brodez									
Platille									
Salempore	405								
" white		56922	19030			24121	23530	35060	21410
" blue		4420						7640	11367

	1717	1720	1721	1722	1723	1724	1725	1726	1728
Salgarn									
Sana	224								
" white		2148	2800			4290	1400	7819	6960
" blue			600						600
Sauvaguzee									
Socrotes	236	1810	480			1140	660	1020	960
Stinquerke		358							
" brodez			1630			4777		2000	
" rayee							11		
Tapchila						400		480	4380
Toile divers					1106				
Toile montee						199	115		
Other									
Coarse									
Bajutapaux									
Beram									
Cotonine									
Coupis		1199	3600			900	2204	696	
Doutis									
Gara		6840							
" white			3040			1926	3530	820	640
" blue			300						
Koratte						1920	1920		
Rasta							70	41	
Other									
Cotton and Silk									
Agabanee						450			
Allibannee									
Atarasoye									
Balacor									
Charconnee									
Chuqueles			200					200	
Dorea	195	3785	5520		101	4036	2186	3722	4103
" brodez						119			
Elatche						490		300	
Fatouye							100		
Montichour									
Nillas			1800			200	620		

Table 4: Contents of Auction Sales of Compagnie des Indes

	1717	1720	1721	1722	1723	1724	1725	1726	1728
Pinasse								270	
Salasoye									
Sirsaca									
Siskrissoy									
Souci			1120			440	404	390	
Tepay			100				190	400	
Toile avec soye									
Other									
Silk									
en caisse									
Armoisin			400			100	345	315	
Attlas									
Bas en soye				1130					
Ceintures									
Challis									
Coanevrive									
Cotonis						100	607		
Damas				1100	109			2765	
" rayee									
Etoffe de Chine									
Etoffe ecorce									
Gaz									
Gilmilis						88			
Gingeras									
Gourgouras				280				1053	
" brodez									
" rayee									
Jamawar						50	202		
Jarretierre									
Katequin									
Kencas									
Lampas									
Line								183	
Longuis							140	72	
Mandarines									
Moguys						80	80		
Mouchoir de soye			2000		157				
Mousseline de soye									

	1717	1720	1721	1722	1723	1724	1725	1726	1728
Nakin									
Pacotile									
Patissoie									
Pekin				880			1 lit	526	
" **brodez**									
" **rayee**								430	
Satin				300				288	
" **broche**				63				121	
" **rayee**				60				560	
Serge de soye								100	
Taffeta									
" **rayee**			240						
Velour				193					
Other									
Other									
Hair									
Hemp			240 mill						
Hides			2501		747				
Jute									
Linen				1706					
Rugs					155				
Other [wool]									
Tobacco							890		
Varnish				1117	1072				16 caisse
Wood									
Ebony									
Sapan			40916				36013	60669	
Red		22867		169900		306000	153117	384614	317700
Wood Products									
Box				2					
Cabinet				2302	1				
Cane				800					
Chest				1	600				
Commode				2				40	
Cup				15200					

Table 4: Contents of Auction Sales of Compagnie des Indes

	1717	1720	1721	1722	1723	1724	1725	1726	1728
Desk				4	4			8	
Fan				4759					
Flower				9800				2263	400 biote
Folding Screen				8				12	
Picture				240	200			98	
Rattan		289	749			2060		400	715
Rottings-Long									
Table				702	2			200	
Tray				3000	4			150	

	1729	1731	1732	1733	1734	1737	1738	1739	1740
Coffee									
Moka	578665	324040	473150	520370	1331577	495700	776180	450000	600000
Bourbon				192000	379260	542000	875950	1440300	1504000
Cowry	99450	371200	450430	657650	300000	51480	217540		279050
Drugs & Spices									
Agaric									
Aloe		326							
Beaume									
Benzoin									
Borax		280					1470		7980
Camphre	360								
Canelle									
Cardamore			3186	3120	5700	16040	6000	3750	6900
Chiampy									
Chincon									
Cornaline									
Ensens	14240								
Esquine		2500	32600	9444	12740	21420	31680	36830	34050
Galange		3500	14070	17060	28300	24920	26510	27600	30590
Galbanum							2000		2 jarres
Gelee de Cerf									
Gerofle									
Grena									
Icquinquin									
Ikin									
Mastaqui									2 jarres
Mirabolan									
Mongistere									
Muscade									
Muse	30		9						
Myrrhe	1440								
Opium				50					
Oreille de Juda									
Orpiment									
Pefouline									
Poismou									
Rhubard	1860	2490	820	33					650
Sagou									120

Table 4: Contents of Auction Sales of Compagnie des Indes

	1729	1731	1732	1733	1734	1737	1738	1739	1740
Sang de Dragon									
Santal									
Senne				3900					
Syricanardy				10					
Tanfao									
Turbit									
Vif-argent		3660	10410						
Vitriol									
Other									
Dyes									
Alum	15099								
Amidon									
Ammoniacum									2 jarres
Cinnabar		3600		245					
Cochineal	1560								
Curcuma			8260		5024	6120	5980	13520	10960
Ecorce Jaune									
Houboua									520
Indigo								73	
Kankou									
Kouankan									
Tumeric									
Vermilion									
Other									
Gum									2 jarres
Arabique									
Lacque									
Senegal									
Gutte	230	1480		273			210		
Other									
Ink		37	36	30		72	200	198	200
Ivory									
Lacquer									
en bois	1650	6450	27710	4040	2531				
en feuille	29044	17230	43230	45330	78240	7270			

	1729	1731	1732	1733	1734	1737	1738	1739	1740
sans bois		5390		42000	77700				
Marble		1211							
Metals									
Copper									
Tin			2017	2017					
Tutenag		45500	241260	245000	158740	122280	86540	101910	98470
Lead									
Mother of Pearl			13900		28000				
Paper		3 caisse		1200	2124	1000			900
Pepper	437024	710000	788660	907660	955600	1183560	645386	485260	382900
Porcelain									
Caisse	71			102	55	62	152	242	277
Rouleau				547	189		350	129	373
	1729	1731	1732	1733					
Bowl									
Covered			63						
Mustard			272						
Shaving									
Sugar		3048	126						
Assorted			252						
Bucket			378						
Candlestick			445						
Cheese mold									
Compote Dish			70						
Cup		4441							
Saucer									
Cup and Saucer		15758	31096						
Decanter									
Flagstone			3600						
Fount									
Goblet		6000							
Goblet and Saucer		115409	31159						
Handle									
Knife			304						

158   Table 4: Contents of Auction Sales of Compagnie des Indes

	1729	1731	1732	1733	1734	1737	1738	1739	1740
Salads			107						
Terrine			126						
Assorted									
Morter									
Oil Lamp			153						
Pagoda									
Plate		14766	19795						
Platter									
Pot									
Butter		489							
Chamber		299	15						
Flower			252						
Ink			480						
Jam			756						
Ointment			434						
Tea		1296							
Tobacco			378						
Water			90						
Other		5332	246						
Salad Dish		598							
Salad & Nest									
Sauce Boat			252						
Service									
Coffee		240	90						
Tea		240	90						
Other		76	63						
Shaker									
Pepper		424	378						
Salt		1669	1260						
Terrines									
Urn			10						
Wash Basin			378						
Other									
Rice									
Saltpeter	686000					151130			
Shells									

Table 4: Contents of Auction Sales of Compagnie des Indes   159

	1729	1731	1732	1733	1734	1737	1738	1739	1740
Sugar									
Cane									
White		84500							
Chrystals		45140							
Tea									
Bouy	231480	414000	254800	273490	514790	590830	686770	910340	695017
Green									
Hayfven	18490	13450	15250	4260	11528	7590	9900	5130	3209
Imperial	18000	15080	30300	12250	32306	9110	12150	3610	
Kamphou	15332	18700	27510	12250	36726	62140	40140	8950	7462
Pekeau	11820	1180	33150	11870	41099	3980	13680	3760	7332
Sactchaon	6357	7500	6480	24500	24559	14240	11730	7000	
Sonlo	34800	260200	309500	35830	141351	95130	13180	160240	268467
Other	113								
Textiles									
Raw Cotton									
Raw Silk	22600	76480	50850	87517	81509	23690	61880	38380	73188
Raw Wool									2 balle
Cotton Thread	4669	470		10350				12150	9600
Silk Thread									
Cloth									
Muslin									
Adatis		615	1242	2104	1773	1584	3000	1000	3482
Alliballies									
Betilles	8680	11700	11710	19803	9958	4060	5180	12360	12330
Casses	9611	25657	84525	44188	22406	21114	41057	13580	21752
Chavonis	3800	1600	1918	4200	2565	2600	3200	8000	2800
Doussoutis									
Jamdanis				208	604	301	202		323
" brodez									
Mallemolles	3753	14407	17100	27344	22119	22482	26785	8360	20492
" brodez				431	351				
Mamandis									
Mouselline									
" brodez	1625								
Serbatis	166	420	537		1692	500	200		457
Tangeb	547	13174	10114	15819	8547	8143	11533	3440	6680

Table 4: Contents of Auction Sales of Compagnie des Indes

	1729	1731	1732	1733	1734	1737	1738	1739	1740
" brodez				1420	924				
Tarnetanne	3240	5160	8260	11370	9136	80	820	1160	2760
Terindanne	4786	3861	6672	11695	10906	6913	13030	4240	8576
" brodez				1603	1720				
" rayee									
Toque	2970		2152	5607	3329	2929	2800	1100	1760
Other									
Finished, finer									
Allegies									
Broderies						1109	1761	480	2774
Chite					1281			603	201
Cravate	2356	1800	1045	1871	3245				
" brodez		495	3372	2462	3365	80			
Darin				100	436				200
Limace	3220	1684	2040	3780	2940				
Other									
Unfinished, finer									
Ambertes									
Organdis	3840	5500	5190	6730	4624	600	60	4020	2180
Percale	1744	3280	3095	5520	4571	382	900	2040	3120
Toile, superfine									
Touvis									
Other									
Finished, coarser									
Baramete									50
Caladoris			1659	3119	1621	1000	3000	200	2917
Calarides									
Chaperconne									
Chelas					97				
Chillies									
Chuckeree									
Fottamoura	721	511			160				
Fottes	3634	3020							
Guinee									
" white	12495	19985	19494	50064	38756	52294	83358	94582	56315
" blue	990		1920	7416	3960	60	3960	2760	12540
Neganepaux	100			500	2860	80		1840	1165

	1729	1731	1732	1733	1734	1737	1738	1739	1740
Nekanias					2440				580
Tapsel		1324							
Toile carreaux									
Other									
Unfinished, coarser									
Aman									
Annabas									
Bafta									
" white	6600	4454	4789	13604	18564	28290	32700	9200	16625
" blue			3200	3000	4800	3300	800		
Basin	3243	5860	10892	16381	9000	480	2600	1000	6202
Begagis					120				
Boelan									
Camelot					230				
Chalbat			297	348		184	300		799
Chander									
Chazelas	300			2800	7860	400		2240	2938
Cirsakes				300					
Contelinea									
Couvevrives									
Deriband					1600	400			2655
Dissouchaye			600	1792	877	200	200	200	702
Grisette		100							
Guingans	2080	4361	4860	11860	8740	15400	18120	19280	20103
Habassis									
Halibannis	800								
Hamans	1957	7016	4851	13743	9145	4951	6228	2520	4172
Kateguis	3197	2039							
Kichorkay									
Lohoria									66
Manchette					289				
Mouchoirs	17301	43754	28831	37950	37387	42788	45991	34455	49916
Nankin									
Nensougues		767	772	960	1247	343	294		391
" brodez				798	1828				
Platille									130
Salempore									
" white	18400	28110	27788	40226	26290	13500	17970	14060	6630
" blue			6320	6558	2400	5680	9760	22080	4560

Table 4: Contents of Auction Sales of Compagnie des Indes

	1729	1731	1732	1733	1734	1737	1738	1739	1740
Salgarn									
Sana									10754
" white	5297	8536	9770	10589	8287	8698	13967	3200	
" blue	1401								
Sauvaguzee									
Socrotes	840	1440	1320	2330	1914	1456	960	2729	1680
Stinquerke			1276	3030	2172				
" brodez	400	2740	1994	3745	1158		450		437
" rayee					1094				
Tapchila	3921								80
Toile divers							1400	950	5068
Toile montee			15	15	18		600	308	200
Other									
Coarse									
Bajutapaux	100			400	3060	160		1760	1690
Beram									
Cotonine					400				
Coupis			600	914	2000	400	200		835
Doutis				640	1220	1120	520	1980	3180
Gara									
" white	4610	10684	17230	35390	39560	41040	46670	18730	54510
" blue				1240	1120	1440	320		
Koratte	5756	4685							
Rasta									
Other									
Cotton and Silk									
Agabanee									
Allibannee		2111	400	3648	4410		1880	560	1880
Atarasoye		374	192	399	418	402	160	100	378
Balacor							100		
Charconnee									
Chuqueles				521	730	189	300	200	1101
Dorea	4514	11134	12376	15698	12532	9622	14774	4340	12258
" brodez	148	44	112		436				
Elatche			696	1481	554	240	285	400	658
Fatouye									
Montichour				200	100				
Nillas				300	358	200	303	300	971

	1729	1731	1732	1733	1734	1737	1738	1739	1740
Pinasse				903	768	600	884	300	1041
Salasoye			62						305
Sirsaca					300	183	100	300	962
Siskrissoy									
Souci			2100	3190	2049	2021	2300	700	2184
Tepay			295	617	554				543
Toile avec soye									
Other									
Silk									
en caisse		2							
Armoisin					400	402			500
Attlas									
Bas en soye									
Ceintures									
Challis	100								
Coanevrive									
Cotonis									
Damas	307	1100	599	1312	1440	1200	1200	1052	1195
" rayee			100		100				
Etoffe de Chine									
Etoffe ecorce									
Gaz					50				10
Gilmilis									
Gingeras									
Gourgouras	132	994	500	800	900	1000	969	986	1000
" brodez		14							
" rayee									
Jamawar				200	347				356
Jarretierre									
Katequin									
Kencas									
Lampas		107		130	150	100	200		95
Line		590							
Longuis									
Mandarines									
Moguys									
Mouchoir de soye		300		420	350				
Mousseline de soye									

	1729	1731	1732	1733	1734	1737	1738	1739	1740
Nakin									
Pacotile									
Patissoie				130	400	200	200	185	200
Pekin	464	610	1063	400	1050	800	795	734	1000
" brodez			200	450					
" rayee		975	300	250	150				
Satin	269	1050	599	723	800	200	150	174	200
" broche									
" rayee		200	100	100	50				100
Serge de soye									
Taffeta									
" rayee									
Velour		30							
Other		2 caisse							
Other									
Hair									
Hemp									
Hides		400							
Jute									
Linen									
Rugs									
Other [wool]									
Tobacco									
Varnish									
Wood									
Ebony									
Sapan					6167	25730	10450	26560	81380
Red	324892	3290	676700	777390	1000279	545390	702766	623300	535840
Wood Products									
Box									
Cabinet			4884						
Cane		1543							
Chest									
Commode									
Cup									

	1729	1731	1732	1733	1734	1737	1738	1739	1740
Desk		2							
Fan	3115	4790		3000	5000	6000	6100	3137	4590
Flower		25000							
Folding Screen					7	8	2	2	4
Picture									
Rattan	1350	1260	1950	1967	4784	1839	768	1474	4656
Rottings-Long		24400		15190				18	
Table									
Tray		2500		1620	1992	1880	1000	1930	1132

Table 4: Contents of Auction Sales of Compagnie des Indes

	1741	1749	1750	1756	1761	1764	1766	1767	1769
Coffee									
Moka	420000	237000		589114				238664	579124
Bourbon	1960000	2000000		435200	1733040	2615200	1620800	1350000	1054800
Cowry	236522	17294	65642		18057	32160	234398	444798	202500
Drugs & Spices									
Agaric									
Aloe									
Beaume									
Benzoin									
Borax	3271						1174	830	1667
Camphre									
Canelle					2310				
Cardamore			80 caisse						
Chiampy									
Chincon									
Cornaline									
Ensens									
Esquine	39655				18444	61993	84417	58637	
Galange									
Galbanum									
Gelee de Cerf									
Gerofle									
Grena					895				
Icquinquin									
Ikin									
Mastaqui									
Mirabolan									
Mongistere									5070
Muscade									
Muse									
Myrrhe									
Opium									
Oreille de Juda									
Orpiment					1142				
Pefouline									
Poismou									
Rhubard	1175				769		794	780	12284

	1741	1749	1750	1756	1761	1764	1766	1767	1769
Sagou									
Sang de Dragon									
Santal									
Senne									
Syricanardy									
Tanfao									
Turbit									
Vif-argent									
Vitriol									
Other									
Dyes									
Alum									
Amidon									
Ammoniacum									
Cinnabar									
Cochineal									
Curcuma	1316								
Ecorce Jaune									
Houboua									
Indigo					1333				
Kankou									
Kouankan									
Tumeric									
Vermilion									
Other									
Gum									
Arabique					3904				
Lacque									
Senegal									
Gutte	598								
Other									
Ink	70								
Ivory									
Lacquer									
en bois					18188		8100	4571	

Table 4: Contents of Auction Sales of Compagnie des Indes

	1741	1749	1750	1756	1761	1764	1766	1767	1769
en feuille	30 caisse				17598		4500		8025
sans bois							22800	24018	
Marble									
Metals									
Copper									
Tin									
Tutenag	126767								
Lead									
Mother of Pearl							5855		1990
Paper	772					3000	1000		3000
Pepper	570767	32132	454984	120092	29608	15000	266137	334667	704118
Porcelain									
Caisse	198				213	409	553	687	2020
Rouleau					292				
Bowl									
Covered									
Mustard									
Shaving									
Sugar									
Assorted									
Bucket									
Candlestick									
Cheese mold									
Compote Dish									
Cup									
Saucer									
Cup and Saucer									
Decanter									
Flagstone									
Fount									
Goblet									
Goblet and Saucer									
Handle									

	1741	1749	1750	1756	1761	1764	1766	1767	1769
Knife									
Salads									
Terrine									
Assorted									
Morter									
Oil Lamp									
Pagoda									
Plate									
Platter									
Pot									
Butter									
Chamber									
Flower									
Ink									
Jam									
Ointment									
Tea									
Tobacco									
Water									
Other									
Salad Dish									
Salad & Nest									
Sauce Boat									
Service									
Coffee									
Tea									
Other									
Shaker									
Pepper									
Salt									
Terrines									
Urn									
Wash Basin									
Other									
Rice									
Saltpeter			168596						
Shells									

Table 4: Contents of Auction Sales of Compagnie des Indes

	1741	1749	1750	1756	1761	1764	1766	1767	1769
Sugar									
Cane									
White									
Chrystals									
Tea									
Bouy	818004				455897	1363627	2039084	1528652	1546260
Green	1215				142488	290684	430636	354214	188257
Hayfven	42929				9356	12014	39495	36700	57505
Imperial	7892				5086		1820		
Kamphou	53832				27571	27356	59348	46624	83761
Pekeau	40549				10000	2877	13700	13505	6569
Sactchaon	18580				12920	12339	22154	14527	14990
Sonlo	241490								
Other							1851		124350
							960 boite		
Textiles									
Raw Cotton									
Raw Silk	94787		12990	12903	25411	13831	85184	52173	33620
Raw Wool									
Cotton Thread	21390		20 balle		12041				22863
Silk Thread									
Cloth									
Muslin						11436 aun			
Adatis	2368	1606	200	31	1024		34		
Alliballies		360							
Betilles	7350	1267	960	701	899			1935	160
Casses	27960	15969	5640	6680	9622		10380	6304	9326
Chavonis	1200	399						1900	
Doussoutis				200					
Jamdanis							9		
" brodez									
Mallemolles	20991	13391	2300	2526	6088		2702	800	1311
" brodez									
Mamandis									3163
Mouselline									
" brodez									

	1741	1749	1750	1756	1761	1764	1766	1767	1769
Serbatis		100			54		365		
Tangeb	9189	6664		1635	973		3149	480	4046
" brodez									99
Tarnetanne	3504	980		600					
Terindanne	9486	2774	3720	3101	352		4899	880	430
" brodez									288
" rayee									
Toque	1093	281	80	105					
Other									
Finished, finer									
Allegies									
Broderies	1938	3185		496	264		2645		
Chite	871			932	5215				845
Cravate									
" brodez									
Darin	400								
Limace	1200							480	720
Other									
Unfinished, finer									
Ambertes			100		1118				2600
Organdis	900	180		600	300			420	
Percale	1560	1286	240	249	1060			267	400
Toile, superfine					300				
Touvis									85
Other									
Finished, coarser						16974 aun			
Baramete									
Caladoris	2782			393			702		362
Calarides									
Chaperconne					147				
Chelas				141	261		146		100
Chillies									
Chuckeree				182					
Fottamoura									
Fottes				500				486	
Guinee									
" white	30906	10564	5825	3694	8898			10218	13275

Table 4: Contents of Auction Sales of Compagnie des Indes

	1741	1749	1750	1756	1761	1764	1766	1767	1769
" blue	12720		240					5880	2460
Neganepaux	720	481	1440	800				160	640
Nekanias	160	1040	480					1725	720
Tapsel	219								
Toile carreaux									
Other									
Unfinished, coarser									
Aman									
Annabas				320					
Bafta			5300						16028
" white	25425	3105		9068	5888		19687	9200	
" blue		2705			100				
Basin	3937	288	2318	1007			615	1400	600
Begagis									
Boelan				1000				1433	1800
Camelot				54					
Chalbat	528								
Chander			80						
Chazelas	800	485		800	802			2096	720
Cirsakes									
Contelinea									
Couvevrives									
Deriband	1360								500
Dissouchaye	707								46
Grisette									
Guingans	8510	9342	5040	6803	360			8940	2326
Habassis							176		280
Halibannis									
Hamans	6256	1953	1460	1636	773		5435	1320	1700
Kateguis								65	
Kichorkay							183		348
Lohoria	25								1100
Manchette									
Mouchoirs	62759	6547	11700	14511	12810	1297 aune	14892	7100	18473
Nankin							480		4200
Nensougues	84	451	360	1038	4		3024	80	1107
" brodez									
Platille									
Salempore									

	1741	1749	1750	1756	1761	1764	1766	1767	1769
" white	5640	9029	620	960	2700			2934	2584
" blue	4800		320					160	3480
Salgarn									90
Sana	9075	1035	1680	131			343		1100
" white									
" blue									
Sauvaguzee									
Socrotes	1080	118							
Stinquerke			400	204			64	518	
" brodez	1106								
" rayee									
Tapchila				80					
Toile divers	8965		120				120		
Toile montee			1 balle						
Other									
Coarse									
Bajutapaux	1680	750	480					604	160
Beram									
Cotonine									
Coupis	459			70	598				
Doutis	1820							100	
Gara			10200						17056
" white	79716	415			8474		40409	31410	
" blue				300					
Koratte				120	769			1025	240
Rasta									
Other									
Cotton and Silk									
Agabanee									
Allibannee	963				18				
Atarasoye									
Balacor									
Charconnee									
Chuqueles	554		200	292			265		
Dorea	12224	6010	2080	2971	2184		6831	1720	5423
" brodez									285
Elatche	780			1199					
Fatouye									

Table 4: Contents of Auction Sales of Compagnie des Indes

	1741	1749	1750	1756	1761	1764	1766	1767	1769
Montichour									
Nillas	547		400	615			124	200	117
Pinasse	590		200				64		
Salasoye	99								
Sirsaca	732			369			328	1200	
Siskrissoy								80	
Souci	1564			200			444		85
Tepay	296			22					
Toile avec soye									
Other									
Silk									
en caisse									
Armoisin	700			496	125	61 aune			
Attlas									
Bas en soye									
Ceintures									
Challis									
Coanevrive									
Cotonis									
Damas	1011				148	88	72	108	415
" rayee	179				56		32	25	
Etoffe de Chine									
Etoffe ecorce							90		
Gaz							24	100	70
Gilmilis									
Gingeras									
Gourgouras	1038				9	100	38	39	300
" brodez									
" rayee									50
Jamawar	400								
Jarretierre									
Katequin									
Kencas									
Lampas	100				54		29	36	100
Line							150	476	200
Longuis									
Mandarines					13				15
Moguys									
Mouchoir de soye					1074				

	1741	1749	1750	1756	1761	1764	1766	1767	1769
Mousseline de soye									
Nakin								4600	
Pacotile					832				
Patissoie	254				120	30	25	29	348
Pekin	578				193	120	89	85	450
" brodez									150
" rayee	396				52		46	49	300
Satin	266				54	50	25	22	270
" broche					28		19	25	100
" rayee	185						25	27	200
Serge de soye									
Taffeta					813				
" rayee	83								
Velour									
Other									
Other									
Hair					10578				
Hemp									
Hides									
Jute									
Linen									
Rugs									
Other [wool]									
Tobacco									
Varnish									
Wood									
Ebony								40000	
Sapan	97000		50000	12772	3226	72103	135946	53348	85696
Red	418319	730171	143434	13803	108500		91616	179469	327712
Wood Products									
Box									
Cabinet									
Cane									
Chest									

Table 4: Contents of Auction Sales of Compagnie des Indes

	1741	1749	1750	1756	1761	1764	1766	1767	1769
Commode									
Cup									
Desk									
Fan	4560								
Flower									
Folding Screen	1								
Picture									
Rattan	2631				1300	2950	2900	1471	5900
Rottings-Long								53166	
Table									
Tray	520				502	771	1272		1225

	Cargoes from Pondichery	Auction Sales
Coffee		
Moka	400000	
Bourbon		
Cowry		200000
Drugs & Spices		
Agaric		
Aloe		
Beaume		
Benzoin		
Borax	5000	
Camphre		
Canelle		
Cardamore		
Chiampy		
Chincon		
Cornaline		
Ensens		
Esquine		
Galange		
Galbanum		
Gelee de Cerf		
Gerofle		
Grena		
Icquinquin		
Ikin		
Mastaqui		
Mirabolan		
Mongistere		
Muscade		
Muse		
Myrrhe		
Opium		
Oreille de Juda		
Orpiment		
Pefouline		
Poismou		
Rhubard		
Sagou		

Table 5: Contents of Imports from Pondichéry and at Sales, 1735-1743

	Cargoes from Pondichery	Auction Sales
Sang de Dragon		
Santal		
Senne		
Syricanardy		
Tanfao		
Turbit		
Vif-argent		
Vitriol		
Other		
Dyes		
Alum		
Amidon		
Ammoniacum		
Cinnabar		
Cochineal		
Curcuma	2500	
Ecorce Jaune		
Houboua		
Indigo		
Kankou		
Kouankan		
Tumeric		
Vermilion		
Other		
Gum		
Arabique		
Lacque		
Senegal		
Gutte		
Other		
Ink		
Ivory		
Lacquer		
en bois		2500
en feuille		25000

	Cargoes from Pondichery	Auction Sales
sans bois		2500
Marble		
Metals		
Copper		
Tin		
Tutenag		
Lead		
Mother of Pearl		
Paper		
Pepper	1250000	550000
Porcelain		
Caisse		
Rouleau		
Bowl		
Covered		
Mustard		
Shaving		
Sugar		
Assorted		
Bucket		
Candlestick		
Cheese mold		
Compote Dish		
Cup		
Saucer		
Cup and Saucer		
Decanter		
Flagstone		
Fount		
Goblet		
Goblet and Saucer		
Handle		
Knife		

Table 5: Contents of Imports from Pondichéry and at Sales, 1735-1743

	Cargoes from Pondichery	Auction Sales
Salads		
Terrine		
Assorted		
Morter		
Oil Lamp		
Pagoda		
Plate		
Platter		
Pot		
Butter		
Chamber		
Flower		
Ink		
Jam		
Ointment		
Tea		
Tobacco		
Water		
Other		
Salad Dish		
Salad & Nest		
Sauce Boat		
Service		
Coffee		
Tea		
Other		
Shaker		
Pepper		
Salt		
Terrines		
Urn		
Wash Basin		
Other		
Rice		
Saltpeter		400000
Shells		

	Cargoes from Pondichery	Auction Sales
Sugar		
Cane		
White		
Chrystals		
Tea		
Bouy		
Green		
Hayfven		
Imperial		
Kamphou		
Pekeau		
Sactchaon		
Sonlo		
Other		
Textiles		
Raw Cotton		
Raw Silk		
Raw Wool		
Cotton Thread	9000	
Silk Thread		
Cloth		
Muslin		
Adatis		1200
Alliballies		
Betilles	15660	
Casses		35680
Chavonis	2000	
Doussoutis		300
Jamdanis		500
" brodez		
Mallemolles		24340
" brodez		
Mamandis		3200
Mouselline		
" brodez		
Serbatis		1000
Tangeb		22500

Table 5: Contents of Imports from Pondichéry and at Sales, 1735-1743

	Cargoes from Pondichery	Auction Sales
" brodez		
Tarnetanne	6480	
Terindanne		13950
" brodez		
" rayee		
Toque		2700
Other		
Finished, finer		
Allegies		
Broderies		
Chite	600	
Cravate		
" brodez		
Darin		
Limace	3000	
Other		
Unfinished, finer		
Ambertes		
Organdis	3780	
Percale	2000	
Toile, superfine		
Touvis		
Other		
Finished, coarser		
Baramete		
Caladoris		3200
Calarides		300
Chaperconne		
Chelas		100
Chillies		
Chuckeree		
Fottamoura		
Fottes		
Guinee		
" white	83800	
" blue	20000	
Neganepaux	4000	

	Cargoes from Pondichery	Auction Sales
Nekanias	5000	
Tapsel		
Toile carreaux		
Other		
Unfinished, coarser		
Aman		
Annabas		
Bafta		18000
" white		
" blue		
Basin	1500	
Begagis		
Boelan		
Camelot		100
Chalbat		700
Chander		
Chazelas		
Cirsakes		
Contelinea		
Couvevrives		
Deriband	2600	
Dissouchaye		300
Grisette		
Guingans	12600	
Habassis		
Halibannis		
Hamans		7260
Kateguis		
Kichorkay		
Lohoria		200
Manchette		
Mouchoirs	39660	52900
Nankin		
Nensougues		4900
" brodez		
Platille		
Salempore		
" white	10160	
" blue		

	Cargoes from Pondichery	Auction Sales
Salgarn		
Sana		19800
" white		
" blue		
Sauvaguzee		
Socrotes	1400	
Stinquerke		550
" brodez		
" rayee		
Tapchila		1400
Toile divers		
Toile montee		
Other		
Coarse		
Bajutapaux	6000	
Beram		
Cotonine		
Coupis		1200
Doutis	1000	
Gara		
" white		70000
" blue		2000
Koratte		
Rasta		
Other		
Cotton and Silk		
Agabanee		
Allibannee		1200
Atarasoye		
Balacor		
Charconnee		
Chuqueles		1400
Dorea		25250
" brodez		
Elatche		600
Fatouye		
Montichour		
Nillas		1000

	Cargoes from Pondichery	Auction Sales
Pinasse		800
Salasoye		
Sirsaca		2000
Siskrissoy		
Souci		2900
Tepay		300
Toile avec soye		
Other		
Silk		
en caisse		
Armoisin		2400
Attlas		
Bas en soye		
Ceintures		
Challis		
Coanevrive		
Cotonis		
Damas		1000
" rayee		
Etoffe de Chine		
Etoffe ecorce		900
Gaz		
Gilmilis		
Gingeras		
Gourgouras		
" brodez		
" rayee		
Jamawar		
Jarretierre		
Katequin		
Kencas		
Lampas		
Line		
Longuis		
Mandarines		
Moguys		
Mouchoir de soye		
Mousseline de soye		
Nakin		

	Cargoes from Pondichery	Auction Sales
Pacotile		
Patissoie		
Pekin		
" brodez		
" rayee		
Satin		
" broche		
" rayee		
Serge de soye		
Taffeta		1000
" rayee		
Velour		
Other		58200
Other		
Hair		
Hemp		
Hides		
Jute		
Linen		
Rugs		
Other [wool]		
Tobacco		
Varnish		
Wood		
Ebony		
Sapan	110000	
Red	800000	
Wood Products		
Box		
Cabinet		
Cane		
Chest		
Commode		
Cup		
Desk		

	Cargoes from Pondichery	Auction Sales
Fan		
Flower		
Folding Screen		
Picture		
Rattan		
Rottings-Long		
Table		
Tray		

Table 6: Summary of Textile Imports of Compagnie des Indes Orientales

	1687	1691	1699	1704	1710	1712	1714	1715	1716
Muslin	8340	11463	11360	10616	21766	40219	54582	23799	29971
Finer, Finished	59685	3965	35549	772	408	12950	8832	2776	2241
Finer, Unfinished	4059	732		446	6740	4627	15285	8845	3793
Coarser, Finished	5223	808	2625	3989	5900	17936	17287	14591	7295
Coarser, Unfinished	45494	16720	29479	8084	13817	48835	44540	32440	19700
Coarse	45113	17617	22362	1814	298	7320	599	20	976
Mixture	10043	2126	12332	200	2766	2341	4622	380	3504
Silk	6084	3816	5488		280	13050			333
Total	184041	57247	119195	25921	51975	147278	145747	82851	67813

	1720	1721	1722	1723	1724	1725	1726	1728	1729
Muslin	42881	48305	3198	2004	54316	32645	57627	40970	38778
Finer, Finished	7848	4280		1464	14222	8063	8850	4929	5376
Finer, Unfinished	3830	5160	1020	75	7420	5353	5200	1580	5584
Coarser, Finished	22391	16940	690		17609	12995	27450	30084	17940
Coarser, Unfinished	76630	39520		1599	64429	56957	79235	81463	65737
Coarse	8039	6940			4746	6926	961	1440	11062
Mixture	5585	8740		101	5735	3500	4482	4103	3883
Silk		2640	4006	266	418	1375	387		1272
Total	167204	132525	8914	5509	168895	127814	184192	164569	149632

	1731	1732	1733	1734	1737	1738	1739	1740	1741
Muslin	76594	144300	145792	96030	70706	107807	53240	81412	83141
Finer, Finished	3979	6457	8113	10831	1189	1761	1083	3175	4409
Finer, Unfinished	8780	8285	12350	9631	1382	960	6060	5300	2460
Coarser, Finished	24840	23073	61099	49894	53434	90318	99382	73567	47507
Coarser, Unfinished	109177	107575	170029	145070	126070	152340	112222	133978	141057
Coarse	15369	17830	38584	47360	44160	47710	22470	60215	83675
Mixture	13663	16233	26957	23209	13457	20926	7200	22281	18349
Silk	5970	3461	5315	6189	3500	3514	3130	4656	5190
Total	258372	327214	468239	388214	313898	425336	304787	384584	385788

	1749	1750	1756	1761	1766	1767	1769
Muslin	43791	12900	15579	19012	21538	12199	18823
Finer, Finished	3185		1428	5479	2645	480	1565
Finer, Unfinished	1466	340	849	2778		687	4600
Coarser, Finished	12085	7985	5459	9306	848	18469	17557
Coarser, Unfinished	34372	29398	37863	23437	45019	35246	52282
Coarse	1165	10680	490	9841	40409	33139	17456
Mixture	6010	2880	5677	2184	8056	3200	5910
Silk			496	3571	574	5621	3053
Total	102074	64183	67841	75608	119089	109036	121246

Table 8: Summary of Major Imports of Compagnie des Indes Orientales

	1687	1691	1699	1704	1710	1712	1714	1715	1716
Coffee	5500	1449							
Cowry	20500		24000			20700			
Drugs	8200	6370	15616	45803		880	5015		204
Dyes	19000		22000	96		68300			
Gum	1800		1425						
Lacquer			41850				629		5274
Metals				98400	74876				
Pepper	130000	90000	214000	14000	215000	566000	611126	284500	26600
Porcelain	1500			47700					4500
Saltpeter	110000	90000	540000		50290	173000	180000		
Sugar						2800			
Tea	3620			960	2382	27360			3360
Textiles									
Cloth	178026	58440	113262	25921	51975	147278	145747	82851	67813
Thread	21000	19300	16900			65100			
Raw Material	16240	19279	11877	20448	451	4000			
Wood	60000	18900	33300	9000	30000	35000	105220	207700	164200
Woodwork									
Rattan			63000					1537	
Total	575386	303738	1097230	262328	424974	1100418	1047737	576588	271951

	1720	1721	1722	1723	1724	1725	1726	1728	1729
Coffee						952100		433540	578665
Cowry	111343	100000				27737	135500	90000	99450
Drugs	1140		68230	8110	26074	31128	337583	568	17930
Dyes		7600	31165	14141	6738				16659
Gum			999	230000	3120	4560		160	230
Lacquer	29099	37825			7773		35268	5099	30694
Metals			249873						
Pepper	289878	220000	88000		471400	238382	468884	366900	437024
Porcelain			303671	344279		1500	59637	24000	21300
Saltpeter		39670					109752	344700	686000
Sugar			27665	307000					
Tea			219473	104100			112317	60360	336392
Textiles									
Cloth	165404	132525	8914	5112	167115	129655	191614	159969	150415
Thread								4579	4669
Raw Material		16856	67800	3000	15432	10440	97309	48600	22600
Wood	22867	40916	169900		306000	189133	445283	317700	324892
Woodwork									
Rattan	8480	22133			60873		11820	21128	39873
Total	628211	617525	1235690	1015742	1064525	1584645	2004967	1877303	2766793

Table 9: Summary of Major Imports of Compagnie des Indes

	1731	1732	1733	1734	1737	1738	1739	1740	1741
Coffee	324040	473150	712370	1710837	1037700	1652130	1890300	2104000	2380000
Cowry	371200	450430	657650	300000	51480	217540		279050	236522
Drugs	12756	61095	33617	46740	62380	67660	68180	80290	44101
Dyes	3600	8260	245	5024	6120	5980	13593	11480	1316
Gum	1480		273			210			598
Lacquer	29070	70940	91370	158471	7270				3000
Metals	45500	243277	247017	158740	122280	86540	101910	98470	126767
Pepper	710000	788660	907660	955600	1183560	645386	485260	382900	570767
Porcelain	170085	93118	194700	73200	18900	150600	111300	195000	59400
Saltpeter					151130				
Sugar	129640								
Tea	730110	676990	374450	802359	783020	787550	1099030	981487	1224491
Textiles									
Cloth	258372	327144	468239	388164	313498	425496	304788	384714	385788
Thread	470		10350				12150	9600	21390
Raw Material	76480	50850	87517	81509	23690	61880	38380	73188	94787
Wood	3290	676700	777300	1006446	571120	713216	649860	617220	515319
Woodwork									
Rattan	38120	42848	58125	141367	54342	22694	43557	137585	77746
Total	2904213	3963462	4620883	5828457	4386490	4836882	4818288	5355257	5741992

	1749	1750	1756	1761	1766	1767	1769
Coffee	2237000		1024314	1733040	1620800	1588664	1633924
Cowry	17294	65642		18057	234398	444798	202500
Drugs				23560	86385	60247	19021
Dyes				1333			
Gum				3904			
Lacquer				35786	35400	28589	8025
Metals							
Pepper	32132	454984	120092	29608	266137	334667	704118
Porcelain				151500	165900	206100	606000
Saltpeter		168596					
Sugar							
Tea				663318	2609048	1994222	2021692
Textiles							
Cloth	102760	64183	68450	75608	119179	109141	123931
Thread		4375		12041			22863
Raw Material		12990	12903	25411	85184	52173	33620
Wood	730171	193434	26575	111726	227562	272817	413408
Woodwork							
Rattan				38415	85695	43468	174345
Total	3119357	964204	1252334	2923307	5535686	5134886	5963447

Table10: Value of Sales, 1687-1768

	1687	1691	1721	1725	1758	1760	1767	1768
Coffee	5568	1485	1466407					
Moka					449917	1034254	450824	53090
Bourbon					1112328	1115050	1280000	1812650
Cowry	9327		84531		451687	151662	331896	618067
Drugs & Spices				300000				
Agaric	160							
Aloe		740						
Beaume								
Benzoin								
Borax							2954	4472
Camphre								
Canelle		5775						
Cardamore							15560	11117
Chiampy								
Chincon								
Cornaline	153							
Ensens	1728							
Esquine					9765		8300	
Galange								
Galbanum								
Gelee de Cerf								
Gerofle					1022			
Grena								
Icquinquin								
Ikin								
Mastaqui								
Mirabolan								
Mongistere								
Muscade								
Muse								
Myrrhe								
Opium								
Oreille de Juda								
Orpiment								
Pefouline								
Poismou								
Rhubard							6101	4572
Sagou								

	1687	1691	1721	1725	1758	1760	1767	1768
Sang de Dragon								
Santal								
Senne	460							
Syricanardy								
Tanfao								
Turbit								
Vif-argent								
Vitriol	2228	1840						
Other						3217		
Dyes								
Alum								
Amidon								
Ammoniacum								
Cinnabar								
Cochineal								
Curcuma								
Ecorce Jaune								
Houboua								
Indigo								
Kankou								
Kouankan								
Tumeric	3315							
Vermilion								
Other								
						1752		
Gum								
Arabique								
Lacque	968						18900	58124
Senegal								
Gutte	2700							
Other								
Ink								
Ivory								
Lacquer								
en bois						9834		
en feuille								

Table10: Value of Sales, 1687-1768

	1687	1691	1721	1725	1758	1760	1767	1768
sans bois								
Marble								
Metals								
Copper								
Tin								
Tutenag								
Lead								
Mother of Pearl								
Paper					6846		8309	8516
Pepper	86450	101625			170630	53376	1508245	555649
Porcelain					42644		156409	18232
Caisse								
Rouleau								
Bowl								
Covered								
Mustard								
Shaving								
Sugar								
Assorted								
Bucket								
Candlestick								
Cheese mold								
Compote Dish								
Cup	173							
Saucer								
Cup and Saucer								
Decanter								
Flagstone								
Fount								
Goblet								
Goblet and Saucer								
Handle								
Knife								

Table10: Value of Sales, 1687-1768

	1687	1691	1721	1725	1758	1760	1767	1768
Salads								
Terrine								
Assorted								
Morter								
Oil Lamp								
Pagoda								
Plate								
Platter								
Pot								
Butter								
Chamber								
Flower								
Ink								
Jam								
Ointment								
Tea								
Tobacco								
Water								
Other								
Salad Dish								
Salad & Nest								
Sauce Boat								
Service								
Coffee								
Tea								
Other								
Shaker								
Pepper								
Salt								
Terrines								
Urn								
Wash Basin								
Other								
Rice								
Saltpeter	99000	45000					380000	
Shells								

Table10: Value of Sales, 1687-1768

	1687	1691	1721	1725	1758	1760	1767	1768
Sugar								
Cane								
White								
Chrystals								
Tea	7240				1245471			
Bouy							2341700	2413948
Green						54324	654375	533662
Hayfven						10571	193653	319520
Imperial								
Kamphou							204467	240536
Pekeau							66299	43391
Sactchaon						2721	68832	61914
Sonlo								
Other						34206	472931	407322
Textiles								
Raw Cotton								
Raw Silk	80053	13378					844000	2259393
Raw Wool								
Cotton Thread	27300	28560			47015		33309	32387
Silk Thread								
Cloth					6994789			
Muslin								
Adatis				2610			631	800
Alliballies								
Betilles	122357	29263		366006			79443	144272
Casses	3090	158127		234654			1184606	1398792
Chavonis							14410	
Doussoutis								
Jamdanis							3527	
" brodez								
Mallemolles		177262		232824			391909	314712
" brodez								
Mamandis								
Mouselline								
" brodez								
Serbatis								
Tangeb	20550	114143		55922			49455	157618

	1687	1691	1721	1725	1758	1760	1767	1768
" brodez								41927
Tarnetanne								
Terindanne				63961			485922	184402
" brodez								
" rayee								
Toque				103096			2028	
Other							6660	36267
Finished, finer								
Allegies	2305							
Broderies							192176	415419
Chite	105905		1200			29210		39892
Cravate	1424	9913		72862		618		
" brodez								
Darin								
Limace							6501	23085
Other								
Unfinished, finer								
Ambertes								
Organdis				171557		28140	25258	51724
Percale	61049	9998		16830			12672	34746
Toile, superfine								
Touvis	572							
Other								
Finished, coarser								
Baramete								
Caladoris						1944		5751
Calarides								
Chaperconne						28679		
Chelas	1232						6660	
Chillies								
Chuckeree								
Fottamoura								
Fottes							4177	4320
Guinee								
" white	134749	34187	31292	301557		1106085	430688	1442449
" blue	3480		74395			7711	144497	615062
Neganepaux							3319	36704

	1687	1691	1721	1725	1758	1760	1767	1768
Nekanias							33632	143792
Tapsel						980		
Toile carreaux								
Other								
Unfinished, coarser								
Aman	11005							
Annabas								
Bafta		19679				60		
" white	32400						691494	1162107
" blue								
Basin		4541		34466		135	94108	180211
Begagis								
Boelan						14494	7981	8734
Camelot								
Chalbat							3516	4958
Chander								
Chazelas							33622	49063
Cirsakes								
Contelinea		63646						
Couvevrives	34102							
Deriband								
Dissouchaye								2160
Grisette								
Guingans	689					10047	102681	160206
Habassis							9110	32900
Halibannis								
Hamans				62051			212747	224575
Kateguis							485	
Kichorkay							20299	6221
Lohoria								
Manchette								
Mouchoirs	19514		33706	321985		70815	464167	1132007
Nankin							21786	66777
Nensougues						911	129597	
" brodez								
Platille								
Salempore		73959						
" white	370055		79768	422337		858350	52816	137747
" blue			77752			380	4320	47114

	1687	1691	1721	1725	1758	1760	1767	1768
Salgarn								
Sana	11184	155806					37294	90735
" white				31503				
" blue								
Sauvaguzee								
Socrotes				29703				
Stinquerke						10239	9491	34318
" brodez								
" rayee								
Tapchila								
Toile divers	62554		12347				871200	894969
Toile montee								
Other	58034						12285	
Ruined							37738	10556
Coarse								
Bajutapaux							11850	50136
Beram								
Cotonine								
Coupis						7413		
Doutis	295344	231129					1773	1239
Gara		8154					1067521	
" white				49992				1311471
" blue								
Koratte						16482	6536	18080
Rasta								
Other								
Cotton and Silk								
Agabanee								
Allibannee								
Atarasoye								
Balacor								
Charconnee								
Chuqueles	3040						6352	16797
Dorea		82846		142641		26789	509249	472385
" brodez								
Elatche							5978	
Fatouye								
Montichour								

Table10: Value of Sales, 1687-1768

	1687	1691	1721	1725	1758	1760	1767	1768
Nillas	44175						13081	6074
Pinasse							515	5592
Salasoye								
Sirsaca								4536
Siskrissoy							5085	43204
Souci	5270					91	17390	
Tepay	59050						498	
Toile avec soye		5129						
Other								
Silk								
en caisse								
Armoisin	15880	29732						15519
Attlas								
Bas en soye								
Ceintures								
Challis						72		
Coanevrive								
Cotonis						12		
Damas								14030
" rayee								3956
Etoffe de Chine		2010					90086	
Etoffe ecorce		20282					1404	
Gaz		1935						4739
Gilmilis								
Gingeras								
Gourgouras								5367
" brodez								
" rayee								
Jamawar								
Jarretierre								
Katequin								
Kencas	5493							
Lampas								7880
Line								9256
Longuis	865							
Mandarines								
Moguys								
Mouchoir de soye						4048		
Mousseline de soye		25583						

	1687	1691	1721	1725	1758	1760	1767	1768
Nakin								6653
Pacotile								
Patissoie								3938
Pekin						68		
" brodez								
" rayee								
Satin	63590	3696				113		3375
" broche								6311
" rayee								3468
Serge de soye								
Taffeta	8063	15380				9163		
" rayee								
Velour								
Other								19858
Other		99805		184913				
Hair			6070					
Hemp								
Hides					42			
Jute								
Linen								
Rugs	49770							
Other [wool]								
Tobacco								
Varnish					9943			9711
Wood								
Ebony						851	70455	
Sapan	2340	2882			9603	870	12919	28126
Red					54542	146250	114391	95392
Wood Products								
Box								
Cabinet								
Cane								
Chest								
Commode								
Cup								

Table10: Value of Sales, 1687-1768

	1687	1691	1721	1725	1758	1760	1767	1768
Desk								
Fan								
Flower								
Folding Screen								
Picture								
Rattan					6876	15960	34311	
Rottings-Long								19939
Table								
Tray							10096	

	1775	1776	1777	1778	1779	1780
Coffee	1874179	3248376	2037	26878		147512
Cowry	696972	920997				23250
Drugs and Spices	212385	402249	1725			5000
Dyes	538470	125287			30512	77770
Hides	18496					
Gum	47289	82377				
Ink	3600					
Ivory						8060
Metals	123090	90921	61281			
Mother of Pearl	4800					
Paper	3960					
Pepper	5366	2365171	91500	18308		
Porcelain	429000	200750	1250		46500	
Saltpeter	893471	1631680	165750			
Shells	50690					
Tea	9876044	3399315			4764	750730
Textile Cloth	14709236	22199714	894437		105368	279917
Thread					2197	
Raw Cotton	29771	44762				13348
Raw Silk	1091860	1382680	38090		22015	20220
Tobacco				1460727		
Varnish	51900	24300			3300	
Wood	63226	46121			4950	17613
Woodwork					12765	4912
Miscellaneous	3000	1690			5270	1570

Table 12: Value of French Exports to India and China, 1775-1780

	1775	1776	1777	1778	1779	1780
Armament	166856	259241	33934	4500	219030	14972
Coral		48000		260000		
Drugs and Dyes	44625	74130	4000	8775	1800	1200
Equipment	59077	343434	57865	70463	4735	11564
Gilding	15000	66100	20000	13680		
Glass	168638	66269	44692	8212		
Hemp	246766	254164	81224		9200	8786
Hides		1092		1200	1760	
Marble			800000			
Metals	1744032	1363974	470250	117397	14351	2430
Pearls	9010					
Provisioning	56238	202050	214695	137805	16706	24821
Soap	26286	82603	9455	50808	13268	36080
Specie	885398	56968	50138			
Supplies	409095	864551	133088	325700	71051	38610
Textile Cloth	787543	1119102	195615	380539	89676	77497
Thread	87200	21760	1050			2400
Tobacco	68509	1810	2293			
Wine and Liquor	2048911	1393735	443648	721191	103705	416587
Wood	1200	228150		5700		5193
Woodwork	71430	23092				
Miscellaneous	1878732	219871	8000	11448	38064	4220

References for Tables

Table 1: Tonnages of Importations and Exportations, 1665-1709.

Kaeppelin, P. *La Compagnie des Indes Orientales et François Martin.* Paris: A. Challamal, 1908. Reprint, New York: Burt Franklin, 1967, 653-661.

Estienne, René. *Les Armements au Long Cours de la Deuxième Compagnie des Indes (1717 - 1773).* Lorient: Service Historique de la Marine, 1996, 67-131.

Table 2: Values of Importation and Exportation, 1725-1771.

Raynal, G.T. *Mémoire Relatif de Commerce, 1721-1771.* Bibliothèque Nationale, Paris. Fr. 6431/185.

Haudrère, Philippe. *La Compagnie Française des Indes au XVIII Siècle.* Paris: Librairie de l'Inde Editeur, 1989, 14 and 1198.

Table 3: Contents of Auction Sales of Compagnie des Indes Orientales, 1687 – 1716.

1687, October 20: Sale at Rouen. Centre des Archives d'Outre-mer, Aix-en-Provence. C/2/6/57

1691, May 28: Sale at Nantes. Centre des Archives d'Outre-mer, Aix-en-Provence. C/2/16/187

1699, September 22: Sale at Nantes. Archives Départementales de Loire-Atlantique, Nantes. C. 750/27. Sale from cargoes of four ships, the *Princesse-de-Savoie*, the *Phélypeaux*, the *Perle-d'Orient* and the *Marchand-des-Indes*.

Sottas, Jules. *Histoire de la Compagnie Royale des Indes Orientales (1664 - 1719).* Rennes: L'Amateur Averti, 1994, 404.

1704, October 6: Sale at Nantes. Archives Départementales de Loire-Atlantique, Nantes. C.750/35. Sale from cargoes of two ships; the *Maurepas* and the *Pondichéry*. Sottas, 417.

1710, November 5: Sale at Nantes. Archives Municipales de la Ville de Nantes, HH 200/7. Sale from cargoes of two ships; the *Malo* and the *Saint Jean Baptiste*.

1712, May 23: Sale at Nantes. Archives Municipales de la Ville de Nantes, HH 200/19. Sale from cargoes of five ships; the *Maurapas*, the *Lis Brillac*, the *Auguste*, the *François d'Argouges* and the *Nouveau Georges*.

1714, July 7: Arrival of cargoes. Archives Municipales de la Ville de Nantes, HH 201/3. Cargoes from two ships, the *Deux Couronnes* and the *Auguste*.

1715, September 30: Sale at Nantes. Archives Municipales de la Ville de Nantes, HH 201/46. Sale from cargoes of two ships, the *Jason* and the *Saint Louis*.

1716, October 12: Sale of Nantes. Archives Municipales de la Ville de Nantes, HH 202/11. Sale from cargoes of two ships, the *Mercure* and the *Venus*.

Table 4: Contents of Auction Sales of Compagnie des Indes, 1717 – 1769.

1717, September 13. Sale at Paris. Bibliothèque Nationale, Paris, Fr. 21778/72.

1720, November 4: Sale. Archives Municipales de la Ville de Nantes, HH 219/30. Sale from cargoes of two ships; the *Comte de Toulouse* (600 tons) and the *Deux Couronnes* (600 tons) that arrived during 1719 and 1720.

1721, November 12: Sale at Nantes. Archives Municipales de la Ville de Nantes, HH 220/72 and HH 221/47. Sale from cargoes of three ships from India: the *Solide* (450 tons), *Vierge de Grâce* (360 tons), *Amphitrite* (800 tons), and some hemp and hides sold on August 21, 1721.

1722, October 12: Sale at Nantes. Archives Municipales de la Ville de Nantes, HH 222/29 and 30. Sale from cargoes of three ships: the *More* (300 tons), the *Galatée* (260 tons), the *Prince de Conty* (230 tons).

1723, December 1: Sale at Nantes. Archives Municipales de la Ville de Nantes, HH 223/9 to 11. Ships were not identified.

1724, August 28: Sale at Nantes. Archives Municipales de la Ville de Nantes, HH 223/54. Sale from cargoes of three ships, the *Bourbon* (1,000 tons), the *Dianne* (300 tons) and the *Athalante* (500 tons). The *Athalante* had not yet arrived, but its cargo was included in planned sale.

1725, September 24: Sale at Nantes. Archives Municipales de la Ville de Nantes, HH 224/18. Sale from cargoes of three ships: the *Royal-Philippe* (750 tons), the *Lys* (850 tons) and the *Union* (560 tons). Also includes coffee, cowry and tobacco not listed at sale, but are listed in their cargoes.

1726, November 12: Sale at Nantes. Archives Municipales de la Ville de Nantes, HH 224/45, 46 and 51. Sale from the cargoes of five ships: the *Saint Louis* (300 tons), the *Duc de Chartres* (900 tons), the *Neptune* (600 tons), the *Apollon* (600 tons), the *Syrène* (450 tons). *Saint Louis* and *Syrène* explicitly stated as included in auction.

1728, September 30: Sale at Nantes. Archives Municipales de la Ville de Nantes, HH 225/10. Sale from the cargoes of five ships; the *Lys* (850 tons), the *Jupiter* (600 tons), the *Solide* (325 tons), the *Badine* (350 tons) and the *Expédition* (120 tons) that arrived between April and August.

1729, October 3: Sale at Nantes. Archives Municipales de la Ville de Nantes, HH 225/43 and 47. Sale from the cargoes of three ships; the *Mars* (650 tons), the *Jason* (500 tons), the *Bourbon* (850 tons), that arrived at Lorient during May, July and August. Also included is the cargo of the *Mercure* (560 tons) which arrived at Lorient on September 30, and may not have been sold until 1730.

1731, September 17: Sale at Nantes. Archives Municipales de la Ville de Nantes, HH 226/40. Sale from cargoes of seven ships; the *Duc de Chartres* (800 tons), the *Diane* (330 tons), the *Méduse* (300 tons), the *Lys* (850 tons), the *Mars* (650 tons), the *Athalante* (500 tons), and the *Neptune* (600 tons) that arrived in Lorient during May, July and August.

1732, October 1: Sale at Nantes. Archives Municipales de la Ville de Nantes, HH
226/58. Sale from cargoes of eight ships; the *Royal Philippe* (700 tons), the
Badine (350 tons), the *Vierge de Grâce* (360 tons), the *Mercure* (560 tons),
the *Danae* (550 tons), the *Jason* (500 tons), the *Argonaute* (550 tons), and the
Galatée (300 tons) that arrived in Lorient during April, May, June, July and
August. Also includes cargo of the Bourbon expected from Pondichéry.

1733, October 5: Sale at Nantes. Archives Municipales de la Ville de Nantes,
HH 226/83. Sale from cargoes of 10 ships; the *Mars* (650 tons), the *Duc de
Chartres* (800 tons), the *Athalante* (500 tons), the *Philbert* (500 tons), the
Dauphin (500 tons), the *Saint Louis* (300 tons), the *Duc d'Anjou* (550 tons),
the *Griffon* (400 tons), the *Duchess* (500 tons), and the *Reine* (450 tons) that
arrived in Lorient during April, May and August.

1734, October 4: Sale at Lorient. Archives Départementales du Calvados, Caen.
C. 6405. Sale from cargoes of 12 ships; the *Royal-Philippe* (700 tons), the *Argonaute* (550 tons), the *Condé* (600 tons), the *Badine* (350 tons), the *Prince
de Conty* (600 tons), the *Vierge de Grâce* (360 tons), the *Jupiter* (650 tons),
the *Neptune* (600 tons), the *Thétis* (500 tons), the *Amphitrite* (500 tons), the
Cavalier (400 tons), and the *Paix* (650 tons) that arrived in Lorient during
May, June, July and August.

1737, September 23: Sale at Lorient. Centre des Archives d'Outre-mer, Aix-en-
Provence. C/2/281/65 & 68. Sale from cargoes of ten ships; the *Reine* (450
tons), the *Apollon* (600 tons), the *Dauphin* (500 tons), the *Comte de Toulouse*
(600 tons), the *Duchess* (500 tons), the *Phoenix* (700 tons), the *Griffon* (400
tons), the *Thétis* (500 tons), the *Paix* (600 tons) that arrived at Lorient in
October of 1736, and May and July, 1737. The cargo of the *Amphitrite* (500
tons) that arrived at Lorient in August, 1737, was also included.

1738, October 13: Sale at Lorient. Centre des Archives d'Outre-mer, Aix-en-
Provence. C/2/28/123. Sale from cargoes of nine ships; the *Fleury* (800 tons),
the *Philibert* (600 tons), the *Maurepas* (550 tons), the *Condé* (600 tons), the
Prince de Conty (600 tons), the *Chauvelin* (600 tons), the *Héron* (450 tons),
the *Jupiter* (500 tons), and the *Lys* (800 tons) that arrived at Lorient in April,
May, July, August and September. The cargo of the *Triton* (500 tons) was
also included: its arrival was soon expected and its cargo was listed in conjunction with auction sale.

1739, October 12: Sale at Lorient. Centre des Archives d'Outre-mer, Aix-en-
Provence. C/2/281/111. Sale from cargoes of ten ships; the *Reine* (450 tons),
the *Comte de Toulouse* (600 tons), the *Phoenix* (700 tons), the *Saint Géran*
(600 tons), the *Duc de Bourbon* (800 tons), the *Fulvy* (600 tons), the *Penthièvre* (600 tons), the *Amphitrite* (500 tons), the *Apollon* (600 tons) and the
Griffon (400 tons) that arrived in Lorient during April, May, June, July and
August. The company expected the arrival of three other ships, the *Paix* (600

tons), the *Thétis* (500 tons) and the *Duchess* (500 tons) before the sale. Their cargoes were not listed and not included.

1740, September 26: Sale at Lorient. Centre des Archives d'Outre-mer, Aix-en-Provence. C/2/281/243. Sale from cargoes of eleven ships; the *Fleury* (800 tons), the *Triton* (500 tons), the *Paix* (600 tons), the *Thétis* (500 tons), the *Héron* (450 tons), the *Argonaute* (600 tons), the *Chauvelin* (600 tons), the *Condé* (600 tons), the *Duc de Chartres* (600 tons), the *Prince de Conty* (600 tons), and the *Fière* (150 tons) that arrived in Lorient during May, June and July. The company expected the arrival of four other ships, the *Duc d'Orléans* (600 tons), the *Maurepas* (700 tons), the *Jupiter* (550 tons) and the *Duchesse* (500 tons) before the sale. Their cargoes were not listed and not included.

1741, September 25: Sale at Lorient. Archives, Ministère des Affaires Etrangères, Asie. 12/42. Sale from cargoes of nine ships; the *Apollon* (600 tons), the *Hercule* (650 tons), the *Lys* (700 tons), the *Maurepas* (700 tons), the *Saint Géran* (600 tons), the *Neptune* (700 tons), the *Jason* (700 tons), the *Fulvy* (600 tons) and the *Phoenix* (780 tons) that arrived in Lorient during April, May, June, July and August.

1749, November 4: Sale at Lorient. Bibliothèque Nationale, Paris. NAF 9225/108. Ships were not listed.

1750, Arrival of Cargoes. Centre des Archives d'Outre-mer, Aix-en-Provence. C/2/282/52 & 53. Cargoes of two ships; the *Brillant* (550 tons) and the *Dragon* (800 tons), arriving in Lorient during August.

1756, November 8: Sale at Lorient. Centre des Archives d'Outre-mer, Aix-en-Provence. C/2/282/186. Ships were not listed.

1761, September 21: Sale at Lorient. Service Historique de la Marine, Lorient. 1P262/80. Ships were not listed.

1764, October 8: Sale at Lorient. Service Historique de la Marine, Lorient. 1P305/70/123. Sale from cargoes of eight ships; the *Fidèlle* (400 tons), the *Vaillant* (1100 tons), the *Massiac* (900 tons), the *Adour* (800 tons), the *Villevault* (900 tons), the *Duc de Choiseul* (900 tons), the *Beaumont* (900 tons) and the *Paix* (800 tons) that arrived in 1764.

1766, October 13: Sale at Lorient. Service Historique de la Marine, Lorient. 1 P305/150. Sale from cargoes of eight ships; the *Bertin* (900 tons), the *Chameau* (750 tons), the *Duc de Choiseul* (900 tons), the *Paix* (800 tons), the *Duc de Praslin* (700 tons), the *Beaumont* (900 tons), the *Villevault* (900 tons), and the *Adour* (800 tons) that arrived in Lorient during March, June and July.

1767, November 9: Sale at Lorient. Centre des Archives d'Outre-mer, Aix-en-Provence. C/2/50/198. Sale from cargoes of six ships; the *Comte d'Artois* (1200 tons), the *Comte d'Argenson* (800 tons), the *Berryer* (900 tons), the *Duc de Duras* (1000 tons), the *Duc de Penthièvre* (900 tons) and the *Ajax* (600 tons) that arrived in Lorient during 1767.

1769, November 20: Sale at Lorient. Centre des Archives d'Outre-mer, Aix-en-Provence. C/2/53/295. Cargoes from seven ships; the *Comte d'Argenson* (800 tons), the *Condé* (1000 tons), the *Penthièvre* (900 tons), the *Berryer* (900 tons), the *Duc de Duras* (1000 tons), the *Sage* (250 tons), and the *Massiac* (900 tons) that arrived in Lorient during 1769.

Table 5: Contents of Imports from Pondichéry and at Sales, 1735-1743.
Averages for four ships. Centre des Archives d'Outre-mer, Aix-en-Provence. C/2/16/163 & 164.

Table 6: Summary of Textile Imports of Compagnie des Indes Orientales, 1687 - 1716.
Same references as Table 3.

Table 7: Summary of Textile Imports of Compagnie des Indes, 1720 - 1769.
Same references as Table 4.

Table 8: Summary of Major Imports of Compagnie des Indes Orientales, 1687 - 1716.
Same references as Table 3.

Table 9: Summary of Major Imports of Compagnie des Indes, 1720 - 1769.
Same references as Table 4.

Table 10: Value of Sales, 1687 - 1768.
1687. Centre des Archives d'Outre-mer, Aix-en-Provence. C/2/6/57.
1691. Centre des Archives d'Outre-mer, Aix-en-Provence. C/2/16/187
1721: Archives Municipales de la Ville de Nantes, HH 220/141 & 142
1725: Centre des Archives d'Outre-mer, Aix-en-Provence.C/2/16/164
1758: Service Historique de la Marine, Lorient. 1P 262/45/9
1760: Service Historique de la Marine, Lorient. 1P 262/45/12
1767: Centre des Archives d'Outre-mer, Aix-en-Provence. C/2/50/147 & 148
1768: Centre des Archives d'Outre-mer, Aix-en-Provence. C/2/56/127 & 128

Table 11: Value of French Imports from India and China, 1775 - 1780.
Archives Nationales, Paris. F/12/242-248.

Table 12: Value of French Exports to India and China, 1775 - 1780.
Archives Nationales, Paris. F/12/242-248.

Glossary of Textile Terms

Adatays, Addatis, Addaties, Adathaies, Adatais: 1) Muslin or very fine and bright cotton cloth. The best came from Bengal. (Savary, 1, 22). 2) Plain muslin, usually fine quality from Dacca. (Irwin, 57). 3) Plain white muslin, medium to fine quality, fashion wear from Dacca in 17th and 18th centuries. Re-export trade. (Chaudhuri, 503). 4) Fine cotton muslin from India, best grades from Bengal. (Wingate, 6).

Agabance, Agabanee, Aggebance, Agibanis: Cotton fabric embroidered with silk, made in Aleppo. (Wingate, 8).

Agaric: Cotton fabric similar to terry cloth, made with fine warp loop pile formed on wires. Used for dresses. (Wingate, 8).

Ajamis: Calico from the Near East. (Wingate, 10).

Alliballies, Allibatis, Alliabally, Allibali: 1) Very fine muslin. (Irwin, 58). 2) Type of East Indian plain, brocaded or embroidered cotton. Some had selvages made with gold thread. (Wingate, 13).

Alibanies, Allibannees, Allibanis: 1) Cotton cloth carried to Holland from India. (Savary, 1, 66). 2. Mixed silk-and-cotton. Probably striped, superior. (Irwin, 58). 3) Mixed cotton and silk, probably striped. Medium to superior quality. Fashionwear and re-export trade. Dacca. 17-18th centuries. (Chaudhuri, 503).

Allegeas, Allegais, Allejaes, Allejars, Alagia, Elastches, Layches: 1) Fabric from India. Two sorts: some of cotton, and others of herbs woven with hemp or linen. (Savary, 1, 67). 2) Originally a striped cloth of mixed cotton-and-silk, commonly red and white or blue and white, sometimes flowered and embellished with gold and silver thread. Some made entirely of cotton, but striped. Gujarat, Bengal, Coromandel. (Irwin, 7). 3) Striped and checked, red and white or blue and white. Medium quality. Domestic and general use, re-export trade, 17th century, South India. (Chaudhuri, 502). 4) East Indian cotton muslin, made in plain weave; also mixed with silk and other fibers.

(Wingate, 13).

Aman, Amand: Plain weave, blue cotton fabric made in the Near East (Syria). Formerly imported in France for the manufacture of curtains.(Wingate, 16).

Amierties, Ambertees, Amertes, Amertis, Emerties: 1) Cotton cloth from India. (Savary, 1, 90). 2) Superior grade of white cloth, used in lining of quilts. Bihar. (Irwin, 58). 3) Plain white, medium quality. General use, block printing in England, re-export trade. Bihar, 17-18th centuries. (Chaudhuri, 504). 4) Closely woven cotton fabric from Patna.(Wingate, 18).

Armoisin, Azmoisin, Armoitins, Armoilins, Arains: 1) A taffeta made in India, but more weak and lower quality than the armoisins of silk. The color is often carmine and red. There are two kinds: arains which are taffetas and striped, and damask which are flowered taffetas. (Savary, 1, 149). 2) Taffetas made in India. Two kinds: arains which are striped or checked taffetas and flowered damask. Lighter than all the taffetas. (Weigert, 153, 166). 3) Thin, lightweight silk taffeta, now largely obsolete. It was made in France and Italy in stripes, geometric designs or dots: in East India, two types were produced; arain and damaris. (Wingate, 27).

Astarte: French silk dress fabric of fine quality, made in a twill weave and printed with bold designs in brilliant colors. (Wingate, 30).

Attlas, Atlas, Cotonis, Cancantas, Calquiers, Bouilles Chalmay, Charmay: 1) Silk satin made in India. It can be plain, striped, flowered in gold or solely in silk. Kinds of Attlas are Cotonis, Cancantas, Calquiers, Cotonis-Bouilles, Bouilles Charmay or Charmay, Quemkas. (Savary, 1, 184). 2) Warp faced satin and weave fabric with silk warps

and cotton wefts. (Murphy, 199).

Atchiabanes: 1) Plain white. Coarse quality. Domestic and general use. Bengal. 18th Century. (Chaudhuri, 503).

Auguili: Coarse Syrian bagging made of cotton mixed with other fibers. Better grades are dyed blue or are white with another color. (Wingate, 32).

Bafta, Baffetas, Baffoted, Baft, Baftah, Bufta, Baffs: 1) Coarse white cotton cloth, coming from India. Often named after region of origin and called Orgagies, Nossaris, Gaudivis, Nerindes, Dabouis. (Savary, 1, 210). 2) Generic term for plain calico of Gujarat, varying in quality from coarse to fine. Sent to Europe usually white, but for Asian markets they were more commonly dyed red, blue or black. (Irwin, 59). 3) Plain white. Medium to superior quality. Clothing and block printing in England. Bengal. 18th century. (Chaudhuri, 503). 4) White and red dyed, less frequently black or blue. Coarse to fine quality. Western India. Domestic and general use. 17th century. (Chaudhuri, 501). 5) Cotton or cotton and silk fabric derived from Persian wool [i.e. yarn] and employed in African and East Indian trade. Formerly the generic term for all white, gray or colored cottons in the African markets. First made in India. In East Africa, it is applied to white cotton shirting or bleached longcloth. Blue bafta is the West African term for plain weave cloth dyed blue. Bafta originally was fine muslin of western India, also a lower grade brocade made in Bengal. (Wingate, 39).

Bajota: Coarse, bleached cotton fabric formerly sold by the Holland East Indian Trading Co. (Wingate, 41).

Bajutapaux, Bejutapaux, Bayutapaux: Term used in the African trade to describe a coarse cotton cloth with blue and white or red and white stripes. (Wingate, 53).

Balais: Silk ribbons. (Savary, 1, 214).

Balasse: Sturdy, plain weave cotton fabric from Surat. (Wingate, 41).

Balazee (Sauvaguzee): White cotton cloth from Surat. (Savary, 1, 222).

Bandannes: Tie dyed silk handkerchiefs (Murphy, 169).

Baramete, Barawazi, Baroquis, Barraiti: Barawazi: Cotton fabric with dark blue, yellow or red woven checks, with border of red, black and yellow checks. (Wingate, 46).

Basin: Cotton cloth. Made in different qualities and fashions. They come from India, are white and without nap. There are two types: twilled or serges, the others are twilled and open. Made in Bengal, Pondichéry, Ballasar. Used to make corsets, petticoats, curtains. (Savary, 1, 289). 2) Twilled, white cotton fabric made with or without narrow stripes and sometimes napped on one side. French fabric made of linen or cotton and linen, or with a hemp warp and cotton filling in twill weave. (Wingate, 49).

Batolini: Term used in the Near East trade for a fabric made with a hemp warp and cotton filling, usually dyed light blue. (Wingate, 51).

Batistes, Baptiste: 1) Linen cloth very fine and white. (Savary, 1, 302). 2) In cotton, it is a sheer, combed, mercerized muslin. Also a sheer silk fabric, plain or figured, resembling silk mull. (Wingate, 51).

Bengales, Bengal: 1) Kind of piece goods exported to England in 17th century. Bengal stripes were striped gingham. (Yule-Burnell, 86). 2) Women's dress fabrics of silk and hair cloth originally from India. Imitation muslin with printed strips. (Wingate, 58).

Berams: Coarse cotton cloth from Surat. Some are white and some are striped in colors. (Savary, 1, 320).

Betain, Betaine, Beteela: Beteela is obsolete term applied to Indian muslin used for neckties, saris, head coverings. (Wingate, 59).

Bezane: French term for various bleached, striped or dyed Bengal cottons and calicos in 18th century. (Wingate, 60).

Betilles: 1) Muslin or white cotton cloth from Pondichéry. Three kinds: coarser, very fine, bright. Red ones come from Bengal. (Savary, 1, 324). 2) Deccan name for muslin. Sometimes dyed red, sometimes striped or flowered with embroidery, much in demand in Europe as neckcloths. (Irwin, 59). 3) Plain white and dyed, base cloth for fine embroidery. Medium to superior quality. Fashionwear. South India. 17-18th centuries. (Chaudhuri, 502). 4) Plain, checked or figured fabric similar to an open texture Swiss muslin. (Wingate, 59).

Boide, Boi, Boy: Coarse, heavy flannel in a plain, loose weave with cotton warp and wool and noil filling. Used as linings. (Wingate, 77).

Bolsas, Bolzas, Coutil: 1) Kind of coutil, made of cotton thread from India. It is either all white or stripped in yellow with the stripes made from unbleached cotton. (Savary, 1, 400). 2) Coutil imported from India during the 17th and 18th centuries. (Wingate, 71).

Bouille-Cotonis, Bouille-Charmay: Attlas. (Savary, 1, 432).

Bombasin: Silk cloth. Also a cloth woven from cotton thread. (Savary, 1, 401).

Bouracan, Barracan, Barragan, Camelot: 1) Coarse cloth, not twilled. It is a kind of camelot that is coarser than ordinary. (Savary, 1, 272, 442). 2) Cloth, not twilled, near to camelot, but coarser. It is used to make coats, surtouts. (Weigert, 154).

Brocart, Brocard, Brocat: Silk cloth

made from thread of gold, silver or silk, set off with flowers and ornaments. (Savary, 1, 483).

Brocatelle: small cloth in imitation of Brocart. Can be made of silk or cotton or wool. (Savary, 1, 483).

Broché: Cloth with ground decorated in designs and made from gold, silver and silk thread. (Savary, 1, 484).

Caddy: Cheap, plain woven calico. (Irwin, 60).

Caladoris, Catadoris, Caladaris: 1) Cotton cloth, striped, red or black from Bengal. (Savary, 1, 524). 2) East Indian calico with black or red stripes. (Wingate, 96).

Calamande, Calamandre, Calmandre: Cloth made in Flanders and Brabant. (Savary, 1, 524).

Calancas, Calencas: East Indian Calico. (Wingate, 96).

Calico: Inexpensive, brightly printed cotton cloth woven with carded yarns in a plain weave. Originally a plain weave, lightweight printed cotton cloth of Indian origin. Similar to percale which has virtually replaced it in the market today. Early calicos were beautiful, elaborate designs of animals. Later calicos were coarser fabric. Derived from Calicut, where fabric first made and painted and dyed or printed with wood blocks. (Wingate, 97).

Callowaypoose: Cheap, striped and chequered cloth – slave trade. (Irwin, 60).

Calquiers: Attlas calquiers are satins from India. (Savary, 1, 532).

Cambaye: Strong, coarse East Indian cotton fabric resembling linen. (Wingate, 98).

Camboolees, Culbuleys, Cambolees: Woolen blanket, cloth of mixed silk and wool. Sind. (Irwin, 60).

Cambric, Cambrai, Cambaye: 1) Chintzes still figured by an old man at Sadras, the cambric being furnished to him. (Yule-Burnell, 202). 2) Cambaye: strong coarse East

Indian cotton fabric to resemble linen. (Wingate, 98). 3) Cambray (Picardies): White cloth, bright and fine, made of linen (Weigert, 155). 4) Comboy: sort of shirt of white calico. (Yule-Burnell, 237).

Cambraisines: Fine cloth from Egypt. (Savary, 1, 532).

Cambresine: 1) Fine linen fabric. (Savary, 1, 533). 2) French term for fine, plain, lightweight cotton linen fabric. (Wingate, 96).

Cambray, Picardies: White cloth, bright and fine, made of linen. (Weigert, 155).

Camcanys, Caymeconyes: Plain muslin from Patna. (Irwin, 60).

Camelin, Camelotine: Small cloth in manner of camelot. (Savary, 1, 533).

Camelot: 1) Cloth not twilled, made of warp and weft stitch. (Savary, 1, 533). 2) Cloth not twilled, plain or striped, made of warp and weft stitch. (Weigert, 155).

Camlet, Camblet, Cambette, Camblette: Arabic origin, referring to pile or nap and to mohair. Name also applied to a wide variety of high quality, fine smooth fabrics made of wool, silk, etc., in plain or satin weave. Another version is light weight fabric woven of hard spun wool and cotton or linen yarn. (Wingate, 100).

Cancanias: Attlas (Savary, 1, 541).

Cannikens, Canequims, Candequees, Cannequinea: 1) Cheap, coarse calico dyed blue or black. (Irwin, 60). 2) East Indian bleached cotton fabric. (Wingate, 101).

Capperees: Cheap blue and white chequered or striped cloth. Slave trade. (Irwin, 61).

Cardouzille: Small fabric of wool without silk. (Savary, 1, 563).

Carolees: 1) Similar to Capperees. (Irwin, 61). 2) Carole: Obsolete twilled woolen trousering fabric. (Wingate, 107).

Carrelé: Silk fabric. (Weigert, 155).

Casses, Caisses, Cossaes, Cassa, Kassa: 1) Plain muslin, usually of good quality. Those sent to Europe were usually medium quality. Dacca. (Irwin, 62). 2) Plain white muslin. Fine quality fashionwear of re-export trade. Bengal. Dacca – 17th -18th centuries. (Chaudhuri, 504). 3) Soft fine East Indian cotton muslin made with slack twist yarn. (Wingate, 110).

Castagnette: Fabric of silk, wool, etc. (Savary, 1, 586).

Castalogue, Castelogne, Couverture de lit: Linen fabric. (Savary, 1, 586).

Catches, Cattaketchies, Cashees: Calico from South India. (Irwin, 61).

Chablis: Commercial term for wood. (Savary, 1, 610).

Chabnam (Rosé): Kind of muslin. (Savary, 1, 610).

Chacart: Type of checked cotton fabric. (Savary, 1, 610).

Chaddars, Chedars, Chadars, Chuddars, Chadders, Chadurs, Chaddahs: 1) From Hindi, chador, meaning shawl painted cotton. (Irwin, 61). 2) Plain weave cotton fabric with a wide blue or black warp stripe on one side and narrow white filling stripes. (Wingate, 116).

Challis, Chalie, Challie, Challi, Challys, Etamine Glossé: 1) Estamine des Indes: Silk fabric. (Savary, 1, 1911). 2) Soft, supple, lightweight, plain weave fabric made of wool, rayon, cotton, etc. Usually printed in small floral patterns. (Wingate, 118).

Chambray: Derived from Cambrai in France. Broad class of plain weave, yarn-dyed cotton fabrics with colored warp and white filling. Often in plain color, but also available in striped, checked and patterned. (Wingate, 118).

Chandar, Chandereans, Chandeli, Chander, Chandin: Indian general term for unbleached, bleached, dyed or printed cotton fabric imported into India. (Wingate, 119).

Chaperoune, Chaferconne: Painted fabric made in the country of the Grand Mogol – Surat, Number of such kinds. (Savary, 3, 131).

Chappa, Chopped silk: Silk cloth. (Wingate, 119).

Charadaries, Carridaries: Striped or chequered woven cloth, probably mixed silk and cotton. (Irwin, 61).

Charconnaes, Cherconnaes: 1) Striped or chequered cloth of mixed silk and cotton. (Irwin, 61). 2) Charkana: Indian term for checked muslin of cotton and silk or all cotton. (Wingate, 120).

Chasseles, Chasselade, Chazelas: Term used in West Africa trade for cotton fabric. (Wingate, 120).

Chauters, Chowters: 1) Plain white calico, usually of superior quality and used in shirting. Western India. (Irwin, 61). 2) Chowtar: Variety of cotton muslin made in India. (Wingate, 129).

Chavonis: Sheer East Indian cotton muslin. (Wingate, 121).

Chelais: Plain weave cotton fabric with a checked or striped border and a wide heading. Used as loincloth. (Wingate, 121).

Chelas, Chillaes, Chelles, Chelloes, Chelos, Cheiloes: 1) Cotton fabric, checked and different colors, coming from India (Surat). (Savary, 1, 715). 2) Cotton handkerchief, usually striped blue and white. (Irwin, 61). 3) Cheiloes: Striped cotton fabric, medium quality in West African trade from Gujarat (Chaudhuri, 501). 4) Chillae: Striped cotton fabric in blue and white from Bengal. Medium quality. Clothing and re-export trade, 18th century. (Chaudhuri, 503). 5) Chelos: Plain weave, East Indian calico, shirting printed in checks and plaids. (Wingate, 121).

Chellos, Chelos: Cheap cotton cloth

with red, blue or black stripes patterned on the loom, used in West Indian class trade. (Irwin, 62).

Chenille: Silk fabric. (Weigert, 155).

Chercolee: Chuquelas, silk and cotton fabric. (Savary, 1, 717).

Cherconnee, Cherconnaes: 1) Chuquelas, silk and cotton fabric. (Savary, 1, 717). 2) Mixed cotton and silk, striped with checks. Bengal. (Chaudhuri, 503). 3) Striped or chequered cloth of mixed silk-and-cotton. (Irwin, 61).

Cherquemolle: Fabric from India, partly silk and partly bark. (Savary, 1, 717).

Chikan, Chilan: Embroidered fine cotton muslin from India. (Wingate, 125).

Chillas, Chillies, Chellies, Chilli: 1) Checked cotton fabric from Bengal. (Savary, 1, 761). 2) Cheap checked cotton cloth from Madras. (Irwin, 62).

Chin: Brocaded silk fabric from China. (Wingate, 125).

Chine: Kind of taffeta of bergame. (Savary, 1, 762).

Chintes (chintz in modern English): 1) Painted or printed calico. (Irwin, 62). 2) Blocked printed. Medium to superior quality. Bengal. Clothing and re-export trade, 17th- 18th Century. (Chaudhuri, 503). 3) Originally, a glazed, plain weave cotton fabric, generally woven with a handspun fine warp and coarser, slack, twill filling, decorated with brilliantly colored pattern of flowers, stripe. First used in 18th century as wearing apparel. Derived from chint, the Indian name for a broad, gaudy printed fabric of cotton. (Wingate, 127). 4) Brilliant colored and permanently dyed – lightweight but durable. (Murphy, 158).

Chintes – Seronge: White cotton fabric ready to be printed and dyed, made in India. (Savary, 1, 762).

Chirans: Cheap calico usually listed with chequered goods in the category of guinee-stuffs. (Irwin, 62).

Chites, Chits, Chittes, Chite, Chitteie: 1) Cotton fabric from India, extremely good with a long lasting dye that does not lose its luster. From Coromandel in India. (Savary, 1, 766). 2) French word for chintz. (Yule-Burnell, 201). 3) Fabric printed and dyed. (Yule-Burnell, 202). 4) Fine, closely woven East Indian, calico in plain weave. (Wingate, 128).

Chuckerees: Checked calico. (Irwin, 62).

Chucklas, Chuclaes: 1) Striped silk and cotton fabric. (Irwin, 62). 2) Mixed cotton and silk fabric, striped, fine quality fashionwear and re-export from Bengal. (Chaudhuri, 503).

Chuquelas, Chercolees, Cherconnees: 1) Fabric of silk and cotton, striped and made in India. (Savary, 1, 771).

Cirsakas: Fabric from India, usually all cotton. (Savary, 1, 782).

Coan fabrics, Coan robes: Sheer silk fabric, fine and transparent as Dacca muslins. (Wingate, 136).

Comconnaes: Plain cotton fabric of inferior quality. (Irwin, 62).

Contailles: Low grade French silk fabric. (Wingate, 145).

Contance: Strong, coarse French bed ticking. (Wingate, 147).

Coopees: Plain white. Medium to superior quality. Bengal. (Chaudhuri, 503).

Copees: East Indian gingham with fancy check patterns. (Wingate, 147).

Coraline, Coralline: Heavy Italian needlepoint lace. (Wingate, 147).

Cotonis: 1) (Attlas). Silk satin from India. (Savary, 1, 1539). 2) Indian fabric woven with silk warp and fine cotton filling in fancy patterns. (Wingate, 153).

Cotonine, Cotonnine: 1) Coarse fabric – sailcloth. (Savary, 1, 1539). 2)

Heavy, strong fabric made of cotton and hemp. (Wingate, 153).

Coutil, Coutis, Coupis, Courtille: 1) Type of fabric that is very strong and close-knit, usually made from hemp. In India, coutil is called Bolzas and made in Bengal. Some are white and striped, some are striped yellow from unbleached cotton. (Savary, 1, 1592). 2) Strong, firmly woven cotton fabric, used for corsets. Derived from French and means drill. (Wingate, 159). 3) Coarse fabric very strong and close-knit, usually made from hemp. (Weigert, 156).

Crepe: Fabric not twilled, very light and bright like gauze. (Weigert, 156).

Crespe, Crepe, Crespodaille, Crespon: Silk fabric. (Savary, 1, 1607).

Cretonne: Kind of white linen fabric. (Savary, 1, 1608).

Culgars: Silk fabric. (Irwin, 63).

Cummuns: Muslin. (Irwin, 63).

Cussidah: East Indian muslin. (Wingate, 173).

Cushtaes: 1) Striped or chequered cloth, possibly silk and cotton. (Irwin, 62). 2) Striped blue and white cotton fabric. Medium to superior quality. Clothing and re-export trade. Bengal. 18th Century. (Chaudhuri, 503).

Cuttanees, Kootnee: 1) Cloth of silk and cotton in satin weave, striped or flowered. (Irwin, 63). 2) Plain white and striped cotton fabric. Superior to fine quality. Bengal. Fashionwear and re-export trade. 17th-18th centuries (Chaudhuri, 504). 3) Indian fabric made of fine linen or silk and cotton. (Wingate, 75).

Damaras: 1) Taffetas from India. (Savary, 1, 1645). 2) Lightweight, thin silk taffeta with small floral patterns made in India. Similar to armoisins. (Wingate, 177)

Damas: 1) Fabric made of silk. (Savary, 1, 1645). 2) Silk fabric. (Wei-

gert, 156). 3) French word meaning damask, which was fine, silk fabric imported from the Orient in the 18th century. (Wingate, 177-178).

Daridas: Kind of taffata from India. (Savary, 1, 1649).

Darins, Darein, Darain: 1) Fabric from hemp. (Savary, 1, 1649). 2) Lightweight, checked or striped fabric similar to muslin from India in 17th and 18th centuries. (Wingate, 180).

Darnamar : Cotton fabric. (Savary, 1, 1649).

Dauphine: 1) Small piece of fabric very light, not twilled. All wool or wool and silk. (Savary, 1, 1651). 2) Lightweight, plain weave wool upholstery fabric made in France in 18th century. (Wingate, 181). 3) Silk textile. (C.I.E.T.A, 11).

Dekin, Decan, Kenaf: Soft bast similar to jute. Twine. (Wingate, 181 & 326).

Dentelle, Pasement: 1) Work composed of several interlaced threads, gold or silver or silk or linen. (Savary, 1, 1677). 2) Term used in France for lace since 17th century. (Wingate, 185).

Deribands, Deriabads, Deribadis, Deritehdi, Derebands, Deriabad: 1) White cotton fabric from India. Some coarser and stronger than others. (Savary, 1, 1681). 2) Good quality plain white calico. (Irwin, 63). 3) White cotton fabric. Coarse to medium quality. Domestic and general use. From North India in 17th century. (Chaudhuri, 501). 4) Bleached, Indian cotton fabric. (Wingate, 186).

Desooksoy: Indian cotton fabric. (Wingate, 187).

Doreas, Doria: 1) Muslin or white cotton cloth from Bengal. They are coarse and fine, striped and checked. (Savary, 1, 1719). 2) Striped or chequered fabric of mixed silk and cotton. (Irwin, 63). 3) Mixed cotton and silk. Fine to superfine quality. Fashionwear and re-export. Bengal. 17th-18th centuries. (Chaudhuri, 504). 4) Doriah: British made plain weave, bleached cotton fabric with crammed warp satin weave stripe originally made and used in India. (Wingate, 194).

Dorures: Fabric that is a satin ornamented in gold. (Savary, 1, 1723).

Dosooty: Kind of cheap cotton stuff. (Wingate, 186).

Doussoutis, Doussoutin, Doussoutis: Dosooties: Plain white muslin. Medium, fine and superfine quality. Fashionwear and re-export trade. Bengal. 18th century. (Chaudhuri, 504).

Doutis, Sauvaguzes, Sauvagagis: Coarse, white cotton fabric. (Savary, 1, 1737).

Elacha, Elaches: Striped cotton fabric from Sind. Warp in cotton or silk, and filling in cotton. (Wingate, 213).

Elaiche: Handmade, plain weave, yarn dyed. Indian silk fabric made in Agra, in narrow white stripes on rose ground. (Wingate, 213).

Elatches: 1) Fabric from India, silk and cotton. Kind of chuquelas and allegeas. (Savary, 1, 1799). 2) Mixed cotton and silk fabric striped. Fine quality fashionwear and re-export trade. Bengal. 18th century. (Chaudhuri, 504). 3) Handmade, checked Indian dress fabric made of cotton and colored silk yarn. (Wingate, 214).

Eschantillon: Show piece of fabric. (Savary, 1, 1837).

Escru: Unbleached silk fabric or thread. (Savary, 1, 1853).

Estamine, Etamine: 1) Small cloth very lightweight, not twilled. Made or silk or wool or both. Those from India are made from silk. (Savary, 1, 1908, 1911). 2) Lightweight, open weave fabric woven with handspun, coarse yarn. (Wingate, 221).

Estrousoye: Silk fabric. (Savary, 3, 379).

Fautahs, Footaes, Photaes: Indian for cloth worn over private parts. Dyed calico, usually blue or white. (Irwin, 69).

Fayenne, Fayetta, Fayouni: 1) Fayenne: Cotton printed in indigo. (Wingate, 230).

2) Fayetta: Fine, soft, lightweight dress goods in cotton and wool. (Wingate, 230).

Fossy: Type of East Indian cotton fabric. (Wingate, 249).

Fottalangees: Striped cloth from India, made of silk and bark. (Savary, 2, 139).

Fottes, Footaes: 1) Checked cotton fabric from Bengal. (Savary, 2, 139). 2) East Indian striped and checked cotton fabric. (Wingate, 249).

Foulard: 1) Light weight lustrous silk fabric from India. (Wingate, 249). 2) Taffeta foulards: silk neck cloth. (Murphy, 169).

Futaines: Fabric made from cotton and hemp. Made in many qualities and fashions. (Savary, 2, 187).

Gaberum: Checked, East Indian calico. (Wingate, 258).

Gadberum: Indian term for fabric used to make bedding. (Wingate, 258).

Garas, Garras, Gurras, Gurrahs: 1) Coarse white cotton fabric from Surat. (Savary, 2, 210). 2) Plain cotton cloth, comparatively coarse. (Irwin, 65). 3) Plain white coarse to medium quality. Domestic and general use, block printed in England. Re-export trade. Bengal. 17th-18th century. (Chaudhuri, 504). 4) Coarse, handmade cotton fabric from India. (Wingate, 259).

Gaudivis = Baffetas: White cotton cloth. (Savary, 2, 217).

Gauffre, Gauffree: Camelots. (Savary, 2, 220).

Gaz, Gaze: 1) Silk cloth, very bright and light. Plain, brocaded, striped. (Savary, 2, 220). 2) Light and transparent cloth of 18th century, made

of cotton and silk. (Weigert, 159).
3) French term for gauze. (Wingate, 261).
Gilham: 1) Silk fabric. (Savary, 3, 846).
2) Silk dress fabric from China. (Wingate, 264).
Gillsaye, Giselle: Sheer French fabric from wool. (Wingate, 266).
Gingham: 1) Originally cloth of mixed cotton and tusser silk. Later imitated in pure cotton, with main distinguishing feature is usual texture of multiple–stranded warps and wefts. (Irwin, 64). 2) Plain white and dyed. Medium quality. Domestic and general use. Re-export trade. South India and Bengal. 17th-18th centuries. (Chaudhuri, 502). 3) Mixed cotton and silk, striped. Medium quality. Fashionwear and re-export trade. Bengal. 17th-18th centuries. (Chaudhuri, 504). 4) Medium or lightweight plain weave, yarn-dyed cotton fabric. Ginghams vary in quality. Madras ginghams made with fine yarn in fancy weaves. (Wingate, 265).
Gingiras: Silk cloth from India. (Savary, 2, 225).
Glissade: Cotton lining fabrics of silk and cotton. (Wingate, 268).
Gode: Striped white cotton fabric from Gode. (Savary, 2, 251).
Godcellet: Term used in India for inexpensive cotton prints with diagonal rows of black flowers in blue grounds – used as petticoats. (Wingate, 275).
Gondozoletti: Cotton fabric from Levant. (Savary, 2, 255).
Goodzi: Coarse East Indian fabric. (Wingate, 270).
Gorgoran, Gourgouras: Obsolete, heavy East Indian silk fabric with stripes in two kinds of weave. (Wingate, 270).
Gris, Grise: Color between white and black. (Savary, 2, 284).
Grisette: Small light fabric mixed of silk, cotton, etc. made in many colors and fashions. (Savary, 2, 286).
Gudar: Coarse, heavy, striped cloth made in India. Color usually red and gray. (Wingate, 278).
Guerley: East India calico. (Wingate, 278).
Guinée, Guinea: 1) White cotton fabric, fine and coarse from Pondichéry. (Savary, 2, 295). 2) Name given in Marseille to cloth sent to Guinea. (Weigert, 159). 3) Cheap, brightly-colored Indian calicos, mostly striped or chequered – slave trade. (Irwin, 65). 4) Plain dyed, checks and striped, coarse quality. West African and colonial trade. Gujarat. 17th century. (Chaudhuri, 501). 5). French term used in 17th & 18th centuries for cotton canvas in gray or dyed dark blue – from India. (Wingate, 279).
Guingans: Cloth of cotton and hemp. Neither fine nor coarse. Blue or white, from Bengal. (Savary, 2, 295).
Guinguet: Very light camelots. (Weigert, 159).
Guipure: Mixed cloth of silk. Sort of dentelle. (Savary, 2, 295).
Gunnies: 1) Strong coarse calico used for sacking. (Irwin, 65). 2) Strong coarse plain weave made from jute. (Wingate, 280).
Guras: Printed cloth from Bengal. (Savary, 2, 296).
Guzee, Guzzee, Guzzy. 1) Ordinary plain white calico. (Irwin, 65). 2) Very poor kind of cotton cloth. (Yule-Burnell, 405). 3) Garrhe: very coarse, plain weave cotton fabric from Bengal. (Wingate, 260).
Hamans, Hamas, Humhums, Hammons, Hamoenes, Hamac: 1) White cotton fabric, very fine and close knit. Best are Bengaloises. (Savary, 2, 310). 2) Plain cotton cloth of varying qualities of thick stout texture for out garments. (Irwin, 66). 3) Obsolete, strong, bleached East Indian cotton fabric. (Wingate,

283).

Hamedis: Mallemolle. (Savary, 2, 311).

Indienne: 1) Cotton dressing robe. (Savary, 2, 420). 2) Cloth made from silk and wool. (Savary, 2, 420). 3) Cotton cloth. (Weigert, 159).

Jamavas, Jamawars, Jamavers: 1) Indian taffetas flowered in gold or silk. (Savary, 2, 379). 2) Piece goods of silk brocade. (Irwin, 66). 3) Obsolete, lightweight, handwoven brocaded silk taffeta from Madras. (Wingate, 315).

Jamadane, Jamdanies, Jamdannes, Jandanee, Jamdanis, Jamdars: 1) Muslin, brocaded in white or colored silk or cotton usually in floral pattern. Sometimes woven like Doreas. (Irwin, 66). 2) Brocaded with white or colored silk, luxury quality. Fashionwear. Bengal. 17th–18th century. (Chandhuri, 504). 3) Group of costly, fine cotton muslins in elaborate woven design. (Wingate, 315).

Jamis: Cotton cloth from Levant. (Savary, 2, 381).

Japergonsi: Fine muslin with gold selvage. (Wingate, 315).

Jour Zephr: Obsolete French term for plain gauze. (Wingate, 319).

Kattequi, Katequis: Blue cotton cloth from Surat. (Savary, 2, 451).

Katey: Plain weave fabric made of tussah silk yarn. (Wingate, 325).

Kathee: Salembaree: Heavy weight cotton tent fabric from Punjab. (Wingate, 521).

Keeses, Kestes, Quesos, Kesis: 1) Thick cotton cloth – elaborate check in blue and white. (Irwin, 67). 2) Striped or solid colored fabric in brilliant colors – from India. Used for trousers. (Wingate, 327).

Kemeas: Taffeta flowered in silk. (Savary, 2, 452).

Kenari: Indian gold and silver lace. (Wingate, 326).

Kenbas: Coarse, heavy, cotton fabric

from Iran. (Wingate, 327).

Kermichi, Kermiss: British term for cotton dress fabric of inferior quality. (Wingate, 327).

Keryabads: Good quality plain calico. (Irwin, 67).

Kichorkay: East Indian Cotton cloth. (Wingate, 330).

Kien-Tcheou: Silk cloth from India. (Savary, 2, 453).

Korathes, Korottes, Korolz, Korattes, Korotes: 1) Coarse cotton fabric from Surat used to make big neckties. Toques de Kambaye. (Savary, 2, 454). 2) Coarse East Indian calico. (Wingate, 336).

Kora: Plain silk cloth on which patterns are tie-dyed. (Murphy, 199).

Lahariya, Lehriya: Tie-dyed design in stripe or zigzags. (Murphy, 198).

Laize, Layze: Cloth made of gold, silver, silk thread. (Savary, 2, 473).

Lakoris, Lawcowries: 1) Plain white cotton fabric. Coarse to medium quality. Domestic and general use. Re-export trade. 17th–18th centuries. Bihar. (Chaudhuri, 504). 2) Cotton fabric made in India. (Wingate, 340).

Lamé: Cloth interwoven with gold and silver thread. (Savary, 2, 478).

Lamparillas (Nompareilles): Small camelots. (Savary, 2, 478).

Lampasses: Cloth printed in India. (Savary, 2, 478).

Lampas, Lampat: Drapery and upholstery fabrics similar to satin damask made of silk, rayon, wool or cotton. Originally a printed silk fabric made in the East Indies. (Wingate, 343).

Lene: Fabric made of leno weave, generally lightweight open weave, fabric of cotton, rayon etc. (Wingate, 349).

Line: Kind of satin from China. (Savary, 2, 546).

Limace, Limances, Limaconne, Limande, Lemanée: Striped cotton cloth. Fine quality. Domestic use from Gujarat in 18th century. (Chaudhuri, 501).

Lodier, Loudrier: Coarse blanket of wool. (Savary, 2, 581).

Lohi: Coarse, heavy, handwoven cashmere dress fabric of wool from Kashmir. (Wingate, 358).

Loita: 1) Plain white cotton fabric. Medium to fine quality. Block printed in England. Fashionwear and re-export. South India. 17th and 18th centuries. (Chaudhuri, 502). 2) Low count Indian cotton fabric of inferior quality. (Wingate, 358).

Longuis: 1) Taffeta. (Savary, 2, 584). 2) Plain-weave cotton or silk fabric, white or dark blue. (Wingate, 363). 3) Loincloth. (Wingate, 363). 4) Rich silk and cotton fabric. (Wingate, 363).

Longcloath, Longcloth: 1) White or blue cotton cloth from Coromandel. (Savary, 2, 382). 2) White shirting or Lancashire calico. Maybe corruption of Lungi or Loonghes. (Yule-Burnell, 518).

Loonghee, Longyi, Lungi, Loonghie, Loongie, Loongyee, Lungee: 1) In French called pagne (Wingate, 363). 2) Plain weave Indian cotton fabric in white or dark blue or small check with silk or gold border. (Wingate, 363). 3) Natural bleached or dyed cotton fabric – used for loincloths. (Wingate, 368). 4) Rich silk and cotton fabric fabric made in India; sometimes interwoven with silk threads and embroidered. (Wingate, 363).

Luquoises: Silk cloth imitated in France. (Savary, 2, 595).

Mallemoles, Malmal, Mollmol, Mulmull: 1) Muslin or white cotton cloth very light and clear from Bengal. (Savary, 2, 618). 2) Plain white muslin. Fine to superfine. Fashionwear and re-export. Bengal. 17th and 18th centuries. (Chaudhuri, 502). 3) Hindi malmal means muslin. Fine muslin often embroidered

with floral motifs. (Irwin, 67). 4) Original term for mull, derived from the Hindi and Persian term, malmal. (Wingate, 403).

Mamondis, Mahmud, Mamoudi, Mamoudie: 1) Hand woven Indian muslin. (Wingate, 372). 2) General term for Indian calicos. (Wingate, 372).

Mamotbani: Muslin or fine and striped cotton fabric. (Savary, 2, 619).

Mandilla, Mundilla, Mundeels, Mundas: 1) Striped fabric of silk and cotton. (Irwin, 67). 2) Handwoven Indian fabric bordered with silk and sometimes with gold and silver threads. (Wingate, 404).

Mauris, Mouris, Moris: 1) Percale. White cotton cloth. (Savary, 2, 695). 2) 18th century French term for percale imported from India. (Wingate, 378).

Melin, Melis, Meslins: 1) Hemp cloth (Savary, 2, 716). 2) French hemp sailcloth. (Wingate, 380).

Mercooles, Merculees: 1) Plain white calico. (Irwin, 68). 2) Plain white, medium quality. North India, 17th century. (Chaudhuri, 501).

Mogador, Mogadore: Plain weave silk ties fabric. (Weigert, 162).

Mogoys, Muga, Moonga, Mooga, Mounga: Raw silk. (Savary, 2, 753).

Mohabut: Colored cotton cloth. (Savary, 2, 753).

Mohere, Mouaire, Moire: Cloth usually of silk. (Savary, 2, 753).

Molleton, Moleton, Molton: Small wool serge. (Savary, 2, 755).

Moncahiard, Mocayer: Very fine cloth of silk and wool. (Savary, 2, 758).

Mongopoes: Cotton fabric. Cambay. (Savary, 2, 759).

Montassies, Mentasses: Cloth with gold thread. (Irwin, 68).

Montichours: Cloth of silk and cotton. (Weigert, 162).

Monties, Motia, Mota: Thick cotton cloth from India. Plain weave, coarse, durable cotton fabric. (Wingate, 400).

Moquette, Mocade, Moucade: Raincoats made of linen, cotton or wool. (Savary, 2, 786).

Morees, Moorees: 1) Cotton cloth of superior quality, used in chintz making. (Irwin, 68). 2) Plain white. Base cloth for chintz. Medium to fine. (Chaudhuri, 502).

Mouchoirs: Handkerchiefs usually of cotton cloth. (Savary, 2, 806).

Moultans: Printed cloth from Surat. (Savary, 2, 821).

Mouris: Cotton cloth. Fine to coarse, white or red. (Savary, 2, 821).

Mousseline: Cotton cloth. (Savary, 2, 822).

Musulipaten: Cotton cloth. (Savary, 2, 836).

Muslin: Fine transparent curtain cloth. (Murphy, 156).

Muttfoons, Matafons: Low grade, checked calico. (Irwin, 68).

Nainsooks, Nansooks, Nyansooks: 1) Plain cotton cloth of superior quality used for neckerchiefs. Could also be muslin or silk fabric. (Irwin, 68). 2) Plain white muslin. Superfine to luxury quality. Fashionwear. Bengal, 18th century. (Chaudhuri, 504). 3) Soft, lightweight plain weave cotton fabric. Produced like longcloth. (Wingate, 407).

Nakas, Nakh, Nac, Nagus, Naskiz, Nassis, Necidj, Nekh: Rich gold brocade, Marco Polo called it silk cloth. (Wingate, 406).

Nankeens: 1). Cotton stuff of brownish yellow tinge. (Yule-Burnell, 616). 2) Obsolete firm textured, durable cotton from China. (Wingate, 407)

Nankin: 1) Silk fabric made in Nankin. (Wingate, 407).

Nankinet: 1) Like nankin. 2) Fine dyed percale. (Wingate, 407).

Negapore, Nagapore: Brightly colored, lightweight, soft silk fabric from India. (Wingate, 406).

Neganepaux, Neganepants, Nagappat-

tinam, Negapaut: Striped medium quality. West African trade. Gujurat. 18th century. (Chandhuri, 502).

Nekanias, Necanias, Nickanees, Nekhumans, Nicannees: 1) Striped blue or white fabric. (Savary, 3, 1082). 2) Cheap striped calico, patterned in the loom. Bought for slave market. (Irwin, 69). 3) Striped. Coarse to medium quality. West African trade. Gujarat. 17th-18th centuries. (Chaudhuri, 501).

Nessu: East African term for nainsook (Wingate, 413).

Nillas, Nillai, Nillaes: 1) Bast cloth mixed with silk from India. (Savary, 2, 864). 2) Striped cloth of mixed tussur silk and cotton, sometimes flowered. Much exported to Europe. (Irwin, 68). 3) Mixed cotton and silk, striped. Medium to superior quality. Clothing and re-export trade. Bengal. 17th-18th centuries. (Chaudhuri, 504). 4) Nilla: Fabric made of mixture of silk and bast fiber in East India. (Wingate, 415).

Nilsaria: Sturdy East Indian calico with stripes and checks composed of blue cloth. (Wingate, 415).

Nossaris: White cotton cloth from India. (Baffetas). (Savary, 2, 877).

Noyalles: Hemp cloth. (Savary, 2, 880).

Nunno: White cloth from China. (Savary, 2, 884).

Organdie, Organdy, Organdis: 1) Kind of mousseline or cotton cloth. (Betille). (Savary, 2, 917). 2) Fine, sheer, very lightweight cotton fabric made of fine count, combed singles in open, plain weave, with characteristic stiff, crisp, clear finish. (Wingate, 426). 3) Organdis: silk cloth. (Savary, 2, 917).

Padou, Padoue: Ruban of silk. (Weigert, 162).

Palempore, Pallampores, Palampoor: Same as salempore. (Yule-Burnell, 662).

Pagnes, Paignes: Kind of covering

colored blue and used by Blacks in Guinea. (Savary, 2, 949).

Panne, Pane: Silk cloth. (Savary, 2, 959).

Pansay, Pankas, Pautkeys, Pansy, Paukes: 1) Silk cloth from China. (Savary, 2, 960). 2) Plain white and dyed cotton fabric. Coarse quality. West African trade. 17th century. (Chaudhuri, 501). 3) Handwoven, plain weave, coarse East Indian calico. (Wingate, 440).

Passements: Silk fabric. (Savary, 3, 415).

Patissoie, Patiffoye, Patisoie: Chinese silk brocade imported in large quantities by France during the reign of Louis XVI. Used for dresses. (Wingate, 441).

Patola: 1) Silk cloth. (Irwin, 69). 2) Plain weave, richly decorated silk fabric with a tie dyed or hand-brocaded border from India. (Wingate, 441).

Pekin: Warp-striped fabric made of silk, rayon, cotton or mixed. (Wingate, 444).

Pelache, Peluche, Pluche: 1) Coarse velvety cotton fabric. (Savary, 2, 1036). 2) Velvety wool or silk fabric. (Weigert, 163).

Percale, Percallas, Percallaes, Paricals, Parcalles: 1) Percalles-Mauris. White cotton fabric, fine to coarse from Pondichéry. (Savary, 2, 1044). 2) High grade plain white cloth, fine, regular and durable used to make chintz, usually bought red. (Irwin, 69). 3) Plain white, base cloth for chintz making. Coarse to fine quality. Domestic and general use, re-export. South India, 17th century. (Chaudhuri, 503). 4) Plain weave, lightweight, piece dyed or printed cotton fabric. Used for dresses. (Wingate, 446).

Pinasses, Pinaffes, Pinacol, Pinecone, Peniascoes: 1) Cloth from India. Made from bark of trees. (Savary, 2, 1094). 2) Brightly colored, prob-ably mixed cotton-and-silk, usually striped. (Irwin, 69). 3) Mixed cotton and silk striped. Medium quality, clothing and re-export. Bengal, 17th-18th centuries. (Chaudhuri, 506). 4) Indian fabric of brown or yellow color, made from bast fibers. Imported by France in 17th -18th centuries. (Wingate, 458).

Platille: 1) Linen cloth, very white. (Savary, 2, 1110).

Populees: Cheap chequered calico. (Irwin, 69).

Poulangis, Poulangy: Wool fabric. (Savary, 2, 1203).

Ras: Wool fabric. (Savary, 2, 1271).

Rasta, Raftas: French term for trousers.

Ratine: Wool cloth. (Savary, 2, 1272).

Rosconnes: Linen cloth. (Savary, 2, 1415).

Rumal: Handkerchief or head cover. (Murphy, 200).

Ruzzai: Term used in India for quilting. (Wingate, 517).

Saboons: Mixed cotton and silk cloth. (Irwin, 70).

Sacerguntes, Sauerguntes, Saurunch-eras, Sauergentes, Sacerguntes: 1) Cotton cloth, warp and weft tie dyed before weaving, from south India. (Irwin, 70).

Sahans, Sahuns: Superior, strong calico. (Irwin, 70).

Salalas, Sallale: Dyed cotton cloth. (Wingate, 521).

Salang: Very durable coarse wool fabric from the Himalayas. (Wingate, 521).

Salara: Handwoven, thin plaid weave cotton fabric from India. (Wingate, 521).

Salempores, Salempouris, Salam-pouris, Sallampores: 1) Blue and white cloth from Coromandel. (Savary 2, 1450). 2) Staple cotton-cloth from South India. Varied widely in quality and price. Exported to Europe in large quantities. (Irwin, 70). 3) Kind of chintz.

(Yule-Burnell, 784). 4) Plain white and blue dyed. Medium quality. Clothing, re-export colonial trade. South India. 17th-18th centuries. (Chaudhuri, 503).

Sallowes, Sallo: 1) Good quality, fine muslin. (Irwin, 70). 2) Plain white cotton fabric. Domestic use and re-export, 17th century. Dacca. (Chaudhuri, 501). 3) Sallo: Plain weave or twill cotton fabric dyed red from India. (Wingate, 521).

Samis, Samilis: Very rich cloth, woven in gold. (Savary, 2, 1467).

Sanas, Sannoes: 1) White or blue cotton cloth. Neither fine nor coarse. Bengal. (Savary, 2, 1457). 2) Plain cotton cloth of ordinary quality, lots exported. (Irwin, 70). 3) Lightweight, bleached or blue colored cotton fabric exported to France in 17th and 18th centuries. Garments. (Wingate, 523).

Sandaline: Small cloth from Venice. (Savary, 2, 1458).

Sangles: Coarse hemp cloth. (Savary, 2, 1461).

Santal: Same as taffeta. (Savary, 2, 1463).

Sarassa, Sarasses: 1) May be superior silk and cotton mixture. (Irwin, 70). 2) Variety of raw cotton from India. (Wingate, 525).

Sarge: Same as serge.

Satin: 1) Silk cloth, lustrous, plain, brocaded, flowered, striped. From China and India. (Savary, 2, 1471). 2) Silk cloth. (Weigert, 165). 3) Smooth, lustrous silk fabric with thick, close texture. (Wingate, 625).

Sauvaguzee, Saulganshi, Sauvagasi, Savesjes, Sauvezi: 1) White cotton cloth from India. Also called Belazees, Sauvaguzees, Doutis from India. (Savary, 2, 1482). 2) Type of calico. Gray or bleached cotton cloth from India. (Wingate, 522).

Saya: Silk cloth from China. (Savary, 2, 1483).

Sayette: Woolen or silk cloth. (Savary, 2, 1483).

Seerbands: 1) Fine muslin. (Irwin, 71). 2) Plain white muslin. Medium to fine quality, clothing and re-export. Bengal. 17th-18th centuries. (Chaudhuri, 505). 3) Fine muslin with texture between nainsook and mull. (Wingate, 520).

Seerhaudconnaes, Seerhandconal: 1) Cotton cloth of ordinary quality. (Irwin, 71). 2) Term for various Indian cotton muslin. (Wingate, 540).

Seersuckers, Sersukers: 1) Indian cloth of silk and cotton, striped in silk, made like muslin. (Savary, 2, 1544). 2) Striped fabric of mixed silk and cotton. (Irwin, 71). 3) Mixed cotton and silk, striped. Medium to superior quality. Clothing and re-export. Bengal. 18th century. (Chaudhuri, 505). 4) Sirsake, Sirfake, Sirsaces: Term used in Batavia for seersucker. (Wingate, 562).

Serbatis, Serbattes, Serribaffs, Seerbettees: 1) Good quality, fine muslin, sometimes dyed red or blue. (Irwin, 71). 2) Plain white muslin. Fine to superfine quality. Fashionwear and re-export. Bengal. 18th century. (Chaudhuri, 505). 3) Fine muslin with gold selvage, made in India. (Wingate, 542).

Serge, Seryas, Serijas, Seares: 1) Cheap strong calico, either plain or striped. Used in making napkins, flags and sailcloth. (Irwin, 71). 2) Cotton twill has a prominent twill, used for linings. (Wingate, 543). 3) Wool cloth. (Wingate, 165).

Serge de Soye: Ras from St. Maur. (Savary, 2, 1514).

Serpilliere: Cheap, coarse cloth. (Weigert, 165).

Shauf: Baffetas. (Savary, 2, 1544).

Siskrissoy, Sistresay: Fabric made with two warps, one of silk and the other of cotton and a spun silk filling in damask patterns with colored stripes, made in India. (Wingate,

563).

Socrote, Socretons, Socquette, Sorcrote: East Indian calico. (Wingate, 572).

Soucha: 1) Silk crepon from China in blue stripes. (Savary, 2, 1565). 2) Chinese silk crepon with blue stripes. (Wingate, 572).

Souci, Sousee, Soosey, Sousaes, Sousies, Soutis: 1) Silk muslin striped in different colors. From India. Sometimes called mousseline even though not made of cotton. (Savary, 2, 1566). 2) Striped or chequered fabric of silk or mixed cotton-and-silk. Big European demand. (Irwin, 71). 3) Soosie is kind of silk, striped cloth – also mixed with cotton. (Yule-Burnell, 854). 4) Sooseys: mixed cotton and silk, striped fine quality. Fashionwear and re-export. Bengal. 18th century. (Chaudhuri, 505). 5) Soosjes: Light weight, Indian cotton fabric made in colored and white stripes. Uses are for hand covering. (Wingate, 569).

Steinkirkes: Cotton handkerchiefs formerly made in India. (Wingate, 586).

Stinquerkes: Cotton handkerchiefs. (Wingate, 586).

Tabis: Coarse taffeta. (Savary, 2, 1640).

Taffeta: Silk cloth, very fine, strong, light, lustrous from India. Plain, striped in gold or silver, checked, flowered. Also called Calquiere, Arains, Armoisios. (Savary, 2, 1646). 2) Silk cloth, very light and fine. (Weigert, 166). 3) Silk piece goods. (Irwin, 71). 4) Silk piece goods. Fine quality. Fashionwear and re-export. Bengal. 17th-18th centuries. (Chaudhuri, 505). 5) Fabrics in plain weave. Term derived from Persian meaning taftah which means very fine, plain weave silk fabric. (Wingate, 599). 6) Taffeta foulards: silk neck-cloth. (Murphy, 169).

Tanjeb, Tangib, Tanzeb, Taniab, Tanjeere, Tungeb: 1) Muslin or white cotton cloth. Plain or brocaded. (Savary, 2, 1664). 2) Plain cotton cloth, usually superior quality, sometimes embroidered with silk in chainstitch. Petticoats, dress. (Irwin, 72). 3) Plain white muslin. Fine quality. Fashionwear and re-export. Bengal, 17th - 18th centuries. (Chaudhuri, 505). 4) Lightweight, plain weave, cotton fabric, embroidered or printed. (Wingate, 603).

Tapchile, Tappe, Tapichindaes: Plain weave cotton fabric. (Irwin, 72).

Tapsel: 1) Coarse striped cotton cloth usually blue. Bengal. (Savary, 2, 1675). 2) Striped, medium quality. West African trade. Gujarat. 17th-18th centuries. (Chaudhuri, 502).

Taquis: Cotton cloth from Levant. (Savary, 2, 1675).

Tarare: Kind of cloth taken from place name. (Savary, 2, 1676).

Tarnetannes, Tarlatanne, Tarlatan: Ternantane-Chevonis is muslin or white cotton cloth, very clear. Pondichéry. (Savary, 2, 1681).

Tayelles, Tayottes: Kind of belt made of cotton or wool. (Savary, 2, 1687).

Tepays, Tepis, Thepays, Thepis, Thebois: 1) Cloth of silk and cotton from India. (Savary, 2, 1714). 2) Mixed cotton and silk. Fine quality. Clothing and re-export. Bengal. 18th century. (Chaudhuri, 505). 3) Tapis is plain weave, inexpensive fabric made of cotton mixed with a small amount of silk. (Wingate, 610). 4) Tepis is coarse, East Indian fabric made of cotton and silk. (Wingate, 611).

Terindanne, Terrindams, Turundams: 1) Plain muslin, usually of superior quality – Dacca. (Irwin, 72). 2) Plain white muslin. Fine to superfine quality. Fashionwear and re-export. Bengal. 17th-18th centuries. (Chaudhuri, 505). 3) Fine. East Indian cotton muslin. (Wing-

228

ate, 611).

Tiretame: Cloth of cotton and wool. (Weigert, 167).

Tondu: Drapery, serge. (Weigert, 167).

Toque: 1) Muslin or white cotton cloth from Bengal. (Savary, 2, 1786). 2) East Indian cotton muslin. (Wingate, 624).

Torade: Cotton muslin from India. (Wingate, 624).

Touanse: 1) Silk cloth from China. Plain, flowered, figured. (Savary, 2, 1791). 2) Strong satin fabric made in solid colors in China for export to France in 18th century. (Wingate, 625)

Toukris, Tuckeryes, Tuckrees: 1) Striped silk piece goods from Bihar. (Irwin, 72) 2) East Indian cotton fabric (Tuckeryes). (Wingate, 632)

Treillis: 1) Cloth from hemp. Very coarse and strong. (Savary, 2, 1813). 2) Kinds of cloth from hemp. Coarse and strong. (Weigert, 167). 3) Strong, coarse French canvas made of unbleached hemp. Work pants. (Wingate, 628). 4) French term for ground in handmade lace. (Wingate, 628).

Tuf: Coarse cloth from hemp. (Savary, 2, 1829).

Tukri: Indian fabric. (Wingate, 633).

Tune: Term used in Canton for coarse silk fabric. (Wingate, 633).

Vane: Padded French quilt made of piqué or calico. (Wingate, 647).

Velour: 1) Rich cloth made entirely of silk. (Savary, 2, 1848). 2) French word meaning velvet. (Wingate, 652).

Select Bibliography

Ames, Glen Joseph. "Colbert and the Elusive Quest for Mercantile Power in the Indian Ocean, 1664 - 1674." *Proceedings of the Annual Meeting of the French Colonial History Society* 16 (1972): 126-141.

Archives de l'Arrondissement Maritime de Lorient. *Inventaire des Archives de la Compagnie des Indes*. Paris: Imprimerie de la Marine, 1978.

Barbier, J. "La Compagnie Française des Indes." *Revue Historique de l'Inde Française* 3 (1919): 5-96.

Barrett, Ward. "World Bullion Flows, 1450-1800." In *The Rise of Merchant Empires*, edited by James D. Tracy, 224-254. Cambridge: Cambridge University Press, 1990.

Beauchesne, Geneviève. "Les Matelots de la Compagnie des Indes." *Cahiers de la Compagnie des Indes* 3 (1998): 55-70.

Begue, Daniele. *L'Organization Juridique de la Compagnie des Indes*. Paris: Domat-Montchrestien, 1936.

Bembatoum, François. *Glossaire Anglais-Français de la Définition des Textiles*. Montreal: Université de Montreal, 1975.

Benoist, P. *La Compagnie française des Indes Orientales de 1642*. Paris: Rousseau, 1933.

Bérinstain, Valérie. *Indiennes et Palampores à l'Ile Bourbon au 18 Siècle*. Saint Louis: MFMC, 1994.

Bérinstain, Valérie. "Les Toiles de l'Inde et la Compagnie des Indes, XVII – XVIII Siècles." *Cahiers de la Compagnie des Indes* 2 (1997): 25-32.

Bertin, Gilles. "Les Aspects Comptables et Financiers du Commerce Colonial de la Compagnie des Indies entre 1719 et 1730." *Revue d'Histoire Economique et Sociale* 40 (1962): 449-483.

Beurdeley, Michel. *Porcelaine de la Compagnie des Indes*. 4th ed. Fribourg: Office du Livre, 1982.

Blancard, Pierre. *Manuel du Commerce des Indes Orientales et de la Chine*. Paris: Bernard, 1806.

Blussée, P.H. and Gaestra, F. ed. *Companies and Trade: Essays on Overseas Trading Companies during the Ancient Regime*. Leiden: Leiden University Press, 1981.

Bonnassieux, Pierre. *Les Grandes Compagnies de Commerce*. Paris: E. Plon, Nourrit et Cie, 1892.

Boudriot, Jean. *Compagnie des Indes, 1720 - 1770*. Paris: Boudriot, 1983.

Boudriot, Jean. "Les Vaisseaux de la Compagnie des Indes, 1720 - 1770." *Cahiers de la Compagnie des Indes*. 3 (1998): 15-20.

Boxer, C.R. "The Third Dutch War in the East (1672 - 1674)." *Mariner's Mirror* 16 (1930): 344-386.

Brennig, Joseph. "The Textile Trade of Seventeenth Century Northern Coromandel; a study of a Pre-Modern Asian Export Industry." Ph.D. diss., University of Wisconsin, 1975.

Carfeuil, Gaspar. *Etat General de Toutes les Marchandises dont on fait Commerce à Marseille*. Marseille, 1688.

Castonnet des Fosses, Henri. *L'Inde Française avant Dupleix*. Paris: Challamel Ainé, 1887.

Castonnet des Fosses, Henri. "La Chute de Dupleix, ses Causes et ses Conséquences." *Bulletin de la Société de Géographie de Tours* (1888).

Chaudhuri, K.N. *The Trading World of Asia and the English East India Company, 1660 -1760*. Cambridge: Cambridge University Press, 1978.

Chaudhury, Sushil. "The Imperatives of the Empire: Private Trade, Sub-Imperialism and the British Attack on Chandernagore, March 1757." *Studies in History* 8 (1992): 1-12.

Chaudhury, Sushil and Morineau, Michel, ed. *Merchants, Companies and Trade*. Cambridge: Cambridge University Press, 1999.

Charpentier, François. *Relation de l'Etablissement de la Compagnie Française pour le Commerce des Indes Orientales.* Paris: Sebastien Cramoisy et Sebastien Marbre-Cramoisy, 1664.

C.I.E.T.A. *Vocabulary of Technical Terms.* Lyon: Centre Internationale d'Etude des Textiles Anciens, 1964.

Clark, G.M. *The Dutch Alliance and the War against French Trade.* Manchester: Manchester University Press, 1923.

Cole, C.W. *Colbert and a Century of Mercantilism.* 2 vols. New York: Columbia University Press, 1939.

Cole, C.W. *French Mercantilism, 1683 - 1700.* New York: Columbia University Press, 1943.

Conan, J. *La Dernière Compagnie Française des Indes (1785 - 1875). Avec la Liste des Principaux Actionnaires de cette Compagnie.* Paris: Librairie des Sciences Politiques et Sociales, 1942.

Cotton, Evan and Fawcett, Charles. *East Indiamen.* London: The Batchworth Press, 1949.

Coural, Jean. *Paris, Mobilier National Soieries Empire.* Paris: Editions de la Reunion de Musées Nationaux, 1980.

Cousseau, Henry-Claude. *La Route des Indes.* Somogy: Editions d'Art, 1999.

Dalgliesh, W.H. *The Company of the Indies in the Days of Dupleix.* Easton: Chemical Publishing Co., 1933.

Delumeau, J. "Le Commerce Extérieur de la France au XVII Siècle." *XVIII Siècle* 70-71 (1966): 81-105.

Dermigny, Louis. *Cargaisons Indiennes. Solier et Cie., 1781 - 1793.* 2 vols. Paris: S.E.V.P.E.N, 1959-1960.

Dermigny, Louis. *La Chine et l'Occident: Le Commerce à Canton au XVIII Siècle, 1719 - 1833.* 3 vols. Paris: S.E.V.P.E.N., 1964.

Desroches, Jean-Paul. *Compagnies des Indes.* Paris: C.P.I.P., 1975.

Dodwell, Henry. *Clive and Dupleix: the Beginning of the Empire.* New Delhi: Asian Educational Services, 1989.

Doursther, Horace. *Dictionnaire Universel des Poids et Mesures, Anciens et Modernes.* Amsterdam: Meridan Publishing Co., 1965.

Dresner, Stephen. *Units of Measurement.* New York: Hastings House, 1971.

Dupleix, Joseph-François. *Mémoire pour le Sieur Dupleix contre la Compagnie des Indes*. Paris: Imprimerie de P.Al. Leprieur, 1759.

Dupont de Nemours, Pierre. *Du Commerce et de la Compagnie des Indes*. Paris: 1769.

Estienne, René. *Les Armements au Long Cours de la Deuxième Compagnie des Indes (1717 - 1773)*. Lorient: Service Historique de la Marine, 1996.

Estienne, René. "Tableau des Armements de la Compagnie des Indes de 1717 à 1773." *Cahiers de la Compagnie des Indes*. 2 (1997): 33-34.

Fabre des Essarts, L.E.J. *Dupleix et l'Inde Française*. Paris: Charavay Frères, 1883.

Fresne de Francheville, Joseph. *Histoire de la Compagnie des Indes*. Paris: 1746.

Froidevaux, Henri. "Le Commerce Français à Madagascar au XVII Siècle." *Vierteljahrschrift fur Social-und Wirtschaftsgeschichte* 3 (1905): 41-111.

Froidevaux, Henri. "Les Derniers Projets du Duc de Meilleraye sur Madagascar (1663)." *Revue de l'Histoire des Colonies Françaises* 3 (1915): 401-430.

Froidevaux, Henri. "Les Débuts de Carrière de François Martin (1665 - 1674)." *Revue de l'Histoire des Colonies Françaises* 19 (1931): 1-34.

Froidevaux, Henri. "François Martin et Pondichéry de 1674 - 1686." *Revue de l'Histoire des Colonies Françaises* 20 (1932): 193-216.

Furber, Holden. *John Company at Work; a Study of European Expansion in India in the Late Eighteenth Century*. Harvard Historical Studies, vol. 55. New York: Octagon Books, 1948.

Gerbier, Pierre Jean Baptiste. *Mémoire pour le Marquis de Bussy*. Paris: Imprimerie de Louis Cellot, 1767.

Girard, Albert. "La Réorganization de la Compagnie des Indes, 1719 - 1723." *Revue d'Histoire Moderne et Contemporaine* 11 (1908): 5-34, 176-197.

Glamann, K. *Dutch Asiatic Trade, 1620 - 1740*. Copenhagen and the Hague: Danish Science Press, 1958.

Grayson, Martin. *Encyclopedia of Textiles, Fibers and Non-Woven Fabrics*. New York: Wiley, 1984.

Grolous, Henri. *La Compagnie Française des Indes Orientales de 1664*. Paris: Librairie Nouvelle de Droit et de Jurisprudence, 1911.

Gupta, Ashin Des. *Malabar in Asian Trade, 1740 - 1800*. Cambridge: University Press, 1967.

Guy, John. *Woven Cargoes: Indian Textiles in the East*. New York: Thames and Hudson, 1998.

Hatalker, V.G. *Relations between the French and the Marathas, 1668 - 1815*. Bombay: Bombay University Press, 1958.

Haudrère, Philippe. *La Compagnie Française des Indes au XVIII Siècle (1719 - 1795)*. 4 vols. Paris: Librairie de l'Inde, 1989.

Haudrère, Philippe. "Jalons pour une Histoire des Compagnies des Indes." *Revue Française d'Histoire d'Outre-mer* 77 (1991): 9-27.

Haudrère, Philippe. "La Route des Indes au XVIII Siècle." *Cahiers de le Compagnie des Indes* 3 (1998): 7-14.

Herpin, Eugène. *Mahé de la Bourdonnais et la Compagnie des Indes*. Saint Brieuc: R. Prud' Homme, 1905.

Higman, B.W. "The Sugar Revolution." *The Economic History Review* 53 (2000): 213-236.

Hirsch, Pierre. *Textile Glossary: English-French*. Paris: Editions Olifant, 1989.

Houben, Henri. *Finances et Politique sous la Terreur. La Liquidation de la Compagnie des Indes (1793 - 1794) Le Faux Décret. L'Instruction. Le Procès*. Paris: Felix Alcan, 1932.

Irwin, John. *A Select Bibliography of Indian Textiles*. Ahmedabad: Calico Museum of Textiles, 1975.

Irwin, John and Brett, Katharine B. *Origins of Chintz*. London: Her Majesty's Stationary Office, 1970.

Irwin, John and Schwartz, P.R. *Studies in Indo-European Textile History*. Ahmedabad: Calico Museum of Textiles, 1966.

Jacq-Hergoualch, Michel. "La France et le Siam de 1685 à 1688. Histoire d'un Echec." *Revue Française d'Histoire d'Outre-mer* 317 (1997): 71-92.

Jewel, Paul. *Dictionary of Textiles*. New Delhi: Anmal Publishers, 1998.

Jouveau-Debreuil, G. "Le Commerce des Cotons à Pondichéry aux XVII et XVIII Siècles." *Le Seigneur*, 1938.

Kaeppelin, P. *La Compagnie des Indes Orientales et François Martin*. Paris: A. Challamal, 1908. Reprint. Burt Franklin Research and Source Works Series. no. 157. New York: Burt Franklin, 1967.

Lally, Thomas-Arthur, comte de. *Mémoire contre le Procureur-Général.* Paris: G. Desprez, 1766.

Lande, Lawrence M. *John Law: Banque Royale and Compagnie des Indes.* Montreal, 1980.

Law, John. *Money and Trade considered with a Proposal for Supplying the Nation with Money.* London: W. Lewis, 1720.

Le Bouedec, Gérard. "Les Approvisionnements de la Compagnie des Indes (1737 - 1770): L'Horizon Geographique Lorientais." *Histoire, Economie et Société* 3 (1982): 377-412.

Le Bouedec, Gérard. "La Rade de Lorient." *Historiens et Géographes* 78 (1988): 191-204.

Le Bouedec, Gérard. *Le Port et l'Arsenal de Lorient.* Paris: Librarie de l'Inde, 1994.

Lepotier, Adolphe. *Lorient: Porte des Indes.* Paris: France-Empire, 1970.

Leroy, Charles. À *la Compagnie Royale des Indes Orientales au Havre de 1664 à 1670.* Rouen: A. Lestringant, 1931.

"Liste des Souscripteurs a la Compagnie des Indes Orientales (1664-1665)." *Revue de l'Histoire des Colonies Françaises* 13 (1927): 431-434.

Luthy, Herbert. "Necker et la Compagnie des Indes." *Annales: ESC(Économie, Sociétés, Civilisations)* 15 (1960): 852-81.

MacGregor, John. *Commercial Statistics.* 5 vols. London: Charles Nott, 1843-1850.

Mahé de la Bourdonnais, Bertrand-François, comte. *Mémoires Historiques.* Paris: Pelleler et Chatet, 1827.

Malleson, George Bruce. *Final French Struggles in India and on the Indian Seas.* London: W.H. Allen, 1884.

Malleson, George Bruce. *Dupleix.* Oxford: Clarendon Press, 1890.

Malleson, George Bruce. *History of the French in India.* Edinburgh: Grant, 1909.

Manning, Catherine. *Fortunes a Faire: the French in Asian Trade, 1719 – 45.* Aldershot: Ashgate Publishing, 1996.

Martin, Gaston. "Nantes et la Compagnie des Indes (1664-1769)." *Revue d'Histoire Économique et Sociale* 14 (1926): 401-446; 15 (1927): 25-65 and 231-253.

Martineau, Alfred. "Mémoire de Dupleix des Gardes sur les Etablissements de la Compagnie des Indes (en 1727) et sur son Commerce dans les Indes Orientales." *Revue Historique de l'Inde Française* 1 (1916): 81-122.

Martineau, Alfred. "Le Commerce d'Europe et les Armaments pour l'Inde de 1741 à 1749." *Revue Historique de l'Inde Française* 5 (1921-22): 71-122.

Martineau, Alfred. *Dupleix et l'Inde Française*. 5 vols. Paris: Champion, 1920-1929.

Mathiez, Albert. *Un procès de corruption sous la Terreur: L'affaire de la Compagnie des Indes*. Paris: Libraire Felix Alcan, 1920.

Mollat, Michael. *Sociétés et Compagnies de Commerce en Orient et dans l'Océan Indien*. Paris: S.E.V.P.N. 1970.

Montagne, Charles. *Histoire de la Compagnie des Indes*. Paris: E. Bouillon, 1899.

Morellet, Abbé. *Mémoire sur la Situation Actuelle de la Compagnie des Indes*. Paris, 1769.

Moreland, W.G. "Indian Exports of Cotton Goods in the 17th Century." *Indian Journal of Economics* 5 (1925): 225-245.

Morineau, Michel. *Les Grandes Compagnies des Indes Orientales (XVI - XIX Siècles)*. Paris: Presses Universitaires de France, 1994.

Mukherjee, Rila. "The French East India Company's Trade in East Bengal from 1750 to 1753." *Indian Historical Review* 17 (1990-1991): 122-135.

Murphy, Antoin E. *John Law: Economic Theorist and Policy-Maker*. Oxford: Clarendon Press, 1997.

Necker, Jacques. *Réponse au Mémoire de M. l'abbé Morellet sur la Compagnie des Indes*. Paris, 1769.

Nussbaum, F.L. "The Formation of the New East India Company of Calonne." *American Historical Review* 38 (1933): 475-497.

Parish, Richard J.A. "Contemporary Account of Embassy to Siam in 1685." *Revue Française de l'Histoire d'Outre-mer* 64 (1977): 293-307.

Parkinson, C. Northcote, ed. *The Trade Winds*. London: George Allen and Unwin, Ltd., 1948.

Pfister, R. *Les Toiles Imprimées de Fostat et l'Hindoustan*. Paris: Editions d'Art et d'Histoire, 1938.

Picard, Robert. *Les Compagnies des Indes: Route de la Porcelaine.* Grenoble: Arthaud, 1966.

Pigeonneau, Henri. *Histoire de Commerce de la France.* 2 vols. Paris: Leopold Cerf, 1885 and 1897.

Pommepy, René. *Les Compagnies Privilegiées de Commerce de 1715 à 1770.* Bordeaux: Imprimerie de l'Université, 1922.

Priestly, Herbert I. *France Overseas through the Old Regime; a Study in European Expansion.* London: D. Appleton-Century Co., 1939.

Rapson, E.J. *The Struggle between France and England.* London: Trubner & Co., 1887.

Ray, A. "The Crisis of the French East India Company at the End of the 17th Century." *Proceedings of the Indian History Congress* 54 (1994): 361.

Ray, I. "The French Company and the Merchants of Bengal, 1680 - 1730." *Indian Economic and Social History Review* 8 (1971): 41-55.

Ray, I. "Dupleix Private Trade in Chandernagore." *Indian Historical Review* 1 (1974): 279-94.

Raynal, G.T. *Mémoire Relatif de Commerce, 1721 - 1771.* Bibliothèque Nationale, Paris. Fr. 6431.

Rennefort, Souche de. *Histoire des Indes Orientales.* Leide: F. Harring, 1900.

Rogal, S.J. "John Wesley Takes Tea." *Methodist History* 32 (1994): 222-228.

Roncière, Charles de la. "Les Précurseurs de la Compagnie des Indes Orientales-La Politique Coloniale de Malouins." *Revue de l'Histoire des Colonies Françaises* 1 (1913): 39-72.

Roques, Georges. *La Manière de Négocier aux Indes, 1676 - 1691.* Edited by Valérie Bérinstain. Paris: Maisonneuve and Larose, 1996.

Roy, Charu Chandra. "Le Commerce Particulier des Française au Bengale." *Revue Historique de l'Inde Française* 3 (1919): 350-387.

Saint-Méry, Moreau de. *Mémoires sur Compagnie des Indes, 1746.* Paris. Archives Nationales, F3/46/1-61.

Samboo, Gopaljee. *Les Comptoirs Français dans l'Inde Nouvelle de la Compagnie des Indes à nos jours.* Paris: Fasquelle, 1950.

Savary des Brulons, Jacques. *Dictionnaire Universel de Commerce.* 3 vols. Paris: Jacques Estienne, 1723.

Sen, Siba Pada. *The French in India, 1763 - 1816.* Calcutta: University of Calcutta Press, 1958.

Sinha, A. "Anglo-French Collaboration in Europe and the Floating of the Nouvelle Compagnie des Indes in 1785." *Proceedings of the Indian History Congress* 54 (1994): 714-721.

Sottas, Jules. *Histoire de la Compagnie Royale des Indes Orientales (1664 - 1719).* Paris: Plon-Nourrit, 1905. Reprint. Rennes: LaDecouvrance, 1994.

Steensgaard, Niels. *The Asian Trade Revolution of the Seventeenth Century.* Chicago: The University of Chicago Press, 1974.

Symson, William. *A New Voyage to the East Indies.* London: J. Wilford, 1732.

Tapie, Victor L. *France in the Age of Louis XIII and Richelieu.* Translated by D. McN. Lockie. New York: Praeger Publishers, 1975.

Tarrade, Jean. *Le Commerce Colonial de la France à la Fin de l'Ancien Regime: L'Évolution du Regime de l'Exclusif de 1763 à 1789.* 2 vols. Paris: Presses Universitaires de France, 1972.

Taylor, George V. "Types of Capitalism in Eighteenth Century France." *English Historical Review* 74 (1964): 478-94.

Treguilly, Philippe le and Moraze, Monique. *L'Inde et la France. Deux Siècles d'Histoire Commune, XVII - XVIII Siècles.* Paris: CNRS Editions, 1995.

Tuloup, François. *Bertrand-François Mahé de la Bourdonnais et la Compagnie des Indes.* Blainville-sur-Mer: L'Amitié par le livre, 1967.

Vigie, Marc. *Dupleix.* Paris: Fayard, 1993.

Vignols, Léon and Sée, Henri. "Les Ventes de la Compagnie des Indes à Nantes (1723 -1734)." *Revue de l'Histoire des Colonies Françaises* 13 (1925): 489-500.

Villers, Lydie. "Voyager aux Indes à la Fin du XVIIeme Siècle." *Histoire, Economie et Société* 6 (1987): 485-494.

Vincenti, Renate. *Elsevier's Textile Dictionary.* Amsterdam: Elsevier, 1993.

Wake, C.H.H. "The Changing Pattern of Europe's Pepper and Spice Trade, ca 1400 -1700." *The Journal of European Economic History* 8 (1979): 361-403.

Weber, Henry. *La Compagnie Française des Indes (1607 - 1875).* Paris: Rousseau, 1904.

Weigert, Roger-Armand, *Textiles en Europe sous Louis XV.* Fribourg: Office du Livre, 1964.

Wingate, B.J. *Fairchild's Dictionary of Textiles*. 6th ed. New York: Fairchild Publications, 1979.

Yule, Henry and Burnell, A.C. *Hobson-Jobson: The Anglo-Indian Dictionary*. 1902. Reprint. Ware: Wordsworth Editions Ltd., 1996.

Zupko, Ronald Edward. *French Weights and Measures before the Revolution. A Dictionary of Provincial and Local Units*. Bloomington: Indiana University Press, 1978.

N.B.
Numerous boxes of manuscripts and papers were consulted at archives throughout France and in London. When appropriate, full references are made to these in the text.

Index

Fontenay, marquis de, 45
Forde, colonel, 87
Foucquembourg, Jean de, 8
Frotet de la Bardelière, Nicolas, 4, 5
Godefroy, Antoine, 5
Godeheu, Charles-Robert, 81, 82
Gonneville, Paulmier de, 4
Goupil, 80
Gournay, Jean-Claude Vincent seigneur de, 92
Grout de Clos-Neuf, François, 4
Haye, Jacob Blanquet de la, 26, 29, 30
Henriquès, Georges, 5
Holderness, Robert Darcy, earl of, 81
Jourdan, sieur, 44, 46
La Caza, 29
La Choue, Briand, 5
La Forest des Royers, 9
Lally-Tollendal, Thomas Arthur, comte de, 87, 88
Laval, François Pyrard de, 4, 5
Law, Jean, 79
Law, John, 49, 50, 51, 52, 53, 55
Lawrence, Stringer, 78, 79, 81
Le Pelletier, 35
LeFer, 5
Leyrit, Duval de, 82, 87
Maissin, 81
Mahé de la Bourdonnais, Bertrand Francis, 74, 75, 76
Mainville, 81
Martin, François, 30, 31
Martin de la Chapelle, sieur, 46
Martin de la Parisère, Armel, 5
Martin de Vitré, François, 4, 5
Mazarin, cardinal Jules, 9, 11
Mazarin, duc de, 12, 28
Meilleraye, Charles de la Porte, duc de la, 9
Mir Jafer, 85, 86, 87
Mirepoix, Charles Pierre Gaston François de Levis, duc de, 81

Mondevergue, François-Lopis, marquis de, 21, 24, 25, 26
Moreau de Séchelles, 92
Morellet, André abbé, 92
Morse, governor, 75
Moutaubon, de, 24
Muhammed Ali, 78, 79, 82
Muisson, Jacques, 5
Muzaffer Jang, 78, 79, 80
Nasir Jang, 78
Necker, Jacques, 92
Nizam of Hyderabad, 74, 78
Orléans, Philippe, duc d', 49, 56
Pallières, baron de, 45
Paradise, captain Louis, 77
Parisière, Armel Martin de la, 5
Parmentier, Jean, 4
Parmentier, Raoul, 4
Partab Singh, 78
Paulmier de Gonneville, 4
Pépin, Jean, 5
Peyton, commodore, 75
Phaulkon, Constance, 39
Phélypeaux, Jerome, 43
Pocock, admiral, 87
Pocquelin, Robert, 35
Pontchartrain, Louis Phélypeaux comte du, 43
Pronis, Jacques, 8, 9
Raja Sahuji, 78
Real, Laurent, 6
Rennefort, Souche de, 24
Rézimont, Gilles, 8
Richelieu, cardinal Armand Jean du Plessis de, 3, 4, 7
Rigault, Nicolas, 8
Roy, Girard de, 5
Ryckloff van Goens, admiral, 30
Saint Germain, Renault de, 85
Saiyid Lashhar, 80
Salabat Jang, 79, 80, 82, 87
Saunders, governor Thomas, 82